In Death's Waiting Room

CARE & WELFARE

Care and welfare are changing rapidly in contemporary welfare states.
The Care & Welfare series publishes studies on changing relationships
between citizens and professionals, on care and welfare governance, on
identity politics in the context of these welfare state transformations, and
on ethical topics. It will inspire the international academic and political
debate by developing and reflecting upon theories of (health) care and
welfare through detailed national case studies and/or international com-
parisons. This series will offer new insights into the interdisciplinary
theory of care and welfare and its practices.

SERIES EDITORS

Jan Willem Duyvendak, University of Amsterdam
Trudie Knijn, Utrecht University
Monique Kremer, Netherlands Scientific Council for Government Policy
  (Wetenschappelijke Raad voor het Regeringsbeleid – WRR)
Margo Trappenburg, Utrecht University, Erasmus University Rotterdam

PREVIOUSLY PUBLISHED

Jan Willem Duyvendak, Trudie Knijn and Monique Kremer (eds.), *Policy,
  People, and the New Professional. De-professionalisation and Re-professio-
  nalisation in Care and Welfare*, 2006 (ISBN 978 90 5356 885 9)
Ine van Hoyweghen, *Risks in the Making. Travels in Life Insurance and
  Genetics*, 2007 (ISBN 978 90 5356 927 6)

IN DEATH'S WAITING ROOM

ROOM

Living and Dying with Dementia in a
Multicultural Society

Anne-Mei The

AMSTERDAM UNIVERSITY PRESS

Cover illustration: © Marcel van den Bergh / Hollandse Hoogte

Cover design: Sabine Mannel, NEON Design, Amsterdam
Lay-out: JAPES, Amsterdam

ISBN 978 90 5356 077 8
NUR 740

Contents

Part I   Park House

Part II The Blauwbörgje Case

Acknowledgements

Without the help and the hospitality of the staff, the residents and the visitors at Park House I would not have been able to study the hidden world of the nursing home. I have learned much from them and I am grateful.

I would also like to thank those involved in the Blauwbörgje case who shared their thoughts with me, and the many experts who discussed various aspects of nursing home care with me.

There are also many who helped to make this book a reality, but I would like to mention a few who made a substantial contribution: Herman Ader, Erik van Aert, Martin Boekholdt, Jan Eefsting, Faye Cossar, Judith Coutinho, Mariel Croon, Dries van Danzig, Robert Eggink, Sjaak van der Geest, Magdelena Hernas, Cees Hertogh, James Kennedy, Bert Keizer, Cilia Linssen, Forough Nayeri, Roeline Pasman, Rissa Philip, Irene Schenker, Marjan Verkerk, Hendrik Jan de Vries, Gerrit van der Wal, Fons van Wanroy, and of course Onno Zijlstra.

The observations in Park House were part of a study of *versterven* commissioned by the Dutch Ministry of Health (VWS), the Dutch edition of the book, *In de Wachtkamer van de Dood: Leven en Sterven met Dementie in een Verkleurende Samenleving*, was made possible by a grant from Het Zonnehuisgroep. I carried out the research and wrote the book while I was a senior research fellow in the Department of Social Medicine and the EMGO Institute at the Free University in Amsterdam. The translation was made possible by a grant from The Netherlands Organisation for Scientific Research (NWO).

I would like to thank Robert Pool for translating the book into English.

Preface

People living in care homes are probably the most vulnerable and least powerful individuals in society. Being dependant on someone else for all your health, social and care needs can result in the individual being silenced and marginalised.

Despite a positive increase in research and practice interest focusing on this area in attempts to provide more positive relationship centred care practices general understandings and knowledge of care home practices remain limited.

What is essential is that the often very difficult and sensitive concerns inherent in providing institutional (and institutionalised) care responses to silenced and vulnerable people should be voiced, debated and given priority. *In Death's Waiting Room* is an accessible and detailed account of the experiences of residents, staff and relatives in a care home setting especially in relation to the complex issues and decisions that come with the dying process.

In the telling of sad, distressing and difficult stories Anne-Mei The highlights many key theoretical concerns but in a manner that makes clear the complexity of how such concerns are played out in practice. The presentation of life and death in Park House engages the reader with these lived complexities in ways that are both fascinating and challenging. The reader is drawn into demanding and thought-provoking questions on urgent issues for society and for our own lives.

The book is an essential and stimulating read for all of us trying to improve the lives of residents, relatives and staff in care homes. It is not only about how to understand better the challenges to providing better care but also how to understand and improve the processes and practices of supporting a good death.

Dr Heather Wilkinson
Centre for Research on
Families and Relationships Dementia Services
Edinburgh University

Colm Cunningham
Dementia Services
Development Centre
University of Stirling

Introduction

The hidden story

This book tells a hidden story. It is a story that concerns us all, but one that we would rather not hear, about a subject we would rather not think about. It is the story of the life and death of old people with dementia. It is a topic that we try and avoid as long as we can, until we are confronted with it when a loved one is admitted to a nursing home. The story does emerge occasionally, however, when an incident reaches the mass media. That is what happened in the Netherlands in the summer of 1997, when the family of a man with dementia accused a nursing home of attempted murder, claiming that they deliberately allowed him to dehydrate and refused to rehydrate him.

The study

The study was part of a project on *versterven* – refraining from artificially feeding and hydrating nursing home residents with advanced Alzheimer's disease.[1] In order to explore and understand what happens to those with dementia who end up in nursing homes, I carried out two years of anthropological research in a nursing home in the Netherlands. Anthropologists study social phenomena through participant observation: by being present and observing what people do and by participating in daily activities. The researcher gradually gains the trust of the group members and becomes an 'insider', while simultaneously noting as an 'outsider' the things that the real insiders do not notice because they have become routine and internalised.[2] Contrary to quantitative survey research the questions in this type of ethnographic research are not all formulated before the fieldwork starts, but rather are developed during the fieldwork. The assumption is that you do not always know beforehand what all the relevant questions are going to be until you start the research and are exposed to the phenomenon in question. Important questions are discovered in conversation with the study population in practical situations. Some of the most important information, especially relating to sensitive and taboo topics, tends to surface in informal conversations in corridors or coffee rooms rather than in formal interview settings.[3] If I had used different methods I would probably have learned little about the rough treatment of residents, the cultural gap between different ethnic groups or carer's double jobs. Participant observation is the only way to study certain topics.

It took time to penetrate the life of the nursing home and establish the necessary degree of rapport. However, when this had been achieved, people came to me and started offering me information. The conversations I had changed over time. Initially it was important for me to gather as much information as possible, whereas later the emphasis was more on collecting different opinions on the same events and comparing the views of the various people involved. Later the conversations developed a more reflective character and I tried to form interpretations and explanations through dialogue with my informants. The most difficult phase in my relationship with my informants started when I left the nursing home. I then had to try and distance myself from the people and experiences I had been involved with in order to be able to write about them critically.

In the nursing home that I will call 'Park House' I was present a few days a week. I attended staff discussions about residents and discussions between staff and relatives. I assisted with simple tasks such as cleaning, feeding and washing residents. When it wasn't busy I asked questions about things that had happened. Most of the time I spent in informal conversation with staff – drinking coffee and chatting. It took time to win their confidence, but they got used to my presence and increasingly they came to me and offered me their stories. In this way I came to understand life in a nursing home, and those who live, work and visit there.

In this book I describe both the nursing home I have called 'Park House' and the Blauwbörgje case, in which relatives accused a nursing home of attempted murder when they abstained from feeding and rehydrating a patient. In doing so I have not meant to suggest that the two nursing homes involved are the same. There are differences. They are in different regions, for example, and as a result Park House was much more seriously affected by labour shortages. Having said that, it can be concluded that the similarities are greater than the differences: the emotions of relatives when they have to hand over the care of a loved one to a nursing home; the communication with relatives; the work of the carers; the increasing workload; the dependency and power relationships between residents and carers; the gap between the expectations of the family and what can actually be realized in practice; the way in which end-of-life decisions are made; the reorganizations; the supervision and management problems; and the ignorance of the wider society about what life in the nursing home is really like.

My description of Park House does not necessarily apply to all nursing homes in the Netherlands, but what I describe is also not based only on my observations in that particular home. I also spoke to more than twenty staff members in another home in the east of the country, and with another forty experts. These additional interviews were carried out to check the findings from Park House and place them in a broader context. Information from these interviews has not been presented explicitly in these pages, but it has been integrated into the narrative.

This book is not just a selection of events, but also a concentration. I have taken a magnifying glass to both the timeline and the main issues. Most of the time events in the nursing home unfold as described in the early chapters. As the book develops it focuses on a few specific incidents. There is a danger that this gives a negative and one-sided view of things. But researchers are meant to problematise and to question, and using extreme situations sometimes makes it easier to understand the phenomenon being studied.

Although in writing this book I have been strongly influenced by those I got to know in Park House, it is not they I describe. In order to make the narrative readable I have created composite characters based on my experiences and the information obtained from the additional interviews. I also use terms such as 'white' and 'black' to refer to those of Dutch origin and those whose origin is in the ex-Dutch colonies in the Caribbean because this fits with the way in which the participants themselves spoke. I have also chosen to use first names for the carers and first and second names for the doctors and other professional staff. This also reflects local usage.

The nursing home and the carers

In Park House scarcity reigned. The home was in financial crisis, as a result of which there was no money for many essentials. Due to a shortage of staff, residents did not receive the required level of attention. During recent years the number of trained nursing home carers in the Netherlands has decreased and the level of training has declined. At the same time, the burden of work has increased because old people are being admitted to nursing homes later and therefore in a more developed stage of their illnesses. Carers who can no longer cope with the burden of work suffer burnout. Work piles up and no matter how hard they work, they never seem to get on top of things. This leads to feelings of helplessness and indifference, and as a result motivation suffers.

As a result of this combination of factors, carers often cannot do much more than get the residents out of bed and feed them. This is not just the case in Park House. According to one study, two thirds of nursing home carers in the Netherlands have insufficient time to care for residents properly, and one in five carers admits to making residents wear 'incontinence gear' – a sort of nappy – because they don't have time to help them go to the toilet. Another study has shown that 80 percent of Dutch nursing homes do not comply with the minimum requirements that the sector itself identified in 2001.

The situation is worst in the Randstad – the Amsterdam-Utrecht-Rotterdam conurbation – where Park House is situated. Nursing homes in this area have undergone a striking transformation in recent years. The largely white Dutch residents are cared for by black carers from the former Dutch Caribbean colony of Surinam. In Park House more than 60 percent of the staff is black. In the department that takes care of residents with dementia, the percentage is even higher, and there are units operating with an entirely 'black team'. For many residents this is a situation that takes some getting used to. They have had little contact with people from Surinam and know nothing of their culture.

The Surinamese carers also have to bridge a cultural gap. They insist that they would never 'dump' their elderly relatives in a nursing home, and so they are doing a job that goes against the grain of their cultural norms and values. There are other problems as well. They regularly feel discriminated against by both the residents and their relatives. There are also socio-economic differences. The Surinamese carers are usually single mothers who have to work very hard just to survive. They usually have to juggle several jobs. Due to the heavy work burden and having to take care of a family single-handed, they are often tired.

Nursing homes seek to solve these problems through reorganization, restructuring, mergers, and privatisation. There is talk of stricter rules and sanctions. Managers want to make the organization less hierarchical, so supervisors are included in the management team, but as a result they are taken away from day-to-day tasks and the distance between supervisors and carers becomes even greater.

These problems – which are by no means unique to the Netherlands – are only likely to increase. With an ageing population in many developed countries, the number of those with dementia will increase, and the urgent question is: How are we going to cope? This book shows that this is a problem that is already upon us.

How It All Started

A phone call from the newspaper

'Have you read in the paper this morning about what's been happening in the Blauwbörgje nursing home?' my friend says when I answer the phone. She is a journalist with one of the national papers. If you have a minute I'll tell you,' she says. 'I'd really like to know what you think. The relatives of a man with dementia have charged the nursing home of deliberately allowing him to dehydrate – not giving him enough to drink. They call it *versterven*. Apparently that's their policy in cases like that.'

'I'm not sure whether I can comment on that,' I say guardedly. 'I don't know anything about nursing homes or about dementia.'

'But what do you think?' she asks enthusiastically. 'His relatives knew absolutely nothing. They found out just in time and managed to get him to hospital. There they put him on a fluid drip and he recovered. He's now sitting up in bed and eating. The doctor says that they were just in time otherwise he'd have had it. Now that's really something.'

'Strange,' I say, 'I always thought that in nursing homes they had such good communication with relatives; better than in hospitals. I can hardly imagine that they wouldn't have discussed this with the relatives.'

I had once been in a nursing home, to visit Mrs Schilling. She had been a patient in the hospital where I was doing an anthropological study and she had been transferred from the hospital to a nursing home. When I arrived, the receptionist took me aside and asked carefully whether I was a relative. It turned out that Mrs Schilling had died a few days earlier. I made an appointment to speak to the doctor who had treated her. During the interview I was struck by they very different approach that he had toward his patients compared to what I had become used to in the hospital. He described in detail how everything had been done to make Mrs Schilling as comfortable as possible. They had spoilt her he said, and she didn't have to get out of bed if she didn't want to. The doctor also described the support given to her family. He described how her condition had deteriorated slowly during the three weeks that she had been in the nursing home. He knew more about her, her family and her dog than any doctor in the hospital knew about a patient, even those who had cancer patients they had been treating for years. And even then, he still gave all the credit to the carers because, he said, they did all the real work while the doctor stood on the sideline.

I had twice encountered patients with dementia. One was a jolly woman who poured herself shots of gin from a bottle hidden in her bedside cupboard, which she described as 'the fridge'. Once she attacked 'intruders' with a computer screen she had taken from the doctor's office. The other was ferried to the hospital, from the nursing home where she had lived for years, to say goodbye to her husband, who was dying of cancer. She sat next to his bed in her wheelchair, in a world of her own. He was happy with her visit and stroked her hand, even though she did not recognise him. He died the next day.

I try to imagine those two demented ladies on a fluid drip. And I try to imagine the nursing home doctor talking to the relatives. What is it like on a nursing home ward populated only by the demented? This new setting after years of observation in hospitals intrigues me. It seems strange that I had hardly ever been in a nursing home, given the increasing relevance of issues relating to ageing.

I look out across the concrete towers of the university complex where I have been working for the past few weeks. It is July 1997. It is boiling hot and the windows don't open.

'Is this really about *versterven*?' I ask. 'If I understand you rightly then it might just have been a communication problem. When emotional issues are involved, the message often gets distorted. I know about the problems of communication between doctor and patient from the bad-news meetings in the hospital, in which the doctor informed the patient of the death sentence of their cancer diagnosis. This often led to misunderstandings by patients and relatives. It's a different situation, I know, but they are both about life and death. If the relatives are not yet ready for death then the bad news is not absorbed.'

There is silence on the other end of the line, then she asks: Can I quote this in the paper?

In the following weeks the papers are full of the Blauwbörgje story. Nowhere is there a response from the nursing home or the doctor responsible. 'No comment from Blauwbörgje,' the papers say. Experts explain, columnists give their opinion. The discussion is about *versterven* – the final phase in the gradual process of deterioration that people with dementia go through, when doctors and relatives decide that is not longer in the patient's interest to prevent 'nature taking its course' with infusions and drips. The dying do not eat and drink well, experts report in the media; so *versterven* is simply part of the process of dying. But this explanation does not calm public opinion. People are not familiar with the process of dying and they worry about what is happening in nursing homes.

In the tram, on my way to the university I encounter Gerrit van der Wal, Professor of Social Medicine and my boss. The conversation turns to what is now generally referred to as the Blauwbörgje affair. We speculate about the precise chain of events and wonder whether such things are common in nursing homes. 'You would need to do some participant observation to find out,' I say.

'Do you think so?' he asks.

'Yes, and you can only understand what happens if you have had direct experience, if you know how people work and what the circumstances are. Then you can understand the experiences and statements of those involved. I wouldn't be surprised if the issue here wasn't *versterven* at all. It would be interesting to find out.'

'It's funny you should say that,' he says. There have been questions in parliament about what is happening in nursing homes with regard to dementia and *versterven*. There will probably be a call for research, and it's quite likely that we will be asked to do it.'

Versterven

Basically *versterven,* as it is used in this book, refers to abstaining from giving food and liquid to patients who refuse or who do not experience sensations of hunger and thirst due to old age or advanced Alzheimer's disease. The word *versterven* is a verb; the noun is *versterving* It does not translate into English unproblematically as 'terminal dehydration'. *Versterving* has been controversial in the Netherlands because of the ambiguities and connotations of the term itself, ambiguity about the nature of tube feeding, uncertainty about whether or not it is painless and the extent to which the dying person is in control, and uncertainty about what constitutes natural death. Many interpreted *versterven* as a transitive verb (a kind of killing) when it is in fact an intransitive verb (a kind of dying). *Versterven* is not something you can do to people, it is something that happens to them. In the media discussion, however, *versterven* was equated with terminating hydration or feeding, or actively not initiating artificial feeding and hydration in patients who did not spontaneously abstain from eating and drinking. A brief consultation of a few dictionaries reveals further sources of ambiguity: (1) To die (out), to wither, to wilt; (2) To descend (in the sense of 'to pass on by inheritance'), to devolve; (3) To hang (meat); (4) To fast, mortify the flesh, renounce earthly pleasures. The associations with 'hanging meat' and with terms like 'wither' and 'wilt' obviously spoke to the imagination of those who bothered to look it up. The term also has strong currents of religious meaning. Indeed, B. Chabot, the psychiatrist who first used the term in the discussion of terminal dehydration, claimed that he had been motivated in his choice of the term by *Job 14:8*: 'Though the root thereof wither old in the earth, and the stock thereof die in the ground' (*Indien zijn wortel in de aarde veroudert, en zijn stam in het stof versterft*). Fasting, mortification of the flesh, renunciation, all suggest voluntary choice and control, as well as some higher end to which these sacrifices are a means. Although this resonance with Christian tradition and belief was only a minor thread in a secular discussion, it was nonetheless present, and it contributed to the ambiguity.[4]

PART I
PARK HOUSE

Life in Park House

Smoked salmon and hard apples

The opening of Park House after the renovations was festive. The Friends of Park House Foundation, which counts prominent members of Dutch society among its members, organised things. The Mayor opened the new building officially in the presence of more than two hundred guests. The building had been decorated and preparations took days. During the ceremony the Mayor praised the nursing home. He would prefer to spend his own old age at home but, if he had to spend it in a nursing home, then this would be the one, he told the guests. There was smoked salmon and eel and champagne. There were important people. Big shots, the carers said, as they turned their noses up. None of the residents were invited; nor were any of the carers.

They still talk about the opening. Even the doctor, Rutger Varenkamp, who is generally positive about everything, gets angry when he remembers. He described it as Dickensian: while the Mayor and his guests stuffed themselves below in the restaurant, the residents were pressed against the upstairs windows trying to get a glimpse of the dignitaries. The doctors were invited, but Varenkamp declined. He thinks it illustrates where management's priorities lay.

The official opening did indeed stand in stark contrast to the reality on the wards, where every cent counts. The De Stadhouder section, for example has a fruit budget of fifteen euros a week for sixty-five residents. Residents can't have more than two pieces of fruit a week. And they can't eat the apples anyway because they are too hard. The nutritionist can't make fruit drinks, because the blender has been stolen. The residents like the bananas most, but the nutritionist locks them in her cupboard, otherwise the non-residents eat them.

'Proletarian shopping!' Anna van Raalten, the care manager says. 'You'd be surprised at the things that disappear here: videos, televisions, toilet paper, soap, everything. It's as though people are coming here to do their shopping.' She's had to have locks put on the cupboards. Only the heads of departments have keys.

Park House is in financial trouble and the problem is only getting worse: a result of privatisation, uncontrolled new building and the use of temporary staff. There doesn't seem to be money for anything: tablecloths, coffee biscuits or flowers. Van Raalten saves ten euros a week to buy tablecloths and artificial flowers. She wants to cheer up the living rooms.

Unrest and absenteeism

Park House is situated next to a park at the edge of town. A month earlier the residents had been moved from an older building further down the road. The new building smells of paint and linoleum. From the entrance there is a long glass corridor to the garden house where the director's office and the support services are situated. This part of the House has all the modern amenities: leather chairs, flat computer screens. I learn later that the garden house is referred to as 'the Gold Coast'.

I wait in the restaurant. There is also a hairdresser and a coffee bar. There are numerous chairs and tables and many coffee-drinking and smoking people. Carers in white coats crisscross the open space, in groups, chatting and laughing. Some push residents in wheelchairs, or support residents who are unable to walk independently: frail old women with neat white hair. More than half of the carers are coloured. When I enquire in Personnel as to the exact percentage of non-indigenous carers, I am told that they are not allowed to keep such records.

The atmosphere in the restaurant is agreeable. No one seems to be in a hurry. Voices are loud: 'No Mrs Bosch, we are going to the hairdresser. No the *hairdresser.*' I have come to meet the care manager and the doctor in charge of the psycho-geriatric ward that is called De Stadhouder, where I want to come and spend the next two years doing participant observation. Park House is a 'mixed' nursing home: there are psycho-geriatric wards for the demented and somatic wards for those with physical disabilities (although the latter also usually have some mental problems as well).

Anna van Raalten arrives for the introductory meeting. She is a small blond woman in her forties with a firm handshake. Together we stroll to De Stadhouder. To get onto the ward you have to push a red button to open the glass sliding doors. To get out you need a code. It is meant to keep the residents with dementia inside. There is a note stuck on the door asking visitors to make sure that Witje, one of the resident's cat, does not escape.

'Is this the best time for you to come and work here? No not really,' she says, rhetorically, when we get to her office. Rutger Varenkamp, the doctor, is also present. 'There is a lot of disruption at the moment. The decision was made before my time and I will honour it,' she says, looking me straight in the eye, 'but you must understand that I am not keen on even more disruption.'

Van Raalten's predecessor was transferred to another post against his will. He was very fond of the carers and they of him. But the board decided to tighten up the administration and he didn't have the right formal qualifications, so he had to go. Van Raalten has worked on De Stadhouder a few months. She has the brief to professionalise the care provided. 'It is really necessary,' she says.

'In this department there is a close-knit team,' Rutger Varenkamp says. He shifts around uncomfortably in his chair. He is about the same age as Van Raalten but looks younger in his jeans, lumberjack shirt and Timberlands. Varenkamp says that the core group of carers has been in De Stadhouder for years. During the last few months many staff have left, partly due to the departure of the previous care manager. There is also substantial absenteeism – almost 20 percent. That puts enormous pressure on those who remain at work. 'The work pressure is high,' says the doctor. 'Too high.'

Locked up

Eight o' clock in the morning. It's my first working day in Park House and I enter De Stadhouder. There are voices in the distance. It is doctor Varenkamp and Mrs Venema, a petite little woman of ninety-seven, with long white hair, sunken cheeks and eyes looking out from deep sockets that give her a permanently surprised look. She shuffles along, in her nightdress and bare feet, behind her walking frame. She is lost in a corridor she has traversed for the last ten years.

'Come along now Mrs Venema,' the doctor says, as he offers her his arm.

She turns her large eyes on him. 'Is it far?'

'Your room is at the end of the corridor. It's not far.'

'I'm used to better treatment than this,' she says, her voice mildly angry.

'But Mrs Venema, what about all the nice sisters who take care of you?'

'That's true.' She puts her arm through his. They move, step by step, down the corridor toward her room.

When the doctor returns we go and sit in the office. He tells me that her anger didn't last long. 'When we got to her door she cuddled me and said she wanted to marry me.'

Mrs Venema is one of the few residents who realises that she is shut up in a nursing home. She mentions the fact regularly. 'I don't deny it either,' Varenkamp says. 'You have to be truthful, even to those with dementia. It is awkward, because they are really shut up, but it's for their own good...' He shrugs and opens his diary.

The food has been paid for

Rutger Varenkamp has just picked up the phone when Mrs Prins comes into the office. She is an 84-year-old woman with short hair. She is wearing trousers and a sweater. Her eyes are full of fear and dismay. Her body is tense. Her movements are slow and remind me of Tai Chi exercises. She is sweating and moaning softly. She stops in front of the doctor and stares at him.

'Mrs Prins has serious dementia. She is loosing her grasp of reality,' he whispers. 'It's very unpleasant for her.' He takes her hand. 'Come and sit down,' he says as he holds her hand. Varenkamp tells me he has reduced her medication because it made her drowsy, but now this is the result. He thinks he should probably resume medication.

When Mrs Prins first moved to Park House she became good friends with Mrs De Bie, Rutger Varenkamp tells me. They always shared a table and later adjacent rooms were organised for them. But then Mrs Prins's condition started to deteriorate. She lost track of where she was and started to worry about who was paying for the food. The carers used to put a receipt in her handbag saying that the food had been paid for and that calmed her down. But after a while even that didn't work any more. The friendship became difficult and Mrs De Bie found a new friend, Mrs Walker. 'You must know her,' he says, 'she's one of The Walkers'. I had seen The Walkers: four or five women who spend the whole day walking up and down the corridor, with the little Mrs Walker in the lead. She always says hello but can't stop for a chat because she has a lot to do: the kids will be home any minute and she still has to tidy up and put the potatoes on. Sometimes she passes by with a pile of towels in her arms.

'Mrs De Bie thinks that Mrs Walker is her sister,' the doctor continues. 'The good thing about places like this is that some people discover a whole family again.'

During my first weeks in Park House I see Mrs Prins pass by, fear in her eyes. Sometimes she is calm, but easy to anger, turning aggressive, spitting and pinching and kicking. Often she lets herself sink to the ground, only to get up again and walk on. She seems to be looking for something. But what?

Femke is Mrs Prins's main carer. She shows me an old photo of Mrs Prins. I hardly recognise the woman with full cheeks and curly hair who stares calmly from the photo. She was a tram conductor and lived with her friend Janny. After Janny's death Mrs Prins started to show the first signs of dementia. Her neighbours kept an eye on her, but this was soon inadequate. She started to boil her knickers in milk and crept through the garden hedge at night looking for her mother. Home care also soon proved inadequate and Mrs Prins was put on the waiting list for a nursing home. Finally she was admitted to Park House. Since then she has been searching the home in vain for Janny.

When she sees Mrs De Bie she cheers up. Femke tells me that Mrs Prins used to be a jolly and sociable woman. She used to chat to the staff on night shift and smoke cigarettes with them. Femke used to go on tram tours with her, and Mrs Prins taught her all the routes. That was five years ago. Now she no longer recognises her former neighbours, her only outside contacts, as she no longer has any family.

Nappies are for babies

Mornings are the busiest time in Park House. The carers have to get the residents out of bed, wash them and dress them. In the mornings the enclosed spaces in the House are warmer and more stuffy than usual. The smell is predominantly of urine and faeces. Carers hurry back and forth between bedrooms and bathrooms. In De Stadhouder there are single, double and triple rooms, each with a washbasin. The beds have adjustable railings. Each resident has a bedside table, a shelf on which to put a bowl of water, a wardrobe and a small notice board with photos. The curtains, wallpaper and linoleum are all marbled salmon pink. Some rooms have been furnished by relatives, with a single piece of the resident's own furniture – usually old-fashioned and much too large for the room. Other rooms only have House furniture, the only personal items being the photos on the notice board, or a bottle of perfume on the shelf above the washbasin, which is usually a present from the carers.

The corridors are lined with washing trolleys piled with towels, basins and the net underwear used to keep the assortment of 'incos' in place. These are 'incontinence systems,' I am told, when I ask about nappies. Nappies are for babies. During my early days in Park House my choice of words was frequently corrected. 'Feeding is what they do in the zoo,' the nutritionist said curtly one morning when I offered to help her with the lunch. And shortly after that one of the carers pointed out: 'We don't talk about cleaning residents, but about *drying* them. You can also say *do the toilet*.' I have the biggest problem with the doctor, Rutger Varenkamp, when I insist on speaking of patients and the day-care centre. 'No,' he says firmly, 'they are residents, not patients; they *live* here, patients don't live in hospitals. And it's a *living room*. You don't call your living room a day-care centre, do you?'

Waitress! Waitress!

In the living room the assistant nutritionist is buttering bread and pouring tea and coffee. From about eight o' clock residents begin to arrive, assisted by carers, who place them at grey Formica tables, on urine resistant plastic chairs. Mrs Van Dam has been wheeled in in her bed and placed in a corner. She had refused to get up. Along the walls there is an assortment of old fashioned oak furniture, the remains of residents' households, that contrasts with the plastic tables and chairs and the linoleum floor. The radio spews Christmas songs, and mixed in with the music there are snatches of carers' voices as they sing along. Someone calls: 'Miss, miss, waitress! I'm thirsty.' Her cup is filled. 'That's nice, thank you'. And before drinking the coffee in front of her, she calls again: 'Waitress, I'm thirsty'. She is Anneke Bloem and she used to be in cabaret. 'Della Distel was my stage name,' she says. 'Much nicer than my real name.' She is one of the few present in the living room with whom it is possible to have a normal conversation, according to the carers. Up to a point, though, because she has the tendency to become repetitive. She is strapped to her chair. Not only does she forget that her cup has just been filled; she also forgets that she can't walk.

She was on the stage for more than fifty years. She didn't spend much time at home, but that didn't matter because there were no children. She would have liked to have had children, but she couldn't, and you can still hear the disappointment in her voice. These days the doctors can find out the cause, but what use is that. I try and pursue the conversation further but notice that I have lost her attention. She leans over and whispers: 'You've such a nice face; you're the nicest.' Then she turns away and calls: 'Waitress, waitress, I'm thirsty.' After a while her message changes: 'Waitress, I need to go to the loo.' When no one takes any notice her voice becomes more urgent: 'Help! Help! I need the loo.'

'Calm down,' Tanja, the assistant nutritionist says, 'I'll get help.'

'Help' Help!' Mrs Bloem keeps calling.

Tanja, fifty years old, short black hair with blond plucks, ten silver rings in each ear, explains later that as nutritionist she is not allowed to help residents with the toilet. Femke arrives with a trolley and with much effort Mrs Bloem is lifted onto it, still strapped to her chair. Femke hauls the trolley off in the direction of the toilets. When they get there Mrs Bloem no longer needs the toilet.

The other residents eat their sandwiches. It is nearly Christmas. Carers are busy with the decorations: holly, red bells, and artificial snow.

Mrs Van Dam Dies

A second mother

Mrs van Dam moved to Park House in the spring. She is eighty-nine and used to live alone with her dog Cazemier. Her son-in-law didn't like the dog and she knew that he would be put down as soon as she went into a nursing home. Rutger Varenkamp did everything in his power to get the dog admitted to Park House together with his owner. This included negotiations with everyone from the doggy-walk service to the director of Park House. 'Everything was arranged,' he says. 'He was going to have a trial weekend, but then he was put down anyway.'

Lately Mrs Van Dam has not been well. Leukaemia is suspected. Varenkamp wants to be sure, so he can give her the right treatment. Because in cases of dementia and cancer the treatment is solely palliative: that is, symptom alleviation only. He doesn't think she will last long. The main thing is to make sure she is comfortable, and that is the job of the carers, he says.

In the living room, Colette, a carer in her mid-thirties and wearing a white coat over her jeans, is stroking Mrs Van Dam's head. Mrs Van Dam is moaning softly. Occasionally she takes the carer's hand and strokes her cheek with it. Colette had been off for three days and was shocked when she saw Mrs Van Dam this morning. Mrs Van Dam had not been eating for a few days. She gestures to a glass of water on the table. 'We are trying to get her to drink,' she tells me. She sighs and tears well in her eyes. 'I will have to let her go,' she says. 'It's terrible. She's such a darling.' Colette says that Mrs Van Dam has become a second mother to her. She has better contact with her than with her own mother. And she is sure that Mrs Van Dam has a better relationship with her than with her own daughter, who never comes to see her. 'Unbelievable, isn't it?' She says. 'I don't understand how she can abandon her mother like that,' she says.

The end of the line

On Wednesday mornings the staff hold a 'multidisciplinary consultation' during which they discuss individual cases, adjust treatment strategies and make plans. Anna van Raalten, the care manager, chairs the meetings.

'Things are not going well with Mrs Van Dam,' she says, opening the meeting one Wednesday. 'It's basically the end of the line for her, and we have to decide how we can make it as easy as possible for her.'

Rutger Varenkamp reports excitedly that he has spoken to her son-in-law on the phone. He wanted to know exactly when she was going to die, because they had booked a holiday and wanted to know whether they would have to cancel. 'He really did say that,' Varenkamp says. I told him: 'I'm sorry. I can't tell you: people just come and go'.

'We have left her in her room today,' says Femke. 'The living room was noisy and it frightened her.'

'Good,' the care manager nods. 'How is she eating?'

'No, she just refuses.'

'Does she ask for food?'

'No, not even biscuits and lemonade as she used to.'

'What about her skin? Are there red blotches?'

'Haven't noticed.'

'Can she turn over in bed?'

'No.'

'Is she being turned over?'

'I assume so,' Femke hesitates. 'She can get halfway.'

They fall silent. The care manager looks at the carers questioningly. 'Well?'

'Well, I think it would be good to change her around,' Femke says awkwardly.

'Are you writing this down? Can you make sure it gets done?' The carer nods, her cheeks red. She takes off her glasses and wipes the lenses.

'What about religion?' asks the doctor. 'Does she need spiritual support?'

Anna van Raalten leafs through Mrs Van Dam's medical file. 'I don't see anything about religion here. We could ask the pastor to come and speak to her.'

Tidy up! Isn't that what you're paid for?

Later that morning Mrs Van Dam is in her bed in the living room again. Vanessa – just twenty, a trainee carer originally from Surinam, wearing a crocheted beret – is helping her to drink. Mrs Van Dam smiles. 'Dear,' Vanessa says as she cuddles Mrs Van Dam.

Mrs Koster, a neat old lady with white, permed hair, is sitting at the table. She is from a good family and had been married to an accountant. She feels that she is better than the rest of the residents. 'Tidy up!' she keeps ordering the carers. 'That's what you're paid for.' Suddenly she turns around and peers through her butterfly-shaped spectacles at the bed in the corner. 'I say, girl,' she calls to Vanessa, 'the person in that bed: how old is she really?'

'Ninety-one,' Vanessa answers, and continues, 'and how old is that person sitting at the table.' Everyone laughs.

'I'm ninety,' says Mrs Koster with a serious expression, 'I was born in 1912'.

'Then you must be ninety-one, just like Mrs Van Dam.'

'Well, I wouldn't want to change places with her, I can tell you.'

Morphine

The next morning Mrs Van Dam is shaking and Femke and Vanessa are trying to give her an injection of Valium. Mrs Van Dam is emaciated and her chin sticks out. Her tongue is blue. They tap her cheek to try and get a response: 'Sister Van Dam! Sister Van Dam!' No response.

Later Vanessa says that Mrs Van Dam's daughter had phoned. When she was told that her mother's condition was deteriorating, the daughter had said that she wanted to be updated about her mother's condition, but that she was not planning to come and see her at the moment; perhaps tomorrow. Vanessa had drunk a cup of tea with Mrs Van Dam and told her that her daughter might come the next day. It is then that she started to shake, and Vanessa had called the doctor. She was worried: 'I thought: Is it what I said about her daughter?'

'I think that the relationship with her daughter isn't very good,' says Femke. 'I remember when she was admitted: the daughter couldn't cope with the situation at all. She left in tears. It was the son-in-law who spoke to Rutger. Mrs Van Dam was angry with her daughter, because she had the feeling that her daughter was having her put away. And she blamed her for having the dog put down.'

That afternoon there is a meeting to discuss Mrs Van Dam's condition. 'Femke says that Mrs Van Dam has reported feeling pain, and I think she is in pain,' says the doctor. 'I phoned the family because I want to put her on morphine. They agree. They said they might come this evening. I said they might be too late, that morphine is a powerful drug... It might reduce her breathing.' He looks at Femke and Vanessa. 'Sometimes carers don't like to administer morphine, especially if there is a chance that it is likely to be the last injection before the patient dies.'

'It's not a problem,' Femke says quickly. The doctor nods. 'Of course. You're an experienced carer.' Femke nods proudly. 'Yes, and I'll tell you something: they always go three at a time.'

The doctor raises an eyebrow: 'Really?'

'Yes, just wait and see. Mrs Van Ris died yesterday, and Mrs Van Dam will follow.'

Rutger mentions that there is another resident upstairs that is dying. He says that she is dying a good death, with her son at her bedside, talking about old times and fond memories. He doesn't think that Mrs Van Dam's death is going to be a good one. 'I'm not making a value judgement,' he says, 'it's just an observation.'

Colette has the evening shift. She is upset when she hears that Mrs Van Dam is dying. But she is also happy that she has the evening shift. She hopes that Mrs Van Dam will die in her shift, or in the morning shift with Femke; not in the night shift with someone she doesn't know. Rutger Varenkamp tells her about the decision to give morphine. He says she can administer Valium if Mrs Van Dam becomes restless.

They always go three at a time

The following morning I hear that Mrs Van Dam passed away during the night. Colette was with her. The carers are busy getting the residents out of bed and don't have time to talk about it. In the office there is a grey bin-liner full of clothes. The label says: 'Mrs Koster'. Anna van Raalten comes through the door, a bundle of papers under her arm. 'A lot's been happening,' she says. 'Three deaths in two days.'

'Three?' I say, surprised. 'Mrs Van Dam, Mrs Ris. Who else?'

'This morning they found Mrs Koster dead in her bed. Heart attack. It happens. Sorry, have to rush.'

I watch her walk down the corridor. In my mind I hear Femke: 'They always go three at a time.' And I also hear Mrs Koster: 'I wouldn't want to change places with her, I can tell you.'

The Family

Football season ticket

The Donkers – husband and wife – shuffle down the corridor. They moved into Park House the previous day. Their son spent the whole weekend decorating their room. There are two armchairs and a table with a large television. There are paintings on the walls and on the noticeboard photos of the highlights of their life with children and grandchildren. During the introductory interview with the doctor and Femke, the son described how difficult the previous years had been: his mother 'officially' has dementia. His father is still mentally all right, but has difficulty keeping track of things. They both hardly eat, but drink too much alcohol. There have been serious incidents: falls, fights, doors left open at night. The son and his wife could no longer cope. With great sadness he had his parents admitted to Park House. His father will not forgive him for this.

Rutger Varenkamp asks about their lives. The son says that his mother is fond of nice clothes and his father likes to read the sports pages. Rutger says that another resident subscribes to a newspaper and that maybe they can share. Femke says that if his father likes football there is a season ticket for the local football team that he could use. The son nods emotionally, and when Rutger offers to put his parents in the guest room because that would be more comfortable than a standard room, the son bursts into tears.

'That's really nice of you,' he says, as he wipes his glasses.

'We want to do what's best for your parents,' says Rutger, as he pats him on the shoulder. 'It'll all be okay as long as we communicate. You can call me any time, but for day-to-day issues you should speak to Femke. She works most days.'

Mr Donkers is angry

Trainee carer Vanessa makes a space for Mr and Mrs Donkers at the breakfast table. She explains in a loud voice how things work: 'You get a slice of white and a slice of brown bread; one with something sweet and the other with something savoury.' After breakfast they shuffle down the corridor together.

Rutger tells me that it is always a difficult decision whether to keep couples together or separate them. Among the residents in the dementia section Mr Donkers does not get much mental stimulation, but if they move him to the non-dementia section he will be separated from his wife. 'We always complain about the management here,' he says, 'but they are really quite flexible. There are many homes in which it is policy to separate all couples as soon as they arrive.'

Back in his office he leafs through the report and reads aloud: 'Mr Donkers is angry with his son for having him locked away...' He tells me that residents are often angry with those who send them to the nursing home: usually daughters and daughters-in-law. They almost always leave in tears after the first visit, he says. Torn by guilt. Sometimes the new residents beat on the glass doors with their fists. But let's be honest: it's not the same as home, and everyone has to get used to it. He shrugs and goes back to the file.

Then he looks up and tells me that his youngest son started nursery school this week. When he dropped him off, after the last goodbye kiss, the child began to cry and hold on to his father. 'I don't want to stay here,' he screamed, 'I want to go back with papa.'

'It was terrible,' Rutger said, 'I never want to experience that again. I told my wife: I don't mind picking him up, but I don't want to drop him off. And you know what: it reminds me of the nursing home.'

People almost never move into a nursing home of their own free will. But in most cases there is not much choice. The 94-year-old Mrs Carpentier, for example, ate nothing but oatmeal porridge for three years before she was admitted. She covered herself and her house in her own faeces. She liked playing with the 'brown clay' that she found everywhere. She particularly enjoyed rubbing it into the furniture.

During her first days in Park House the carers put Mrs Carpentier with various residents in the living room so that she can make new friends, but she doesn't get on with any of them. She finds them 'a strange lot'. She listens to classical music in her room, and strolls through the corridors with her walking stick. She only has one desire, which she expresses politely and repeatedly: to go home.

Mrs Post had been looked after by her husband for years and he was exhausted. At nights she prowled around the house. She demanded that he change her clothes several times a day. She hit him, and he couldn't cope any more.

During her first weeks in the nursing home Mrs Post called continuously for her husband. She hit one of the assistant dieticians because she thought the she was flirting with her husband. When the assistant responded that she didn't even know what Mr Post looked like, Mrs Post said that she could borrow him if she liked, as long as she returned him.

Mrs Post was taken care of by Darah, who tried everything to calm her down. 'Your husband will be here later,' she kept telling Mrs Post, but she didn't seem to register. Then Darah said, pointing to one of the male residents: 'Look, there he is.' Mrs Post went over to the man and said: 'Come along, we're going home.' Later that day her husband arrived with a neighbour. Mrs Post went straight to the neighbour and said: 'Karel, at last, you're here.' The tears streamed down Mr Post's cheeks.

A nice afternoon in the park

Rutger Varenkamp talks about Mrs Scharloo, who has just been moved from a care home to Park House. She is gloomy. Varenkamp can understand her mood, because the move had been sudden. Her children had moved her to Park House without consulting her. 'Can you imagine? One day the car arrives, your children ask you to get in, it stops somewhere else, you get out, and suddenly you are sharing a bedroom with three other people and a living room with twelve others. Maybe they have Alzheimer's, but they do know when they are being moved around.'

It's not uncommon that people arrive in the nursing home unprepared, says Varenkamp. He knows of cases in which relatives have said: 'We're going for a nice afternoon in the park,' and then drive their mother to the nursing home. He can understand that it is difficult to break the news to elderly and dependent parents, but it still isn't fair. And all it does is shift the problem of telling them onto the nursing home staff.

Visits

Apart from the first desperate months in which the people with dementia start to lose control over reality, the suffering is not too bad, Rutger Varenkamp thinks. A person with dementia doesn't suffer any more than a person without dementia. It is worse for the family. 'Imagine holding a photo of your mother or father in your hand and watching it gradually fade,' he says.

He thinks that caring for those with dementia is seriously under-valued, because you are not only caring for the people with dementia, but also for their family. The communication and the support sometimes take up half the time, especially if the family is emotionally unstable, according to Varenkamp.

Carers sometimes think that some relatives don't visit often enough. Some have difficulty keeping this view to themselves. Mrs Wielens has a niece who comes once a fortnight. The carers think that this is not often enough. It is easy to judge the relatives, Varenkamp says. The niece lives quite far away, and can't leave her husband for long because he has cancer. But the carers think she isn't a good relative because she doesn't come often enough.

There are residents who have visitors every day, like the Surinamese Mrs Wijntak. The daughters and sons-in-law of the *Indische*[5] Mrs Halie even comes twice a day. They help to take care of their mother; they bring her food in the afternoon, and they come in the evening to put her to bed. They spend many hours in Park House and view this as entirely normal. When Mrs Halie started showing the symptoms of Alzheimer's one of the daughters took her into her home but all contributed to her care. When her condition deteriorated and she had to be moved to a nursing home, they continued their collective care for her there. She always cared for them, now it is their turn to care for her. That is how they explain it.

According to the Surinamese carers it is no coincidence that the coloured residents receive the most visitors. For them it is obvious that you care for your relatives when they are old. You even care for those you don't know very well. You take them into your home and you support them financially if necessary. You don't normally have them admitted to an institution, though that is changing these days.

In Surinam there is always an auntie at home who can take care of the children and the old granny, explains Surinamese carer Christa. But in Holland the women all work, so there isn't anyone to keep an eye on things. The houses here aren't suitable either; how can you take care of a mother with advanced dementia when you live in a small third floor apartment? Many of the Surinamese carers want to return to Surinam when they are old. Then at least they won't end up in a nursing home.

It does indeed seem as though the few coloured residents get more visitors than the white residents. But it isn't that clear cut. There are also white residents who have visitors every day and coloured ones whose relatives don't care. A poignant example is the Surinamese Mrs Japur. She has four children who almost never visit her. When she turned seventy her youngest son was supposed to come to dinner. She had her best dress on and was really looking forward to it. She had the food all laid out in the family room. He arrived late at night, drunk.

Mrs Japur tells Femke – her favourite carer – about it the next morning. 'It wasn't very nice of him,' she keeps repeating. Femke organises a new party, with the carers as guests. Mrs Japur is the beaming centre of attention. She is pleased with her present: a beauty case full of lipstick and nail varnish.

Later it turns out that the same son has been sluicing his mother's pension into his own bank account for years. Because she had no money she was always unable to go on trips with the other residents or buy new clothes. When this all comes to light the legal responsibility for Mrs Japur is taken away from the son by the court and given to Femke. She now does this with enthusiasm.

My husband doesn't want to come here

The 93-year-old Mrs Blauw has lived in Park House for more than ten years. Her husband died in the autumn, and about the same time Mrs Blauw had had a minor cerebral infarction; then last week a second one. Rutger Varenkamp arranges a meeting with her daughter-in-law, who says that it would be better for communication to go through her rather than her husband. Varenkamp tells her that Mrs Blauw's mental condition is bad – she is suffering from advanced dementia, and her physical condition isn't too good either: the infarctions were a blow to her system. He says that it is important to make decisions about what they are to do if her condition continues to deteriorate. Mrs Blauw has to be assisted with eating and drinking. And even that is becoming more and more difficult. It won't be long before she is unable to swallow her food. The question is: what to do then.

'We could feed your mother-in-law through a tube, the doctor explains. 'The question is: are we helping her by doing that? We have our ideas about this. You must have your own.'

'Certainly.'

'Tell me first, so I don't influence you.'

'I don't think we should do it.'

'Then we agree. One other thing: what do we do if she gets pneumonia? It could kill her. I could give her antibiotics. But you could also see pneumonia as an opportunity to die. It's not called the old man's friend for nothing. If we decide not to treat her if she gets pneumonia then we are talking about a symptomatic approach. That means doing everything possible to make your mother-in-law as comfortable as possible without unnecessarily extending her life. If she were to get a urinary tract infection then we would treat that, because that is an unpleasant illness that doesn't kill you.'

'I agree.'

'We'll put this in writing in her file, but we will discuss it again if the situation changes. Actually we should discuss this with your husband, but you're representing him, so it should be okay.' She nods, and red patches become visible on her neck.

'We try and make her as comfortable as possible. She has a simple life, and perhaps it seems shallow to us, but we have the impression that she isn't suffering,' the doctors says.

'In the beginning it was difficult,' says the daughter-in-law. 'When we tried to leave after a visit she tried to come with us. It was horrible; as though we had had her locked up. That has improved, because she no longer notices. I don't think she is suffering. I can live with the situation. But my husband can't. He can't bear to see his mother like that. And the atmosphere here has a bad effect on him. It makes him aggressive. When he manages to force himself to come, he gets angry at the slightest provocation. When we were here last Saturday he was unhappy about absolutely everything. There were stains on his mother's blouse and her hair hadn't been combed. He gave the carers a hard time. He even considered making an official complaint. It took me a whole day to persuade him to drop the idea. When he is in one of those moods I hardly recognise him. And we argue about it as well. I tell him that it is his mother, but he says she isn't his mother any more.'

'You are both right in that regard,' the doctor says in a friendly tone. 'She is still his biological mother, of course. But she is no longer the same woman she was. It's difficult.'

'You know,' she says, her voice emotional, 'when my husband doesn't come, I feel guilty towards her. As though he is abandoning her. But I can't force him to come.'

'I can imagine,' says the doctor. There are children who come every day and there are children who never come. That's how it is.'

She sighs. 'I'm glad you see it like that, because I worry about it terribly. I've come here secretly, and I don't know whether I can tell my husband about this talk. It would put him into a bad mood for days.'

Eating Problems

Stewed pears

During the multi-disciplinary consultation the discussion turns to Mrs Boshard. Carer Piet mentions that she is not eating well. He has mentioned this before, he says. She hardly eats because she doesn't enjoy it. Piet suggested that it might taste better with a bit of salt, but she insisted that that isn't the problem. Piet tasted the food, and had to agree with her: there was nothing wrong with the ingredients really, it just wasn't very tasty. 'Food is one of the few pleasures that the residents have,' he says. 'Why can't they have some choice as to what they eat?'

Van Raalten shakes her head: 'That's the policy, and I'm not involved in those decisions.'

If they could cook themselves, that would be best, Piet continues. He describes how, when they sometimes make pancakes, Mrs Boshard eats all hers without a problem; and she loves stewed pears. So we save them for her, and sometimes, after a few days, she says: 'Do you think I'm crazy? I know you've been giving me pears for days.'

The care manager says she will ask the kitchen whether the food could be more varied, but she can't ask them to prepare it differently. She asks about Mrs Boshard's financial situation. 'Not very good,' Piet replies.

Van Raalten: 'Then it will be difficult.'

The occupational therapist offers to bring leftovers from home: she could cook a bit more. Van Raalten shakes her head again. It wouldn't have been prepared and cooled according to official guidelines.

'Well', the occupational therapist protests, 'it's not as though it'll make her sick. We do eat fresh food at home.'

'I don't doubt it, but I have to stick to the rules.'

You have to put the spoon in his mouth

Half past twelve is lunchtime for the residents. This is a labour-intensive time of day in units D and E, where the serious Alzheimer's residents are housed, and I am giving a hand. In the corridor is a large trolley full of food trays. The round blue lids are removed from the steaming plates and the food is mashed with some gravy. Mrs Melkman can eat by herself. Her knitting and the church photo book are put aside. A white bib is tied round her neck and the tray is put in front of her.

Mrs Brugsma does need help. She gazes at me from her wheelchair. There is dried orange juice on her chin. I mash her food and lift a spoonful to her mouth. She stares at me. All around I hear the loud voices of

carers: 'Open your mouth, Mrs Koning.' 'Uncle Wijnand, open wide.'
'Come on now Sientje, be a dear and open.'

I raise my voice and I hear myself saying to the adult opposite me:
'Now doesn't this look tasty?' Mrs Brugsma continues to stare at me.
Next to me Sylvia is feeding two residents simultaneously. Her plates
are soon empty, while I haven't managed to get a single spoonful into
Mrs Brugsma's mouth. I never realised how difficult it was to feed some-
one. 'Maybe you should try sitting on the other side,' Sylvia suggests.
'She eats better when the spoon is coming from the left.' But this doesn't
help either. She closes her mouth tightly.

'Shall I do it?' Sylvia asks, finally.

'Please,' I say, relieved.

Mrs Brugma eats her food. I move to another resident, who also refuses to eat. Again Sylvia comes to the rescue.

'It might work if you try with Mr Koning,' she says, pointing to a tall,
thin man in a grey three-piece suit. He is hunched up in a wheelchair,
his head almost in his lap. I struggle to get my head on the same level as
his, and hold the spoon in front of his mouth. He drools and seems to be
in another world.

'You have to stick the spoon in his mouth, just like a baby,' says Sylvia,
who has just had her fourth baby. I timidly push the tip of the spoon
between his lips. 'Further, further,' she commands. It works. Mr Koning
opens his mouth and swallows.

Alzheimer's disease and eating problems

As Alzheimer's disease advances, sufferers find it increasingly difficult
to eat and drink. They forget how to, and their sensation of hunger and
thirst becomes less acute. When they are no longer able to eat themselves, they have to be assisted. Sometimes they are given dietary supplements.

In the disease's advanced stage there is the danger of choking. In order to prevent this, patients are given liquid or mashed food. When they
reach the final phase of their illness, staff accept that they will eat and
drink insufficiently. However, tube feeding is almost never initiated. If
they have a treatable illness, such as pneumonia, when they are in a less
advanced stage of Alzheimer's, they are given fluid through a tube. This
also facilitates the effect of the medication, which would be less effective
if the patient were dehydrated. In this way, a temporary physical breakdown, in the wider and gradual process of mental decline, can be over-
come.

In the nursing home, fluid is usually administered through hypodermoclysis: the subcutaneous infusion of fluids through needles inserted
into subcutaneous tissue, an easy hydration technique for mildly to mod-
erately dehydrated adult patients, especially the elderly. Fluid and food

can also be administered through a catheter, or through percutaneous endoscopic gastrostomy (PEG), a procedure for placing a tube into the stomach through the abdominal wall.

Nursing home doctors agree that that it is best to use a hypodermoclysis in the case of Alzheimer's patients who suffer from an additional physical illness. But some initiate this process earlier than others. In Park House, for example, Rutger Varenkamp is a supporter of the use of hypodermoclysis. During my stay in the House he initiated this intervention five times a year, while other doctors only did this three times a year on average.

Needles in your leg

In the corridor I run into Rutger Varenkamp. He is on his weekly 'wound rounds'. It is the only time he wears his white doctor's coat. He is on his way to see Mrs Scharloo, an 87-year old Surinamese woman who was admitted to Park House a few weeks ago. She is finding it difficult getting used to the nursing home. The meals are the biggest problem. She refuses to eat or drink, and the reasons are unclear.

The doctor has sought frantically for an underlying medical cause. He has considered all kinds of possibilities, but in vain. Finally he put her on anti-depressants because she seemed sad. This often happens with new residents.

Varenkamp wants to wait and see whether the anti-depressants work. Because the medication can only work if she is not dehydrated, and because she is not drinking, she is receiving hypodermoclysis.

Mrs Scharloo observes us through large eyes when we enter her room. She is in bed and her black frizzy hair is tied back tightly. In her ears there are long gold earrings.

'Good morning Mrs Scharloo,' says the doctor. 'I'm going to give you new needles. Is that okay?'

She nods.

'The needles used to be enormous,' he says. 'We used to have to make a cut in the leg in order to be able to insert them. It was a rather painful exercise. The older carers remember it well. Now the needles are much smaller. Just a little prick, no more.' He goes outside to get some needles. I remain behind with Mrs Scharloo.

'How are things?' I ask.

'Not good,' she mumbles. 'No, not good at all.'

Staff Vicissitudes

Black nurses are so rough

Darah enters Anna van Raalten's office. 'I'm all alone on C. Can you give me a hand?' The Surinamese carer is in her mid-forties. She is wearing a white nurse's uniform and white clogs. She has a broad yellow and red striped scarf covering her frizzy hair. Due to staff shortages Van Raalten, a nurse by training, sometimes helps out. I sit at the meeting table and write notes. Anna van Raalten stands up and gestures me to accompany them. We follow Darah to unit C, where the mid-stage Alzheimer's residents are housed.

In one of the triple rooms Mrs Das is waiting patiently. She is afraid of falling out of bed, Darah warns us. Meanwhile the 90-year-old Mrs Wijntak is sitting in front of a bowl of water in the middle of the room, naked, washing herself with a face cloth. She nods condescendingly as we enter. She is erect and proud and looks self-satisfied. Normally she wears colourful garments and matching beads.

Next to Mrs Wijntak is Mrs Heering, a heavy woman who has to be hauled out of bed with a lift. Together with Anna van Raalten I look for soap, hairbrushes and other toilet articles. The care manager complains: 'Everything here disappears. I keep repeating that things should be tidied up and kept in their proper place, otherwise you can't find anything.'

Mrs Das shivers as she is washed. She is cooperative: put your arm up, put your arm down, turn around. She takes the towel to dry herself. There are photos above her bed. She points to the pictures and explains who's who. 'That's Henk. It's Geert, my nephew. No, it's Kees, Henk, my son, my father...' She shakes her head. 'I don't know any more.'

Anna turns round and whispers to me: 'she doesn't have any children, and she's never been married. She always lived with her parents and took care of them until they died. The photos are all of her sister's family.' Mrs Das nods, as if confirming the words of the care manager. Suddenly she says: 'It's nice to be washed so gently. Those black nurses are so rough.'

The lift to Coroni

Ten thirty is coffee time. But because the carers want to have everyone out of bed before their break, it is often eleven or later before they have coffee. Then the smokers disappear into the restaurant with a mug of coffee and their cigarettes. The others drink their coffee in the office or in the residents' living rooms.

In the living room of unit A and B trainee carer Vanessa is handing round cassava crisps. Her mother sent them over from Surinam. 'You can get them here as well, you know,' trainee Cindy, also Surinamese, informs the group.

The conversation is about colleagues and acquaintances in Surinam. Whenever a name is mentioned, someone says: 'From Para? No from Coroni. Oh yes, of course.'

'So funny,' Vanessa says. 'Mrs Chocolaat from upstairs was waiting for the lift, and she asked me: Nurse, does this lift go to Coroni? I said: It certainly does, come on board.' Vanessa gets up and embraces one of the residents while she sings a Surinamese song. The resident sways with the tune and calls, 'Vanessa, Vanessa.'

Later I ask Vanessa about Mrs Scharloo. She tells me that Mrs Scharloo is not eating and drinking properly. She used to at least eat bread, but now she spits that out as well. A bit of custard, that's all she'll eat now. Mrs Scharloo keeps saying she doesn't want to go on. Vanessa doesn't ask what she means, because she is scared of the answer.

Vanessa laughs shyly. She says that Mrs Van Dam also wasn't eating well last year. She explained the consequences to her. First she said: if you don't eat, you'll get thin. Later she said: If you don't eat, you'll die. Mrs Van Dam didn't want to die, so she started eating again. A few weeks ago she stopped eating again. Vanessa repeated what she had said the previous year. This time Mrs Van Dam said calmly: 'Yes, I know l will die.'

'Are you afraid that Mrs Scharloo will say that as well?' I ask.

She nods vigorously.

'Does it make you feel bad?'

'I worry about it. I wonder whether we couldn't have done more.'

'How is she different from Mrs Van Dam?' I ask.

Vanessa thinks they are very different. Mrs Scharloo has just moved into the nursing home and Vanessa thinks it sad that she has already lost her will to live.

Black teams

Rutger Varenkamp is sitting in his office in unit C updating residents' files. In the corridor radio Salto, the Surinamese station, blares. Today all the carers in the House are Surinamese or Antillean. Loud voices can be heard; too loud. And they are not speaking Dutch. Without looking up from his notes, the doctor says: 'Officially they're not supposed to speak Surinamese in here,' he says, 'but it happens nonetheless, and I don't want to have to keep saying so.'

Many of the carers in Park House are Surinamese. Five years ago this was 40 percent. It was decided then to limit the recruitment of foreign carers in order to achieve some semblance of balance, as most of the residents were indigenous. The generation to which the residents belong is not used to people from other ethnic groups, and this sometimes leads to funny situations, but also to unpleasant confrontations. Coloured workers sometimes feel they are being discriminated against by residents and, especially, relatives – all reasons for keeping an eye on the ethnic balance.

But in the current climate of the labour market there is little choice. Currently 60 percent of carers in Park House are foreign. The figure is slightly biased, because almost all the temps are coloured. And they are not spread evenly: some units have greater concentrations of coloured staff than others. Some units have entirely 'black teams'.

Enquiries in other nursing homes reveal that there also more than half of the carers are coloured. There is also a correlation between the colour of the carers and the affliction of the residents. Residents with treatable physical afflictions that require technical skills have relatively more white carers. In revalidation departments there are also more white staff. In departments with many people with Alzheimer's three quarters of the carers are coloured. This is related to the level of schooling required: staff in Alzheimer's departments generally have lower levels of education than in other departments.

Cultural differences

When I enquire about cultural differences both groups shrug: no, there is no difference between working with white and black colleagues. They won't say any more. I don't believe them, because they hardly mix socially, in the restaurant, for example.

'We know each other, so we tend to sit together,' the Surinamese carers tell me. 'It's easier to chat.'

'We sit with those we know best,' a white carer says.

'Come on,' I say, 'don't tell me there are no differences.' They smile and shrug. Honestly, but also provocatively, I say to a group of Surinamese carers: 'I enjoy being with you; it's good fun.' They laugh and nod in agreement.

Then one of them says: 'We attach more importance to eating.' And indeed, in the breaks they spend a lot of time discussing what they are going to cook and where to buy the best ingredients. Everyone has an address where they can buy a tub of peanut sauce for a discount. It's way up in the north of the city, but worth it if you have to prepare *saté* for a whole crowd coming to a birthday party.

I enjoy participating in these culinary discussions. Someone asks how I make saffron rice. I feel pangs of hunger as Christa describes her chicken marinade. The next day she brings me some to try. The Surinamese carers often bring their own meals. Sometimes their children bring them food. In the weekend they often cook themselves in the activity centre. They all bring a few ingredients. It is striking, they remark, that the 'Hollanders' enjoy eating with us, but never bring anything themselves.

When I have been in Park House longer I find out more about black-white differences. Regarding differences in the way they work, the Surinamese carer Justine tells me: 'Dutch carers are more consistent. If we're with a white colleague and she says we have to dress residents, we do it, we don't say: Let's do that later. If it's a Surinamese colleague who says that, no one gets up.' But Justine thinks that Surinamese colleagues do a better job at bodily care. They will make an extra effort to use body lotion and deodorant, and will spend time selecting clothes for the day. 'Hollanders just go bam! bam! bam! and they're finished.'

Justine also talks about the sensitive issues between the Dutch and Surinamese carers. For example, the rule that Surinamers are not allowed to speak Surinamese. The person responsible for that rule is referred to as a 'shit-head'. Why shouldn't they be allowed to speak their other tongue? Though Justine herself does think this might upset residents.

And then there are the celebrations marking the abolition of slavery on the 1st of July, a day that Surinamers often want to take off. If a white colleague has a comment about the celebration, or wants to know why it warrants a day off, the situation can become tense, says Justine. Whenever Surinamers feel hard done by, they immediately draw parallels with slavery, and they accuse the Dutch of having exploited their ancestors.

Justine thinks that the reference to slavery in the twenty-first century is exaggerated. Of course you should respect your culture and know your heritage. Of course you should be allowed to celebrate days that are important and wear traditional clothes on those days. But she thinks it wrong to treat all Dutch people of all historical periods in the same way.

Too few carers

Anna van Raalten is sitting behind her desk. The phone rings continually: staff reporting sick. The calls all sound the same: 'What a pity. So what is wrong exactly? When do you think you'll be able to come back? Okay, well, get better soon.'

The same happens with those on long-term sick leave, who have to report regularly on their condition: 'How are things now? Why don't you call in and we can have coffee? Yes, that would be much better, because the longer you're away, the more difficult it is to come back. No, let's make an appointment *now*, otherwise we'll never get round to it. How about next Tuesday? I'll put it in my diary, and tell the others. We'll be expecting you. All the best.'

She is often on the phone to the temp agency trying to organise staff for holidays and to cover sick leave. And she often complains about temp staff that don't show up. On the door of her office there is a notice:

Do you want to earn 50 euros? Then work at Christmas and over the New Year and you'll get 50 euros extra.

When she notices me reading it, she tells me that she can't get staff any other way. She is now busy organising transport for Christmas, as there will hardly be any public transport, and staff would have to come in by taxi, which is expensive and unreliable, she says. She is trying to get Paul, from physiotherapy, to pick up the carers with a mini-bus. Fortunately they all live quite close together.

We talk on. I tell her that I think it a pity that Cindy has to interrupt her training as a carer because she won't be able to afford the train fare when she moves. 'Interruption? What interruption? She will just give up, of course,' Van Raalten says decidedly.

'Yes, it might be difficult to pick things up again,' I say. 'Especially if she has a child.'

'She'll never have the discipline to start again,' Van Raalten continues. 'She'd probably have stopped anyway. She isn't the only one. It's as though the trainees don't have any sense of responsibility. The training is all paid for, and they've already done part of it. When you've got that far you don't just stop.' I nod bewilderedly and swallow what I was going to say about considering lending her the money.

No evening shift

At the end of the day shift, at half past three, Anna van Raalten says that she can't get anyone for the evening shift for unit D, and for unit E she can only find one assistant nurse. She has been trying all day. 'I'll leave it with you,' she says to the group, as she gets up to leave. After she has gone there is much mumbling.

Ten minutes later a group of carers has assembled outside the care manager's office. They suggest solutions. Mildred recommends a friend and tries to call her on her mobile. 'Here is the boss,' she says, handing the phone to Van Raalten, who is ten years her junior. Van Raalten takes the phone, stony-faced. Everyone laughs.

The phone call provides someone for the evening shift. But that doesn't solve the problem. A bit later Colette calls in, at the end of her day shift and with her coat on ready to go home. She offers to do a double shift, and the offer is accepted without hesitation. She phones her children: 'There is some food in the fridge. If you want to eat something else, you can order something.' As she hangs up, she says: 'They're used to having everything ready for them.'

A week later I run into Colette in the corridor. She is busy putting away residents' clothes that have come back from the laundry. She tells me that she finished her training as carer three years ago. When her twins were about thirteen, she drove them mad at home. They said: 'Mum, please find something to do.' She had always wanted to be a carer, and she enjoys her work, especially the interactions with the residents. 'They're such dears, and you really feel that you mean something to them.' When she is on the evening shift she often brings sausage, cheese and fruit juice for the residents. She wants them to have a nice time.

Colette says that she has been accepted for training as a nurse in the hospital, but has decided to stay in the nursing home instead. She is attached to 'her' residents and would miss them. And anyway, so many of the carers are leaving. She is genuinely concerned for the residents, and tells me that continuity is very important for them, especially those with Alzheimer's. Mrs Sterk, for example, is very sensitive to change and to strangers. She gets very upset if she doesn't know the person who is putting her to bed. Then the new carer tends to think she is being difficult. It's a problem for her, but also for the regular carers, who have to give her extra attention to calm her down again. 'It's because of things like that that I sometimes have to report sick. If I've been doing double shifts, as I often do, then an incident like that is the final straw. It's worst in the summer, when many of the permanent staff are on leave.'

Mrs Scharloo Doesn't Want To Go On

A miserable wretch

Mrs Scharloo is the Surinamese lady who was brought to the nursing home without anyone telling her where she was going. For weeks she is the major topic of discussion during the multi-disciplinary consultation.

'Mrs Scharloo is eating a bit better now,' says Darah during one of these meetings. 'But you have to keep an eye on her, because as soon as you turn your back she spits it out again. Or she empties her plate behind the radiator.'

'It's something between her ears,' sighs Rutger Varenkamp. 'There's no physical cause. We've looked at absolutely everything.'

'Yesterday she was in bed by seven, and kept pulling out the hypodermoclysis needles,' says Darah. 'I had to keep sticking them back.'

'Maybe we should use tape to keep them in place?' says the doctor. 'It's difficult to know what she wants. Initially she said she didn't want hypodermoclysis. But when I told her about the possible consequences she decided she did.'

'But Rutger, is she really capable of making a decision like that?' asks Anna van Raalten.

'It's difficult to say,' the doctor hesitates. 'She is capable of deciding about minor issues, but not about whether or not she wants to die.'

'Her children hope she will recover,' says Darah.

'That's to be expected,' Varenkamp retorts. 'They feel guilty, don't they.'

Darah says that Mrs Scharloo keeps pulling the blankets over her head and saying: 'I don't want to go on, I don't want to go on.'

Anna van Raalten proposes consulting a psychologist in order to find out how best to deal with her. It will also help her to 'get her own thoughts in order'.

'We have to avoid becoming despondent,' she adds. 'It must be difficult for you all. Do you talk about it among yourselves?'

Darah says that some of the carers have had enough of it. Mrs Scharloo says 'yes' when she means 'no', and she doesn't have any contact with the other residents. She just sits by herself, a miserable wretch.

'But she *is* a miserable wretch,' says the doctor. 'She wants to live, but not like this, in a nursing home, and without anybody consulting her. That's the cause of all this yes-no business. I hope the anti-depressants start working, otherwise she will really die.'

The physiotherapy department and the activity centre have taken Mrs Scharloo into their care. 'We are trying to keep her busy, but she is easily overwhelmed,' says Marga, of the activity centre. 'As soon as there are more than three or four people in the centre, she wants to leave. When we had her by herself the other day, she drank two cups of tea.'

'What does she like?' asks Anna van Raalten.

'We put on the Surinamese radio channel,' says Darah. 'But she didn't respond.'

Rutger Varenkamp makes notes: 'I'll ask the psychologist to call in.'

He looks at Darah: 'It's difficult for you all to get her to do what you want, but you have to assume that she's depressive, and that we can't take everything she says at face value. She has to have medication, and she needs to drink, in order to get out of that rut. We'll keep the hypodermoclysis in at night as well.'

Swallow! Mouth open! Drink!

A few days later I go and see Mrs Scharloo in the living room of unit C. She is sitting alone at a table. Above the table there are two paintings of Surinamese rice paddies, sent by her family and hung up by Rutger Varenkamp. An attempt has been made to make the place more like home, as advised by the psychologist. One painting is not quite straight; the other is partly obscured by the salmon-coloured curtain.

A carer is feeding Mrs Scharloo: 'Here, have another spoonful. It's really tasty.' Mrs Scharloo opens her mouth. 'Well done dear. One more spoon.' When the carer is distracted by another resident and turns her head, Mrs Scharloo quickly takes the food from her mouth and puts it on the plate of the resident next to her. This process is repeated several times. Then a tremendous stench rises, and on the floor, between Mrs Scharloo's feet, a pool of diarrhoea gradually spreads outwards. As it runs down her legs the carer continues to feed her.

Later that afternoon Mrs Scharloo's eldest son and his wife come to visit. They are already in their late sixties. The son is wearing a jogging suit and a baseball cap. 'Ma has to get used to the place,' the daughter-in-law says. 'She says: The nurses are nice, but the home isn't. You know, she lived in another home for years. She had to leave. We couldn't do anything about that. We do our best, but it's very time consuming.'

'Everything will be okay,' the son says.

Darah has been trying all morning to give Mrs Scharloo her anti-depressants. She now gives the pill to the daughter-in-law. 'Maybe you'll succeed,' she says.

'Swallow!' the daughter-in-law commands. 'Mouth open, let's see whether you've swallowed it.' Mrs Scharloo still has the pill in her mouth, but keeps her mouth tightly shut. 'Drink! Swallow! Mouth open! Come on, let's see,' the daughter-in-law commands, holding the cup of water to Mrs Scharloo's mouth and pushing her head back. Mrs Scharloo resists and keeps her mouth closed. Her son takes her hand and speaks to her softly, but firmly, in Surinamese. She looks at him with large, innocent eyes. Then she opens her mouth and the pill has gone.

In the corridor Darah grabs my arm: 'Did you see that? They're forcing those pills down her throat. She didn't want them; she resisted. They're threatening not to visit if she doesn't eat and drink. It's terrible how they treat her. It's not nice looking after her, because you don't get anything in return.'

No porridge

I look in on Mrs Scharloo every day. The situation remains critical. Rutger Varenkamp has been keeping track of what she eats: liquid food - banana flavour – rice pudding, no porridge! He has also been noting how she wants it: only from a normal cup, not a cup with a lid and a spout, like the ones given to babies.

One afternoon I meet Alma in the living room. She is in her fifties and is to assist in the living room as part of a scheme to get the unemployed back to work. It's her first day. Mrs Scharloo is at the table, slumped forward. She has hardly eaten anything, says Alma. She hasn't touched the lemonade all morning. Rutger Varenkamp enters and sits at the table next to Mrs Scharloo.

'Do you want to drink something?'

She nods.

'In this cup,' says the doctor, pointing to the cup with the spout, 'or in an ordinary cup?'

'An ordinary one.'

'I thought so. I'll put it in an ordinary one.'

Mrs Scharloo picks up the cup with both hands and takes a few sips.

'What did she eat this morning?' asks the doctor.

'She spits everything out,' answers Alma from the sofa, as she leafs through a magazine. 'I need a break,' she says. 'Busy morning.'

'What did you give her?'

'Porridge.'

'She doesn't like porridge,' says the doctor, irritated. She only likes rice pudding.

'I've only just started. How should I know? No one told me.'

'It's all in her file.'

'I don't know anything about the file,' says Alma and she continues to page through the magazine. 'They told me to give her porridge.'

The doctor sighs. 'Mrs Scharloo, do you want to eat something? Do you want some liquid food?'

Christa is on the evening shift. She is forty-three, Surinamese, and her hair is a mass of small braids clinging tightly to her skull. She is making soup. When she sees me sitting with Mrs Scharloo she calls: 'You're concerned about her, hey? That woman, yes, that woman has something.

She won't last long. She doesn't have the energy. Everything that gives her energy she spits out.' Christa's voice echoes through the living room.

'What does she have,' I ask, after rushing over to her to prevent her from talking so loudly. I feel uncomfortable talking about Mrs Scharloo in her presence, and that of other residents.

Christa tells me that she has spoken to the temps who looked after Mrs Scharloo in the care home, before she came to Park House. Christa thinks that the sudden change of environment has affected her; that she is angry with her children for having forced her to move, and that she is not happy with her life in the nursing home. So unhappy that she wants to die. But her religion is a problem. She is Roman Catholic, and 'they aren't allowed to ask to be allowed to die. Only the man up there can decide that for them,' Christa says.

Christa has tried her best to repair the relationship between Mrs Scharloo and her children. A lot of the carers have noticed that she is angry, and even the head of the evening shift commented on her angry expression. When her relatives came to visit, Christa took them aside and said: 'Even the head of the evening shift, who is white, has noticed that there is something wrong with your mother. You have to do some-thing. It's not good that you didn't prepare her for the nursing home. You shouldn't have treated her like that. She is an adult woman and you should treat her with respect.'

Christa had given them a calabash of water and taken them to a quiet room, together with Mrs Scharloo, so they could 'do what they had to do'. They all drank from the water and poured some out on the floor. And then they talked. It was the Surinamese way of resolving conflict and achieving forgiveness.

Something to make you less dejected

Rutger Varenkamp pushes Mrs Scharloo's wheelchair into his office.

'How are things?' he asks.

Mrs Scharloo nods and fiddles with the hypodermoclysis needles in her leg.

'Do the needles hurt?'

'Yes.'

'Do you want me to remove them?'

She nods vigorously.

'Then you have to drink properly,' says Varenkamp. 'Look at me, Mrs Scharloo. If you keep refusing to drink you will get weaker and weaker. Do you understand? Look at me, I want to ask you an important ques-tion: are you feeling dejected?'

She looks down at the floor.

'Are you dejected because you are here?'

She nods.

'It wasn't working out in the place you were before. They couldn't take care of you properly there. Understand?'

She turns away.

'Are you not eating because you feel dejected?'

She shakes her head.

'Then why aren't you eating?'

Silence.

'Don't you want to tell me?'

She turns her face away.

He takes her hands: 'Mrs Scharloo, I'll remove the needles. Then I'm going to be away for a few days. During those days you must try to eat and drink. Or would you prefer to be fed through a tube?'

She looks him in the eye and shakes her head.

He pats her arm and moves to his desk. 'I'm going to give you something to make you less dejected,' he says.

The big guns

Later that afternoon Rutger Varenkamp returns to the topic of Mrs Scharloo. He's going to bring in the big guns, he says. In addition to the antidepressant he has already given her, he is going to give her another injectable one. She won't be able to spit that one out. Varenkamp hopes that this will help. He has the feeling that something is upsetting her, but can't find out what it is.

He is agitated and drums his fingers on the table. Mrs Scharloo still hasn't told him what the problem is. He wonders whether he will ever win enough trust to find out. He doesn't think her family are exactly running over with love for her. They visit, but they find it inconvenient. Especially the daughter-in-law, who talks a lot and doesn't listen, says Varenkamp. The children don't get on among themselves either. One daughter phoned Varenkamp to say she wanted to buy new clothes for her mother, but then the daughter-in-law said that her husband was having none of it.

The doctor says he is having a few days off. He hopes that a miracle will happen in those days, that Mrs Scharloo will be laughing and enjoying her meals when her returns. But he is worried that she won't make it. The way she is eating she could suffer for months, he says. If that has to happen then it would be better for her if she died quickly.

Yes, that's how far his thoughts have developed, he says. Her situation is extremely grave. That's why it's important that the carers take feeding her properly seriously. It's not as though it is that difficult. He has written what she wants to eat in her file and in the kitchen notes. And he has hung a list up on the kitchen cupboards. Weeks ago he wrote on the tins of supplements in the kitchen how many spoons each resident should get. 'Nothing can go wrong, you think. But then they don't read what you've written everywhere.' His tone is sarcastic. 'You saw yourself today how things went. Sometimes I'm on the point of exploding.'

And that's not only in the case of Mrs Scharloo. He says he has to remind them a few times a day. Anna van Raalten doesn't agree with this. She thinks that once something has been agreed in the meeting it shouldn't have to be repeated and the carers are responsible for seeing that it is carried out. That is fine in theory, but if it doesn't get done then the residents are the losers, he complains.

Mrs Bos passes the office and looks through the window. She stares at us and says, with her shrill, singsong voice: 'Two people. I can see two people.' The she looks down the corridor. 'Hey, someone's coming.' A woman appears and kisses Mrs Bos. 'Hey, it's my daughter.'

Rutger Varenkamp smiles. After a while he says: 'Maybe I should be less strict with the carers. Maybe they just need more time. You know, I tell my kids a hundred times a day to hang up their coats, and they still don't do it. It's a bit like that.'

The situation round Mrs Scharloo continues to exercise everyone in the department. I notice while browsing through her file that she is a keen churchgoer. However, no one seems to be aware of this. When I raise this with the 'humanist' counsellor,[6] she replies: 'We only get involved when we are asked. This lady obviously hasn't made a request.' She says she will inform her colleague, Pieter Verdoorn, the pastor.

A few days later I notice a note in her file saying that the pastor has been to see her. Assistant carer Jessy comes in and asks what I'm reading. I tell her. Jessy was on shift that day, and she tells me that after the pastor had left Mrs Scharloo had been very talkative. She said she prayed every day for strength. Jessy had never heard her talk so much. She had been looking forward to the church service on Sunday, but she ended up not going because she was still in bed when they came to get her because the carers didn't know they had to get her up early for church. Jessy had put on a tape with church music, but it didn't help. Jessy thinks her physical condition has deteriorated: she is short of breath and wheezes. 'Fluid in her lungs,' Jessy thinks. She is also still hardly eating and drinking. Jessy thinks it is resistance, a kind of hunger strike. Apparently she walked a bit with the physiotherapist. When Jessy or one of the carers tries to walk with her she just lets herself fall on the floor.

Go to the other side, mama

A week later Christa tells me that Mrs Scharloo has passed away. Friday she started coughing up blood. Saturday morning she complained of pain in her chest. The carers had washed her and put her in the living room. 'She didn't look happy,' Christa told me. 'Her breathing was heavy and the whites of her eyes were yellow. We gave her some dessert, but she spit it out.'

Christa tested her blood sugar level. It was much too low. They put her to bed. When they were undressing her they saw that her body was covered with red patches. They called her family immediately and said they had to come at once. They were already on their way; it seems they had had a premonition.

Christa made Mrs Scharloo up with some powder. They spoke in Surinamese, to calm her down. Surinamese colleagues from other units came together. There were six of them. 'Her family wasn't here yet, so we acted as her family,' Christa says.

The dying woman said she wanted to see her children. Christa said: 'They're coming. They're not here yet, but we're your people and we are here, just like your grandchildren. So go to the other side, mama, if you want to, and protect us who remain behind.'

Christa held her hand when she died. She thinks that Mrs Scharloo was a good woman, because she died easily. Christa tells me that Surinamers believe that bad people take long to die.

Christa feels different when she is with Dutch residents compared to Surinamese residents because she is Surinamese. If a Dutch resident dies, she speaks Dutch and strokes her head and says: 'Go to sleep dear and rest.' She feels more involved when a Surinamese resident dies; she has to act like a granddaughter. 'I have a different kind of bond with my compatriots,' she says. 'You see your own grandmother in them. Not that I give them preferential treatment, because we are all the same in the final instance. We all bleed the same, whether white or black.'

Christa laid Mrs Scharloo out in the Surinamese manner. You have to purify yourself by washing your hands and face with alcohol, she explains, because you are no longer the same as the dead person. The dead have become ghosts, spirits, but you are still alive. 'If your spirit is weak, you could sicken.' Christa couldn't find any alcohol in the nursing home so she laid Mrs Scharloo out and then phoned home and told her sister she needed some alcohol. 'My sister had some beer in the fridge. That was much too cold, so she warmed it on the heater.'

Christa went into her house backwards when she got home. 'You have to do that when a ghost is following you. If you look it straight in the eye then it won't follow you in.' When she got home she washed herself with the warm beer. Then she put some perfume, which contained seven spirits, in a calabash. She then washed herself with that as well. As she was doing this she talked to herself: 'Yes, I laid her out. It's all work, I mustn't let anything interfere.'

It is important to approach the dead in the right way, Christa explains. Death is a transition to another world. Relatives have to treat the spirit of the deceased in the same way they would treat the living: with respect; if they don't, the deceased will extract vengeance.

Winti

After the death of Mrs Scharloo Christa spoke often about Surinamese rituals; also about *winti*. Christa liked to talk of these things, she said, though she didn't do so often. 'Hollanders think it's all superstition,' she says. 'I hate it when people say that. I grew up with it. It's my religion. If I accept their beliefs then they should accept mine.'

Winti means spirit. There are different kinds of spirits and they live in the forests. There are also the spirits of the dead. Knowledge of *winti* is passed from one generation to the next. Christa's knowledge of it comes from her mother. *Winti* 'comes on you' and possesses you; but not everyone. Christa's mother had 'it'. When she died it was only Christa and a younger sister, out of eleven children, who inherited it from her.

Winti can 'come on you' when you are in trance. That doesn't just happen. You can create a trance state through music or dance. It can also happen when you are angry. When you get *winti* you do things you wouldn't normally do. You may speak in tongues, or eat broken glass. Sometimes you dance on hot coals or broken glass. If *winti* is in you then you don't feel anything, but if the *winti* leaves you, the shards will cut your feet.

There are *wintis* that are strong, and if you have one you can beat ten men. Christa says she has seen a youth with such a *winti* who pulled a street lamp out of the ground. Some *wintis* need beer or strong liquor. If you provide these then you can ask questions. This usually happens when there are problems. The *winti* will give answers.

Christa is often possessed by *winti*. Last year she was in Surinam and underwent rituals with a medicine woman in the forest. *Winti* possessed her and she started talking about her brother. When she recovered the medicine woman told her that her brother was seriously ill. Christa was unaware of this. If something wasn't done soon, said the medicine woman, then he would die. The only hope was for him to undergo traditional rituals.

Christa went back to the Netherlands and straight to her brother. He wasn't at home and it turned out that he had been admitted to hospital. He had lumps in his stomach and the doctors were baffled. Christa rushed him back to Surinam where the rituals took place. Just in time. He later recovered completely. Someone who wanted him dead had sent the illness, says, Christa.

If you want to harm someone you can go to a medicine man. He sends the victim something, usually a 'basket' containing various substances. This can be placed on a street corner in the neighbourhood where the victim lives, and when he passes, it 'gets' him and something happens to him.

Not all medicine men do this kind of black magic, and it is often disapproved of in the community. It is seen as an abuse of the supernatural powers of the *wintis* to harm others for your own gain. There is also the danger that the spirits will become angry and turn their powers against the perpetrator.

In Park House there are quite a few carers who believe in *winti*. 'If you observe us carefully,' says Christa, 'you'll see we wear certain kinds of jewellery, and special beads. Those are for *winti*. Sometimes your body asks for certain jewellery. Then you have to go and buy it, otherwise things won't go well for you.'

There are also Surinamese carers who are not involved in *winti*. Darah, for example, grew up in a different kind of environment. Her mother was not like that, Christa says. She was Christian. Christa is also Christian, and believes in God, but she doesn't see any conflict between Christianity and *winti*.

Daily Care

Shit

One morning Anna van Raalten accosts me: 'It's really busy today and Sylvia has twelve residents to get out of bed. Can you give a hand?' When I get to the unit I find Sylvia, Rutger Varenkamp and a medical student there. They are all washing and dressing residents. Sylvia accompanies me to Mrs Melkman's room and explains what I have to do: 'She wears a bra, a shirt and an inco. You have to apply this ointment to the lesions on her buttocks as well. She can wash herself, though.'

Mrs Melkman is not in her room. I find the 83-year-old in the living room, in her nightgown, eating fried eggs, hair unkempt. Before I reach her table she stands up and strides past me, cursing, into the corridor: 'You're crazy! I always have to do everything myself.' I follow her and, taking her hand, lead her to her room. She continues to curse.

'You like Mozart, don't you?' I ask.

'Of course.'

'Shall I put on some music then?'

She shrugs: 'Do what you like.'

I sort through her clothes and hold up a blouse: 'How about this?'

'Ugh! That ugly thing. I'd rather wear something plain.'

I hold up another blouse.

'My clothes are all so ugly, horrible.'

She takes off her nightgown and throws it on the bed and starts to scrub her face with a facecloth, as Mozart floats up from the ghetto blaster. This has a calming effect.

Then she crouches slightly and before I realize what is happening she is standing in the middle of a large pool of watery diarrhoea. 'Just look at this!' she exclaims. 'What a mess; my sister's such a slob. I always have to do everything by myself.'

She walks around the room and wipes her hands on the side of the sink. An unpleasant odour fills the room and I retch.

The floor, the sink, Mrs Melkman – everything is covered in shit.

I wonder how I am ever going to clean it up.

I count to ten and then ask: 'How is Maxima, by the way?' (Maxima is the Argentinean girlfriend of the Dutch crown-prince, Willem-Alexander.)

On the table lays Mrs Melkman's collection of well-worn gossip magazines. The cover of the top magazine displays a picture of Maxima.

'Have you spoken to her?' I ask.

'Of course,' she answers, curtly. 'That Willem-Alexander has to decide whether or not he's going to marry her. He's crazy, that lad.'

'I agree,' I say, nodding. 'Is Maxima very sad?'

'Of course she's sad,' Mrs Melkman continues, incredulously. 'She's always sad. She's crazy'.

She stops walking around. I wonder what to do. The shit is everywhere. There are brown footprints all through the room. I guide her to a chair and then, with a wad of paper towels I wipe up the worst of the shit. In the sink I mix some shampoo with warm water and with a towel I clean the floor. Then I wash and dress Mrs Melkman. I open the window and the smell gradually recedes.

Daubing

It is my second experience with shit in Park House. The first time I hadn't realised what was happening. One morning I came into the guest room and noticed a terrible stench. A blocked drain, I thought. Patricia, the cleaner came in - a tall, slim Surinamese woman in her late fifties with a diamond embedded in one of her front teeth. She leaned on her mop: 'Would you mind locking the door when you've been in here. Otherwise the residents come in and do their... you know... in here. Yesterday the room was full: piles in every corner.'

She roared with laughter at my bewildered expression: 'You're not used to this, are you? They're very clever; they go anywhere where the door is open and they crouch.' She crouches in imitation. 'We have to lock the linen room. They do it there as well, right on top of all the clean sheets.'

From that moment on I started to pay more attention to what was said in the handover meeting between shifts. It was not pleasant when carers talked about residents being 'faeces incontinent'. But it didn't sound so bad either, hearing them tell of 'daubing' or treading in shit and slipping. It sounded just like the reporting of eating patterns or medication.

Colette laughs when I mention it to her. 'Daubing keeps us busy,' she says. 'Mrs Vriesma even digs it out of her anus! The nightshift cleans her and her bed every night, but the day shift always have to start again. You smell it in the morning as soon as you enter. She's covered from head to toe every morning; it's in her hair, on her face, everywhere.' I try to imagine Mrs Vriesma, who always has a friendly smile, covered in shit. I can't.

'What do you do?'

'Clean up,' answers Colette.

'Naturally,' I mumble.

'First I get her to sit on the pot. I don't want to touch her like that. Then I get her under the shower and try and soak off the crusts. It's not easy, because it's under her nails and everywhere. It's worse for Mrs Bakker and Mrs Boshard who share the room with her.'

'You must have a hard time,' I say. 'And I thought that I had a hard time with Mrs Melkman.'

'It's terrible in the beginning, but you learn. It's easy if you have one resident covered in shit. It gets difficult when you have to make a choice. What should you do first and what can wait?' She tells me about a trainee who came to her upset because Mrs Vriesma was covered in shit and Mrs Boshard desperately needed the toilet. She didn't know what to do and decided to help Mrs Vriesma first. Mrs Boshard got angry and in protest lit up a cigarette in bed.

This difficult thing about this work, says Colette, is that so much happens at once. She hears herself saying: 'I'll be there in a minute,' but often she doesn't get there because she doesn't have time. And then there are the residents' relatives who also need attention. Some relatives are very difficult and demanding, and that can be frustrating when you are busy.

Colette asks me whether I know the book *No Time To Be Nice*. It describes the pressure under which carers have to work because they always have to do so much at once. Colette lends it to me.

Compensation

Rutger Varenkamp has prepared me: Mrs Molenaar's family is difficult. 'We have our hands full with them,' he sighs. 'Every time they phone – and they phone often – I think: What now? In the past Mrs Molenaar didn't have much contact with her sons, who hardly visited her. The daughters-in-law did. The laundry is a recurrent theme. The daughters-in-law wash Mrs Molenaar's clothes, but sometimes things get mixed up and her clothes are washed in the nursing home. Underwear disappears, or pleated skirts get ironed flat. The daughters-in-law submit an official complaint about everything that goes wrong. They have had various meetings with the director. It takes up a lot of everyone's time to sort things out.'

The doctor has invited the daughters-in-law for a meeting because Mrs Molenaar's condition has deteriorated. Have they noticed? Rutger Varenkamp wonders. They nod when he tells them such things, he says, but then go straight on to complain about something trivial. Mrs Molenaar won't die in the next few days, because her physical condition is reasonable, but he is worried that her Alzheimer's is becoming worse. As a result she often almost chokes. It is time to decide on what to do.

Two well-groomed women in their late forties are waiting in the corridor. They are tanned and gym-slim, with ankle-length skirts and T-shirts. We chat amicably over coffee.

'The reason I asked you to come,' Rutger says, 'is to give you an update. We've spoken a few times on the phone about various problems and sometimes we run into each other in the corridor, but I think it's good to occasionally have a more official meeting. Your mother-in-law's condition is deteriorating and I think it is a good time to talk about...'

'Ma isn't what she was, we can see that. But when you see all the things she still *can* do, it's impressive.'

'How often do they wash her?' the other daughter-in-law asks.

'Every morning,' answers Darah. 'And they change her after lunch...'

'Does she still do that? Incredible!' They both put their hands over their mouths in surprise.

' ...and before going to bed,' Darah continues.

'Your mother-in-law wears an incontinence device,' the doctor says. 'It absorbs the urine, so she doesn't notice, just like a baby. If she does something else in between and the carers smell it, then of course they change her as well. They don't wait for the next toilet round.'

'I don't know who it was,' says one of the daughters-in-law. 'I think it was Sylvia. Last week Ma had really messed herself, and when I got the washing there were her knickers, rinsed and in a plastic bag. Now that's cooperation! She puts it in a bag, and I do the rest. I'm impressed. I agreed to do the washing, so I'm not complaining. As dirty as it is, it's my own family...'

Rutger Varenkamp nods: 'I'm glad you're happy with how things went last week. Now if we could just discuss...'

'I thought I'd mention it. I met Sylvia last Tuesday, and Friday the knickers were in the bag. Lets be honest: things have been different.' Her tone becomes threatening. 'There has been underwear just mixed in with the washing: no plastic bag at all. And then I wonder: Is that really necessary? At least they could put it in a bag.' Her sister-in-law chips in: 'My husband gets queasy when he hears that sort of thing. No, he is not happy at all. He was planning to phone you.'

'Alright,' says the doctor, 'I want to talk to you about your mother-in-law: her condition is deteriorating.'

'I'm glad you mentioned that,' says one of the daughters-in-law. 'I spoke to one of the carers a while ago. I won't mention any names, but you know who I mean.' She nods meaningfully. 'I asked how Ma was and she said, just there in the corridor, that she wouldn't last long. Bang! Just like that. I thought that was really callous. My husband said: That's unacceptable. I was upset. Remember, I called you about it. I thought you should be aware what sort of things happen here.'

The doctor nods: 'I know. Things like that can seem hard. That's why it's good that we have this opportunity to talk, because your mother-in-law doesn't have eternal life.'

'You know,' she interrupts, 'it was more *how* she said it, just like that, so suddenly and coldly. Ma had become worse, but not that bad.'

'She has an illness that is destroying her brain, and eventually it will kill her.'

'Terrible!'

'Well, she doesn't notice...' the doctor tries to say.

'Not for her. Ma has no idea. But for *us*. Yes, I see it in the children. I said to my daughter last week, Rutger from Park House phoned. He wants to talk about Granny, because she is getting worse. She cried all afternoon and I had to comfort her.'

She nods and wipes her eyes with a tissue. 'Yes, my daughter is getting married in December. She said: Oh Ma, maybe Granny won't be there. I thought: How can I solve this one?'

'Yes,' the doctor tries again. 'It is the question whether your mother-in-law will be here in December. I'm being honest with you, because...'

'I said to my daughter: if Granny is still here, then we'll visit her after the wedding. She can't come to the wedding, but we can go to her.'

'Yes,' the doctor nods, 'we can't say with certainty how long it will take.'

'That's really something, you know, really something.'

'The fact is that your mother-in-law is getting closer to the phase of taking leave, and it's good to talk about it. We have already said that drips and infusions will only cause her more discomfort, and it won't help her.' The daughters-in-law nod. 'We think that people shouldn't have to suffer,' the doctor continues. 'We'll give her medication against shortness of breath and pain. I assume you agree with that.' They nod again.

'I'll write it in her file and when the time comes that Mrs Molenaar is in pain or short of breath, we'll call you to discuss the issue again. Do you have any questions?'

'Yes, certainly. Doctor, you know that my mother-in-law's spectacles are missing. They cost more than 400 euros. We submitted a claim for compensation months ago, but we haven't had a reply yet. The glasses are gone, I know, but we want the compensation, so my girls can buy a permanent reminder of their Gran. Doctor, I'm assuming that you are going to cooperate on this.'

Bringing them up by phone

After the meeting with Mrs Molenaar's daughters-in-law I walk with Darah to the living room of unit C. Darah tells me she has applied for the job of care coordinator. Her colleagues persuaded her to. She hopes she will be short-listed. Then she yawns. She has been working for ten days without a break. Tomorrow she is free. Then she will finally have time to clean the house and do the shopping. She is a single mother with three daughters, between nine and thirteen. She travels three hours every day to and from work.

'You must be up early,' I say.

'At five. Then I get breakfast ready and make a start with dinner. I try and do a few household chores as well. This morning I did some ironing.'

Darah tells me that her husband left when her youngest child was three. From that moment she had to support the family financially. It was then that she started working in the nursing home. She is still in contact with her ex-husband, and he occasionally gives her some money for the children, but not much. Basically he gives her something if she is nice to him.

Darah works mostly in the evenings. She tells her children never to open the door to anyone. They don't. Last week they wouldn't even open it for their father. 'They told him they weren't allowed to open to anyone,' says Darah roaring with laughter. 'He just went away.'

'Are they alone at home?' I ask. Darah says that the three of them stay together. When she has evening shift she makes sure the food is pre-pared before she leaves. They have a list for whose turn it is to do the dishes and that sort of thing. And she calls them regularly to check whether they have cleaned up and help them with their homework. She is bringing them up by phone, she says. They also call her. She takes a mobile phone out of her white coat pocket. 'It's much easier these days,' she says.

Our conversation is interrupted by Mrs Goslinga, who calls from the living room: 'Darah, I can hear your voice. Are you there?'

'Yes, Mrs Goslinga, I'm here,' Darah calls from the corridor.

'Listen, Darah, do you still love me?'

'Yes of course, Mrs Goslinga.'

Justine passes with a flask of coffee: 'Do you want a nice cup of coffee, Mrs Goslinga?'

'Look,' Mrs Goslinga says, 'all those girls in front of the window.'

'What's that, Mrs Goslinga?'

'There are girls at the window.'

'What are they doing there?' asks the carer.

'Earning money.'

'By looking out the window?'

'No, screwing.'

'Screwing? What kind of screwing?'

'*Dirty* screwing of course.'[7]

A week later Darah comes into the guest room, where I am writing up my notes, beaming. She has been appointed as the new care coordinator. Her interview went well, she says. The person from the family council asked her easy questions about the residents. The carer on the interview panel asked her what she would deal with first if she were care coordina-tor. She answered that she would try and improve motivation.

After the interview she had to wait in the corridor. When they called her back in they told her she had the job. Anna van Raalten said she was glad that she had applied. She wanted her to start immediately. Darah's eldest daughter screamed when she phoned to tell her the good news. Her daughter had been very supportive; she had always said: 'Mom, you have to believe that you can do it.'

Nice work?

When I ask carers why they are doing this job, they say they 'like caring for people' or that they 'want to do something with people'. Colette says that she always tries to put herself in the residents' position and see things through their eyes. She often thinks about how she would want to be cared for: 'That's the mirror I hold up to myself. When I see that I have made them happy, it makes my day.'

Many carers say that they made a conscious choice to work with people with Alzheimer's. When I ask why, they shrug. When I push them they say that they are so 'helpless and endearing, just like small children'.

Darah thinks the Alzheimer's residents are 'just sweet'. She tells me how the other day Mrs Goslinga asked her if they could pray together. She had said: 'Lord, here I stand in front of you with Darah. Please let her stay with us for a long time, because we need her. Please also keep her children and her colleagues healthy.' Darah said it brought tears to her eyes. 'You don't have that sort of thing with the somatic residents.'

Carers differ in their opinion as to whether they have a good job or not. Darah's children wouldn't ever even consider working in the care sector, she says, laughing. They think it's hard work for little money. Mom is crazy to do it, they say. They want to do something in management or IT.

Darah notices this attitude in the holiday helpers: the schoolgirls who come and help to make the beds in the summer holidays wear rubber gloves because they consider the beds dirty. Darah: 'Then I think: I won't see her back again next year. No, young people today don't fancy working with people with Alzheimer's in a nursing home. It's dirty and it's hard work and you don't get paid much.'

In personnel I enquire about the carers' salaries. A new carer fresh from the three-year training will earn 1400 euros a month. On top of that they get about 17 percent for irregular hours. Nurses with two-years' training get 1200 euros before tax. Unskilled assistants get about the same. One problem is that this salary structure does not motivate staff to do further training, I am told.

Femke says she often hears that her work is badly paid. She doesn't agree entirely. With her payment for irregular hours she gets about 1700 euros a month before tax. That's not bad, she thinks. She earns the same as her husband, so together they have a decent income.

Rutger Varenkamp says that nursing home doctors don't earn much either in comparison to colleagues in other sectors, and they have less status. He chose this specialisation carefully. He came to work in Park House fifteen years ago as part of his military service. He enjoyed it and never left. Varenkamp likes working with the residents and the carers. The friends he studied with, who now work in hospitals, look down at the work he does. He sees that clearly. They often say: 'You don't get any credit working in a nursing home. It's not nice, but you get used to it.'

During a refresher course for nursing home staff I talk about my first impressions in 'death's waiting room'. After the coffee break a doctor tells me that he recognises my descriptions, but that the expression 'death's waiting room' irritates him. 'There we go again,' he thought.

'What's wrong with a good waiting room for death?' I ask, surprised.

'Nothing,' he says, still irritated.

'It's just that we always have to defend the fact that we work in a nursing home,' a psychologist explains.

Another nursing home doctor claims that his work could easily compete with the heroics of hospital work. If a medical specialist says to relatives that the patient is dying, they accept it. They say: 'Thank you doctor, for doing your best and looking after him.' When nursing home doctors give that message then the chance of resistance from the relatives is much greater. Nursing home doctors aren't seen as real doctors, he says. At parties you can brag about your spectacular achievements on the Intensive Care Unit. No one wants to hear about the experiences of nursing home doctors.

'It's as though the misery of the nursing home radiates from us,' the irritated nursing home doctor says. 'Old age, death, degeneration: society looks down on them.'

'The losers' shed,' a colleague says provocatively. 'Who wants to work there?'

Everyday Life

Sitting and waiting

The residents spend most of the day in the living room. They stare and sway to the music, which plays continuously. Sometimes they chat. Rutger Varenkamp brings in magazines that he finds abandoned in the train, but the residents never read. The staff make good use of them, though. Not much happens in the living room during the day, and it is the carers who walk around and chat and laugh.

In the mornings when the residents have been washed they are seated at the table for breakfast. They remain there most of the day. They wait – consciously or unconsciously – until the next major activity of the day is presented to them: coffee, lunch, tea, afternoon soup, dinner. Then it's time to go to bed.

When I mention the long hours that the residents are seated, the carers nod. 'Have you ever tried sitting still in a chair for a whole afternoon?' Piet, one of the carers, asks. 'I have, and it's not easy.'

'Imagine being strapped to your chair the whole afternoon,' says Femke. 'Because they are often restrained as well. And then having to ask to be taken to the toilet.'

'And these are people who did not lead sedentary lives,' says Piet.

'They just sit there and nothing happens,' I add.

'Don't be too quick with a judgement,' says Piet cynically. 'They drink litres of coffee.' The question is, he adds, do they experience it as having to sit still the whole day? Some seem not to want any physical activity. They won't initiate anything; they have to be activated. You see that clearly when they have holidays. Then there are more staff and they get more individual attention. Then suddenly they can eat with a knife and fork, they are interested in their surroundings, and they are concerned about whether their hair has been done. If there was one carer per resident then things would be much better, Piet is convinced, but unfortunately this is impossible.

I notice that much of the conversation is about washing, dressing and going to the hairdresser. All issues relating to bodily care and appearance, whereas I would have thought that other things were more important for the quality of life.

'That's true,' says Piet, 'but the basis is eating, drinking and bodily care. If you have Alzheimer's and you haven't washed for five days then there isn't much quality of life, because your social interactions suffer as a result.' He emphasises each word. 'Imagine that we got them out of bed really quickly. Hup! Bums washed, in the wheelchair, and off for a nice little trip. After a while they'd look terrible. That wouldn't be nice for other people and it wouldn't be nice for them either.'

Arranging flowers and polishing nails

In the activity centre Marga and Joosje, occupational therapists, are busy framing pictures that residents have painted. The room looks modern: linoleum, straight, white walls, Venetian blinds. Against one wall is a large mahogany sideboard containing gilt cutlery. On top are two porcelain dogs. Here and there are old velvet armchairs.

Mrs Wielens is drinking a cup of tea. 'Come on, give me a cigarette,' she says. 'Mine are finished. Roll one for me.' Marga rolls a cigarette for her. Mrs Wielens inhales deeply, smoking with abandonment: 'Really nice, a cigarette. Really.'

'Actually, you're not allowed to smoke here any more,' says Marga. 'But we allow it. It's their home, after all. Imagine not being allowed to smoke in your own living room!' Joosje talks about the Wednesday morning discussion group. She alternates, running it with pastor Pieter Verdoorn one week and with Marga the next. 'We discuss everything. Sometimes we read the papers, or someone brings something in. There are not many who can still participate in things like that, because most of the residents have Alzheimer's.'

The occupational therapists organise group activities for the residents, and are assisted by volunteers and carers, if the latter have time. Individual activities, such as walks outside, or going out for coffee, are the carers' responsibility. That hasn't happened in recent years, say the carers, because they don't have the time.

The activities on offer for the week are recorded on the whiteboard in the corridor: singing, chat groups, making pancakes. Larger activities are also organised in the restaurant: afternoon drinks, music, dance, entertainment evenings and special occasions such as Christmas and Easter. Sometimes activities are organised in the living rooms, such as flower arrangement or nail polishing. Anna van Raalten thinks there should be more activities in the living rooms, to make them 'more lively'. Joosje understands, but she prefers to keep things in the activity centre. 'The atmosphere is different,' she says. 'And as a result the discussions are different.'

I have to agree. I have never seen Mrs Wielens so talkative. Then the door opens and Mrs Donkers enters. She looks good, in her green dress and matching necklace. She laughs and gives Mrs Wielens a friendly pat on the shoulder.

'See that,' says Joosje. 'You don't get that in the living rooms. They really meet each other here. They talk. We don't understand how it works, but they seem to have more contact.'

Pancakes with syrup

Thenext afternoon is the weekly bus trip. Marga gets the residents from the living rooms. I accompany Mrs Sterk, who is wearing her aubergine hat with matching feather. Darah kisses residents and wishes them a nice trip. Paul, the physiotherapist, helps to put the wheelchairs in the bus. Then they have to be secured to the floor.

The bus leaves and Marga hands out sweets, all the while describing the passing scenery; ordinary things, but the residents consider them special: cars, cyclists, buildings, meadows. I sit between Mrs de Vos – 'De Vos-Haverkamp,' she likes to emphasise – and Mrs Boshard. The latter is irritated by the chatter of Mrs De Vos, with whom she shares a table in the living room. 'De Vos-Haverkamp is my name. I've never been sick, you know, and I've never had a headache either, *never*,' she keeps repeating, cheerfully.

'I know someone who has a headache right now,' mumbles Mrs Boshard, giving me a meaningful glance.

We eat pancakes with syrup in Vreeland. At the table it is quiet. The pancakes are gone in no time. Mrs Boshard, who normally eats with difficulty, and whose dietary problems are often the subject of the multi-disciplinary consultation, finishes her plate long before me. Even Mrs Sterk eats with gusto. The syrup drips down her chin. She ignores everyone, and when I try to make conversation, she waves me away with her aubergine hat.

Mrs de Vos sits next to Mrs Heering. When Mrs Heering starts to put on her coat for the trip back, Mrs de Vos becomes restless: 'Please, can I go with her?' she repeats. 'I don't want to stay here alone.'

We take a different route back to Park House. We pass a carer on her bicycle. We wave. She tries to keep up with the bus and to wave at the same time. Marga starts to sing. Paul says dryly: 'When we get back we're all going to hide, just like we used to do when we came back from a school trip.'

Mrs de Vos is silent. She tugs at my sleeve and says that she is not looking forward to coming home alone, because there is no one at home waiting for her. I tell her that we are all going together and that Mrs Heering will be with her as well. 'Tonight as well? Is she sleeping over? Oh good.' But a few minutes later she has forgotten and is worried again. Mrs Boshard gets irritated: 'I have to listen to that all day at the table,' she says.

Mozart and salsa

It's Thursday morning. Willem is playing the piano in the activity centre. He is a volunteer and the husband of one of the residents with Alzheimer's. Residents are sitting round the table drinking coffee from china cups with flowers. Around them is a second circle of residents in wheel-chairs.

Willem plays old Dutch songs. His wife sits next to him. She laughs and sways to the music. She claps her hands and looks happy. Willem is a real performer. He plays and sings, then jumps up and conducts with broad sweeps of his arms. Then he sits down and continues playing. In between he chats to residents: 'Did you say you liked my beard?'

'It's neat,' says the woman he asked, laughing.

'Neat? No one has ever said *that* before!'

Residents clap and sing along, as do the carers and occupational thera-pists. Mrs Melkman marches resolutely past, her handbag around her neck like a necklace, her arms waving back and forth as she walks, like a soldier.

When she runs into volunteer Peter, they start dancing, she moving her head to the rhythm. When she laughs her dentures move back and forth.

Mrs Blauw is brought in in her wheelchair. She has just been to the hairdresser. Because it is Christmas soon she has had silver glitter put in her hair. She is also singing along. It's impossible to have a conversation with her because she is too far-gone, the carers say. But she knows the words of all the songs. Mrs Melkman marches back into the activity cen-tre and joins in again seamlessly. As she swings past me she stabs at my face with her finger: 'Mozart, that's who I like.'

Assistant carer Mildred – small, Surinamese, mid-fifties, in her white coat and tight purple leggings – is holding on to a wheelchair and dan-cing salsa steps, her hips swaying to the music. Willem gets up and claps, and together they sing: 'Because I love you...'

The nursing home doctor and a medical student stand in the en-trance. The student, who hasn't yet decided whether to become an inter-nist or a surgeon, mumbles: 'It almost makes me want to become a nur-sing home doctor.'

Foreigners

'Is living in a nursing home just unpleasant, or is it really horrendous?' I wonder. I don't dare to put this question to those who work in Park House, because it seems like I am the only person who sees it like that. The carers and the doctor cheerfully show me all the possibilities: birth-day parties, resident holidays, coffee mornings.

'How bad is it to have Alzheimer's?' I ask one of the carers. 'If you've had a happy life then it's okay,' says Femke. 'At first it's bad,' Darah thinks, 'but later it's better if you do have Alzheimer's. It saves you all the grief. It's bad for the children, but not for the resident.'

But whose criteria do you use in determining how bad it is? How bad is it, for example, that Mrs Caspers, who used to be a principled anthroposophist and vegetarian, now enjoys her meat? Every day she uncovers her breasts in the living room, bounces them up and down, and shouts: 'Look, here are the foreigners!' Mrs Caspers, with her hair in a tight bun, looks slyly through her small round spectacles. The carers laugh. I feel ashamed for her. What would she have thought of this if she could observe it from the perspective of her younger self? Does it matter? And what would her children think of it? They remember how she used to be. Perhaps that is why they never come and see her. And what does it mean for her that her children no longer come and visit her? Does she notice? Is her daily call – 'Jacob, are you upstairs? Are you there? I miss you' – related to this?

Who said it would be nice?

That afternoon I have an appointment with Rosan Hüsken, the humanist counsellor. On my way I pass Mildred in the corridor. She holds up a packet of liquorice allsorts and shouts: 'Eating sweets, singing and making love: that's what I live for.' Then I run into Marco Burgers. He is the boss of Anna van Raalten and the other care managers. 'Do you ever get to see the other floors?' he asks. 'We were discussing you this morning. Someone died on the first floor after the decision was made not to give antibiotics. We thought it would have been an interesting case for you. There is a new care manager in that department, and you haven't met her yet.'

Burgers tells me that he has been the interim-manager in Park House for a year. They are trying to improve the quality of care. He says that one of the problems is that the staff spend more time looking after themselves than looking after the residents. It's as though some of the carers come to the nursing home for their own enjoyment. And the atmosphere is too informal. Too much 'you scratch my back and I'll scratch yours.' And too much of the opposite as well: 'if you make things difficult for me, then I'll make them even more difficult for you.' It's difficult to change that culture, the manager says.

Rosan Hüsken asks about my first impressions in the nursing home. The humanist counsellor is in her forties, shoulder-length brown curls and wearing a purple velvet dress. Hüsken is white, but her accent reveals years of having lived in Surinam. I tell her that I am shocked by the meagreness of the care, the shortages of funds and the fact that residents spend almost all of their time seated. That the best thing that can happen to them is a visit to the hairdresser or a birthday meal. 'Yes, it's not all roses here,' Hüsken says. 'But then who said it would be nice?'

'But don't you think it's a terrible prospect to have to go to a nursing home?' I ask.

'Yes and no,' she answers. She says she has thought about this question a lot. Her mother died recently after a long illness, during which

Hüsken had taken care of her. During the same period her neighbour was admitted to a nursing home. During these experiences she decided that she wouldn't mind living in a nursing home later. 'I'll survive there. And the alternative – not going to a nursing home – would mean a huge burden on my family. I looked after my mother and I don't regret it, but I don't want my children to have to do that for me.'

And the neighbour was slowly wasting away at home. It was an awful situation, says Hüsken. Finally she ended up in a nursing home. During the first weeks she insisted that she would rather die than stay in the nursing home, because nothing happened there. But there she was washed, fed, and put on the toilet. That didn't happen at home. There she just became more and more filthy and undernourished. At home there was no occupational therapy, no one to talk to. In the home she had her first party and her first trip in many years. So lots of things were happening.

'Then I realised that it all depends on what you compare it to,' says Hüsken. 'With good times in the past, when you were young? Yes, then life in the nursing home is not so great. But when you compare it with how my neighbour was languishing, wasting away in her house, or with people with Alzheimer's wandering the streets, then life in the nursing home is a godsend.'

It'll be great to pray again

As a result of my conversation with Rosan Hüsken I look at life in Park House through new eyes. I notice other things. Through the open door I hear Rutger Varenkamp and Colette speaking to Mrs White, who has had a heart attack. 'No Mrs White, you have to stay in bed.' Mrs White tries to get out of bed, gesticulating with her hands. She whispers something to the doctor. He nods and says: 'Mrs White, really, it's all organised. I've spoken to your boss, the circus manager, and he says it's okay for you to take some leave. He says you've worked so hard during the last months that you deserve a break.' Mrs White lays her head back on the pillows and closes her eyes. Colette takes her hand and sits on the edge of the bed.

At the entrance to the activity centre pastor Pieter Verdoorn shakes the hand of one of the residents who has attended his discussion group. 'I'll see you in church on Sunday then, Mrs de Vos.'

'Yes,' she nods enthusiastically, 'it will be great to pray again.'

'Well, I've never heard it put quite like that, Mrs de Vos!'

'Yes, you close your eyes and you put your hands together like this,' says Mrs de Vos, showing us how it is done. 'And then you pretend to pray but in fact you're having a little nap instead.'

'Oh, Mrs de Vos', the pastor wags his finger at her, 'I'll be keeping an eye on you in church.'

I start to feel at home in the nursing home. When I sit in the guest room making notes on my laptop, Mrs Walker and Mrs Melkman call in often. Mrs Walker joins me at the table and swings her legs like a little girl, because the chair is too high for her and her feet don't reach the ground. Before she leaves she tidies up. She doesn't have time to hang around, she says, because the children will be home any minute and she has to put the potatoes on. If she doesn't hurry her father will give her a thrashing.

Mrs Melkman is always excited when she joins me. Her sentences always start with: 'It's scandalous.' Then follows a series of recurring themes: Maxima, such a dear girl; Willem-Alexander should really make up his mind and marry her; those terrible Catholics; Mozart; her dentures; her daughter Petra, who is a darling.

I no longer notice the leanness in the nursing home. I no longer see the residents as victims. The nursing home is really a way out for many residents: those who were lonely at home have friends, they find 'lost' relatives, they flourish. There are even love affairs. Mrs Carpentier is head over heels in love with Mrs Davids, for example. 'Oh, she's so good looking,' she sighs every time she sees her. Mrs Davids enjoys the attention and smiles back. But no, she doesn't feel anything for Mrs Carpentier 'in that way'. She is in love with carer Robby Casparie, an athletic *Indo* not yet thirty. Giggling and with flushed cheeks, she waves to him whenever he is in the living room.

Sex in the guest room

Anna van Raalten comes into the guest room with a mysterious expression on her face. She closes the door and asks whether I have every noticed anything strange when I come to the guest room to type up my notes. I shake my head, but she keeps looking at me interrogatively. Then she says that she thinks someone has been sleeping in the room.

I tell her that the bed did indeed look as though it had been slept in. I thought that the children of Mrs De Graaf had spent the night here.

'Yes, yes, the bed has been slept in,' the care manager says, stifling a laugh. 'It appears that it is slept in often, by a resident from upstairs, together with a sweetheart.'

'Oh, really,' I mumble.

'I'm not sure how they get the keys,' she says. Colette found out because the sheets were dirty. Maria, the Philippine assistant was also there. She kept saying: 'Screwing, screwing.' We both laugh. The care manager had e-mailed her counterpart: 'Is this coming from your budget or mine?'

In the coffee break Colette also talks about the nocturnal activities in the guest room. Rick van Velzen, the doctor from upstairs, had asked her whether the guest room was being used. She had said: Yes, Anne-Mei uses it. Van Velzen wanted clean sheets for the room. Colette was puzzled, until the doctor explained that the room was needed for a resident who wanted to make love. Colette thinks someone was 'hired in' for the occasion.

Sylvia says that she had had a similar experience during her training. She had been asked whether she could 'organise a lady' for the night for one of the residents. Sylvia thought it was a joke, but it wasn't. So she organised someone. 'There are nursing homes where it isn't allowed,' she says. 'In Park House it's always been possible.'

Femke thinks it's good that it is made possible in Park House. I say that I have sometimes wondered how things like that are organised. Nursing home residents have the same needs as anyone else, after all.

'You can say that again,' says Sylvia. 'Have you ever had Mr Slot after you?' She tells me that Mr Slot can't keep his hands off the carers. Sometimes they have to push him away with force.

Colette leans forward conspiratorially and whispers that a while ago she heard a tremendous racket coming from the room of Mr and Mrs Hak. She went to investigate. Mrs Hak shouted: 'He wants me to kneel like this.' She proceeded to get down on hands and knees to demonstrate. He turned red and pulled the sheets over his head. Colette left as quickly as she had come.

Sex is more common in the somatic departments, says Femke. She once went to help a resident get ready for the night. He was busy in the bathroom and when he heard her he said: Hang on I'm coming. 'Well,' Femke says, 'he was indeed coming, quite literally. So I quickly shut the door again and said: Take your time, I'll come back later. Then he said: Can't you come and help me with this? I said: No Koos, this is something that you will have to do yourself.'

Inadequate Care

Mrs Driessen has convulsions

Rutger Varenkamp stands red-faced in Mrs Driessen's room. He has been called out of the communication course organised by the director. Mrs Driessen moans and is not responsive. She is diabetic and has hypoglycaemia. The doctor wants to give her a glucose injection and needs alcohol to disinfect the skin. Colette is the only carer present who is qualified to assist the doctor. She runs up and down looking for some alcohol. There are a lot of small bottles in the cupboards, but no alcohol.

Rosalie had a fright. She found Mrs Driessen having convulsions in bed. The 50-year-old Surinamese assistant carer stands quietly next to the doctor, arms folded. Rutger Varenkamp pats her on the shoulder: 'She'll be okay.'

To me he says: 'Mrs Driessen has a very variable blood-sugar level. The problem is that I don't know whether she gets what she needs in the evenings. Her food and drink list isn't filled in properly.'

There is a knock at the door. The care manager from one of the other departments sticks her head round he door: 'I have an assistant dietician on offer for a couple of hours. She needs a bit of support; doesn't know anyone here.'

'I won't complain,' says Rutger Varenkamp cheerfully. 'Feel free to bother us if you're offering us dieticians. Thanks.' Rosalie takes the dietician to the living room while Rutger Varenkamp checks Mrs Driessen's blood sugar-level, noting that it has risen again. When Colette returns with a bottle of alcohol, he says: 'You know what I'm going to say now, don't you? Supplies of essentials need to be checked. It's your responsibility. I've also noticed that there isn't any tape.'

Then he adds jokingly: 'You'd almost think you were in a hospital; all that action. Quite unusual.' He doesn't manage with the injection and has to insert a drip. He goes to get the necessary equipment.

'There are not enough of us here today,' says Colette. 'There are only assistants. Then something like this has to happen. Mrs Driessen has her blood-sugar checked five times a day.' To Rosalie, who has just come back into the room, she says: 'Did Mrs Driessen have her blood-sugar checked this morning? She should've seen this coming.' Rosalie shrugs: 'I wasn't here then. No one mentioned it to me. How should I know?'

Mrs Driessen recovers after receiving her medication, and the doctor returns to his course.

In unit C everyone is upset. The carers feel responsible. Later they discuss things with Rutger Varenkamp. Darah says that she had given Mrs Driessen syrup the previous evening. She thought that would be sufficient.

'It's really necessary that she gets the food she needs,' says Varen-kamp. 'It's not for nothing that these people have special diets. It's also not only Mrs Driessen; the other residents need to have their supplements as well. This evening it's Darah's shift, so everything will be okay, but when there are new people we need to make sure that it happens. You all need to make sure that this sort of thing is recorded in the file after every shift.'

Shortcomings

After the doctor has left, the atmosphere in the small office changes. Darah says that Mrs Engel's condition is deteriorating; that she just 'lets it all run' and then makes excuses. This morning she said that a dog had been in her room and lifted its leg. Then after she had 'daubed' she held her hand to Darah's face and said: 'Want to taste? Go on, it's fresh chocolate.' The carers all laugh.

'Well, Mrs Ligthart is another one,' says Jessy. 'I was next to her bed and she looked at me sideways and said: Yes child, it's under the bed. You'll clean it up, won't you? And while I'm cleaning it up she says: You don't mind, do you child?'

'Last week I was on nights,' says Christa. 'Sixty-four people with the shits. What a job!'

Then Jessy imitates Rutger Varenkamp talking about the dietary supplements. She gets up and claps her hands: 'Ladies, ladies, please remember the right amounts; it's very important.' She does a good imitation. In her hand she holds an imaginary tin of supplement. The carers all laugh heartily.

The reality is that they have failed, Jessy tells me later. On the units with the serious Alzheimer's residents it takes a lot of time to feed everyone. That means that there is often no supervision for the residents with less serious dementia. As a result the carers often don't know whether they have eaten or how much. Mrs Walker, for example, always throws everything away. If a resident has a full plate, Mrs Walker will ask: 'Are you finished?' and throw everything in the bin, without waiting for an answer. Jessy says that they are supposed to be more 'resident-oriented', but that isn't feasible. With the current level of staffing they hardly manage to get the residents out of bed.

The carers run the show

During a family interview Mr Molleman says that twice he has noticed that his wife did not have her restraining strap on when she was seated at the table. Fortunately he was around to prevent her falling off the chair, but he is worried that it might happen again when he is not around.

Rutger Varenkamp says he is unhappy to hear this. He explains that the permanent staff know that Mrs Molleman needs to be secured, but that the temps don't. He explains that they have tried all kinds of things to inform the temps about that sort of thing, such as notes stuck on the inside of cupboard doors, for example (they are not allowed to stick them on the outside for reasons of confidentiality).

Mr Molleman nods impatiently. He says that he has submitted an official complaint. Because Varenkamp wasn't around, he went to the 'lady who is in charge'. 'Have you heard anything about it, doctor?' he asks. Varenkamp shakes his head. Mr Molleman says that when he visited at the weekend his wife was covered in porridge. He went to the office to report this. 'There were five or six of these, of these, what shall I call them...' Mr Molleman nods meaningfully to the doctor.

'Members of staff,' suggests the doctor with a straight face.

'...of these people who've been spending too much time sunbathing, shall we say. You know what I mean?' He winks at the doctor. 'Well, they were sitting and babbling in that language of theirs, you know.' Mr Molleman had told them that his wife was covered in porridge and asked them to come and clean it up. 'They all stared at me as though I were mad,' he said. 'Finally one of them said she'd come.'

Mr Molleman went back to his wife's room and waited. But no one came. After a while he went back to the office. They were still chatting and drinking coffee, he says. He asked again: 'Is someone coming?' Finally one of them came reluctantly. She banged doors as she went and made such a noise that a resident came and asked him what was wrong. Once they got to the room the carer told him to leave her alone with Mrs Molleman. He refused. She then demanded that he remove his bag from the bed. He refused to do this as well. The carer then roughly grabbed the wheelchair in which Mrs Molleman was sitting. 'Hey, hang on a minute,' he said, 'there is a human being sitting in that chair.' He tells Varenkamp that he became very angry and said things he shouldn't have said.

The doctor takes a deep breath and closes his eyes. When he opens them and stares silently through the window into the corridor. I follow his gaze. I see Mrs Prins approaching, her expression scared, tormented. She approaches in slow motion, as though in trance. Mrs Bakker comes around a corner, holding her dress up with both hands. She looks as though she is about to crouch down and answer nature's call. She has the expression of a guilty child.

Rutger Varenkamp clears his throat. 'Mr Molleman, that was someone who was not exactly customer-friendly. I'm sorry. Do you know who it was?'

'No. I didn't know any of them.'

Varenkamp explains that they have to use staff from various temping agencies, but that they keep a blacklist of those they no longer want. There are those who only come for a couple of days but who spoil the good name of the nursing home. Unfortunately Mr Molleman seems to have encountered one of those.

After the interview Rutger Varenkamp shares with me his concern about the quality of some of the carers and his inability to do anything about it. 'I'm deeply ashamed when relatives come to me with stories like that,' he says. 'Unfortunately it's not the first time, and I have to listen to them as representative of the organisation, but as doctor I'm really on the sideline, because it's the carers who run the show.'

Mrs Bekkering's children

The son of Mrs Bekkering, a man in his mid-sixties, walks briskly into the unit.

'Is mother not yet ready?' he asks.

'She's coming in a minute, Mr Bekkering,' says the assistant dietician. He visits every Tuesday morning. After a while his mother appears on Jessy's arm.

'Good morning mother.'

'Morning son.'

'You look wonderful, mother.' She smiles and smoothes her blouse. 'Shall we go down and have a cup of coffee?' She nods and takes her son's arm to go downstairs. She walks with difficulty and can hardly keep up with him. I observe them in the restaurant. They sit at a table, coffee and cake in front of them, each looking in a different direction.

Mrs Bekkering has two children who haven't had any contact with each other for years. The only communication between brother and sister is through notes that they leave on their mother's bed. They tried communicating about the care of their mother through the carers, but that led to problems. After various meetings and the intervention of the humanist counsellor, it was decided that staff should not become involved in the family intrigues of residents. It is difficult, because relatives often try to curry favour with carers and then get them to do their dirty work. The situation with the son and daughter of Mrs Bekkering is still difficult.

The daughter thinks that the care in Park House is way below standard and she makes no secret of it. She has even been on local television to complain, revealing in great detail how residents with broken limbs were left untreated. 'And that in the nursing home in which our Mayor recently said he would want to spend his final days,' the interviewer added, delicately.

Staff in De Stadhouder were shocked by the programme. Femke says that Mrs Bekkering actually fell out of bed and broke her wrist, and that this hadn't been noticed for several days. 'Things like that happen occasionally,' says Femke. 'But if the resident isn't in pain then it's difficult to know that anything is wrong.'

The daughter of Mrs Bekkering, the primary contact person and legal representative, requested a transfer to another nursing home. She didn't inform her brother, and staff felt obliged to inform him.

Don't wash one's dirty linen in public

Rutger Varenkamp looks up when I walk into the office. 'Come on, I want to show you something.' He leads the way to the kitchen. When we enter there are three open tins of nutritional supplements on the table. They look used. 'Just when I had given up hope, things are starting to happen,' he says proudly. 'My nagging has had some effect.'

Back in the office I ask whether forgetting to give supplements or forgetting to fill in the fluid and dietary lists is limited to Park House, or whether it is also common in other nursing homes. Rutger Varenkamp doesn't think it would be very different anywhere else. He speaks to colleagues often, and they all complain that they have to ask carers 'a hundred times' if they want to get anything done. And they complain that there is no continuity in care.

The labour situation differs between different regions. In the provinces it is easier to get staff, and in some areas there is less absenteeism. A friend of Varenkamp's works near Zwolle, in the middle of the Dutch Bible Belt, where there is hardly any absenteeism at all due to the dominant Protestant work ethic.

Then I mention Mrs Bloem, who keeps calling for the toilet. Some carers just ignore her. They say that she is very demanding, forgets that she has just been to the toilet, and has an inco anyway. Rutger Varenkamp blanches: 'That's just not acceptable.'

I argue that I can also understand the carers' behaviour, given the burden of work they face. The work of the doctor is limited to medical issues, the carers have to deal with everything else and it is never-ending, and all the time Mrs Bloem is calling for the toilet.

'Carers learn to make choices,' says Rutger Varenkamp severely. 'You learn that beds can wait, but Mrs Bloem can't.' But, he admits, things are more complicated in practice. Carers want to have all the practical issues sorted out first. They know that some things are really unacceptable, but sometimes carers are tired and things happen nonetheless, says Varenkamp. He thinks this is common throughout the psycho-geriatric sector.

I tell him that I recently discussed Park House with a colleague from the university who is also a nursing home doctor. He claimed that such things didn't happen in his nursing home and that my experiences weren't representative. He insisted that I was in the wrong nursing home. Rutger Varenkamp chuckles and tells me about his training as nursing home doctor. His supervisors always had splendid examples of things running as they should. 'There is a taboo on washing one's dirty linen in public,' he says. 'That doesn't do the name of the nursing home or the nursing home sector any good. My colleagues are sensitive about that.'

Versterven

Hypodermoclysis or no hypodermoclysis

I'm having lunch with Rutger Varenkamp in the Restaurant. He talks about residents he thinks will die soon. One of them is the 96-year-old Mrs Bakker. She has had a few bad falls recently. Varenkamp could extend her life by strapping her to a chair and feeding her through a tube. But in consultation with her daughter he has decided not to do that. The daughter thinks that her mother has already been deprived of too much. If she were to be restrained then she would loose the last bit of freedom she has. This means that they accept the risk that Mrs Bakker will fall and injure herself. Since yesterday she has refused to get out of bed, and she is also refusing to eat and drink. She doesn't want anything. 'She's not even taking any notice of me,' he says, smiling. 'I won't be here next week,' he continues, 'but I've asked the locum not to giver her hypodermoclysis.' He shakes his head.

I ask what the difference is between Mrs Bakker on the one hand and Mrs Scharloo and Mrs Driessen on the other, because the latter two had both recently had hypodermoclysis. Varenkamp says that Mrs Bakker's condition has been deteriorating gradually for a long time. She is old, weak and in the final stages of Alzheimer's. Her situation is irreversible and extra fluid wouldn't make any difference to that; it would probably extend her suffering.

Mrs Scharloo, on the other hand, had a temporary physical collapse, probably related to her depression. That depression was treated. In order to give the medication a chance to have an effect it was necessary to make sure that she was adequately hydrated. So hypodermoclysis was necessary. Mrs Driessen was similar to Mrs Scharloo. She was also not yet in an advanced stage of her Alzheimer's. She also had a treatable physical condition – diabetes. And she also needed to be rehydrated in order to make physical recovery possible.

'That's the medical story,' I say, 'but you told me previously that you treated Mrs Scharloo more actively because she hadn't been in the nursing home long.'

Varenkamp confirms that this also played a role. In situations like that it's more difficult to assess the situation,' he says. Moreover, it is possible that the resident is temporarily upset due to the move to the nursing home. And it's more difficult for staff to cope when a new resident dies. Varenkamp prefers it when residents first have the chance of a good period in Park House before they pass away; and that is usually possible, he says. Because Mrs Bakker has been in Park House for years, Varenkamp is sure that she would refuse hypodermoclysis anyway.

The decision to give Mrs Driessen a second hypodermoclysis was not influenced by the fact that she had not been in the nursing home long, says the doctor. 'It's funny, actually,' he muses, 'but I never really think about the differences like that. It all seems so logical. In the case of Mrs Driessen there is also the fact that her family want us to do everything possible. Her daughter-in-law visits every day and wants us to do everything to keep her mother alive.'

Get away from me!

After lunch I go with Rutger Varenkamp to see Mrs Bakker. He wants to give her tranquillising drops. It is a coercive measure that he will have to report, he explains. Not that it is really physical coercion: Mrs Bakker won't take her drops voluntarily, so he puts them in her drinks without telling her.

Mrs Bakker is asleep in bed. The doctor takes her arm gently and wakes her up. Initially she is bewildered and friendly, but as soon as he shows her the glass of water and suggests that she gets out of bed, she becomes angry: 'No, please! Get away from me! Otherwise I'll call the police.' She thrashes about defensively. Then she closes her eyes tightly.

'This is hopeless,' says the doctor. 'I won't be able to get her to take the drops like this.' And he won't be able to check her blood sugar either. That morning Justine had tried to give her suppositories, but it had not been a success. She is still refusing to eat or drink anything. Varenkamp doesn't think she is in pain. 'When I see her like that, I wonder why we don't just leave her alone,' he says. 'Come on, let's discuss it with Darah.'

In the office Darah is working on the residents' files. 'Have you seen Mrs Bakker today?' he asks.

'Yes, a minute ago. I wanted to get her out of bed, but I didn't manage. She doesn't want anything and just gets angry.'

'It worries me,' says the doctor. 'What are we going to do? I don't think she's in pain.'

'No,' agrees the carer, 'she's not in pain.'

'It seems like she just doesn't want to go on,' says the doctor. 'She can go without food and drink for a day or so, but if it lasts any longer then she'll die. Do you have any ideas?'

Darah suggests calling Mrs Bakker's son, Berend. She's always talking about him, and he comes and puts her to bed almost every evening. He was a late arrival and had always lived with his mother. Perhaps he could get her to drink something. She listens to him, Darah thinks.

Rutger Varenkamp phones Berend Bakker. When he hangs up he says that the son will come this evening and see what he can do. Otherwise he didn't say much. He has a strong bond with his mother, the doctor suggests, and may find it difficult letting go.

Mrs Bakker was in the same condition when she first arrived in Park House, says Darah. She was angry and kept walking away. Now she can't walk away any more and just lies in bed angry. Darah thinks she just doesn't want to go on anymore.

'I happens sometimes that people withdraw to die,' says Varenkamp. 'That is indeed what this looks like.'

Decisions about life and death

Later that afternoon I ask Anna van Raalten whether Mrs Bakker is in the process of *versterven*. The care manager thinks so. When someone doesn't want to eat or drink anymore, doesn't want to sit up, and becomes drowsy, then those are signs that point in that direction. The course *versterven* takes differs from one person to another, Van Raalten explains. One person might drink litres of water then suddenly stop from one day to the next, while another might reduce much more gradually.

In the case of Mrs Bakker everyone agrees that she should be left alone. Unfortunately that doesn't always happen. The care manager says that her family sometimes demand all kinds of things, while the doctors and carers wonder whether any of it is useful. Usually they try to keep the family happy, because relatives need time to get used to the fact that their loved one is dying, and the responsibility for decisions about life and death weigh heavily on them. Often it is a question of relatives feeling sure that absolutely everything has been tried. Only then can they think: we've tried that and it didn't work, so no point trying it again.

I ask whether the decision to keep residents alive as long as possible isn't made in the best interests of the relatives rather than those of the resident. Van Raalten thinks I am putting it rather starkly. She prefers to say that they take the relatives' wishes into account. They are still here after their loved one dies, and it is important for how they cope with mourning. Van Raalten: 'Sometimes they need extra time, and we try and give it to them. The question remains, of course, whether this is all in the best interests of the resident. And I'm not always convinced of that.'

Later Rutger Varenkamp tells me that during the weekend he was on call for another nursing home. There he had decided to give a resident tube feeding because the daughter wanted it. She was histrionic and had a pathological relationship with her mother, says Varenkamp. She kept shouting: 'If my mother dies then I want to die as well.' And that influenced him, he said. Afterwards the daughter had kissed him and said: 'You're a wonderful doctor. Thank you.'

Varenkamp says that in the case of this resident no symptomatic policy had been agreed in the nursing home: there was absolutely nothing about it in her file. He would never have given one of the Park House residents tube feeding under those circumstances, he says. It is a radical intervention and it is doubtful that it benefits the resident at all.

'But when you don't know someone then you tend to be more conservative,' he explains. 'In this situation the daughter was the deciding factor. She just wasn't ready to part with her mother.' Varenkamp had tried to prepare her for the inevitable by telling her that if her mother didn't improve then the tube would have to be removed after a few days and that there then wasn't much more that could be done for her. He also told her that there was a possibility that her mother would remove the tube herself. 'Then you have to ask yourself the difficult question why,' he said. 'I think, though, that in the case of this lady it would probably be because of irritation.' Varenkamp says that emotions are roused in the nursing home when a resident removes a hypodermoclysis or a feeding tube. The nursing staff tend to think that they do it as a sign of not wanting to go on. 'They tend to think that much more easily than I do,' says Varenkamp. 'And that leads to tensions.'

Doctors won't let them go

Carer Femke thinks that carers don't have much say in the decision about the use of hypodermoclysis. It is the doctor and especially the family that decides. Rutger Varenkamp does listen to the carers' views, she concedes, and that wasn't the case with his predecessors.

'Rutger does listen to us,' her colleague Piet says. 'But then he does what he wants anyway.' Piet says that on a number of occasions Varenkamp had simply replaced the hypodermoclysis needles after a resident had pulled them out and the carers were convinced that the resident had removed them because she no longer wanted to live. One resident's legs were taped up so that she could no longer remove the needles. Piet says that he 'can feel it' when residents no longer want to live. It starts with them refusing food and drink, he says.

Tanja, the assistant dietician, agrees. She says that sometimes residents plead to be allowed to die.

Piet talks about a resident who stopped eating and drinking. As a result she suffered kidney failure. According to Piet she refused to eat and drink because she wanted to die. According to Rutger Varenkamp her kidneys were the cause of the problem, so the put her on hypodermoclysis. She pulled the needles out a few times. 'Logical,' says Piet, 'because she still wanted to die, and she did die not long afterwards. It often happens like that. For me it's clear when they no longer want to live, but then the doctor gives them an antidepressant or hypodermoclysis. Doctors seem to have difficulty in allowing them to let go.'

A cold nose

Mrs Bakker is dying. I visit her every day. 'She's the same,' says Darah one Sunday morning. 'She is refusing everything and she keeps undressing.' Sitting in the office later I can hear her calling for her mother. I go and see her. She is lying naked on top of her bed with her knees tightly together. She is covered in bruises and her body is just skin and bones. Bed sheets, incos, pyjamas and turds are scattered about the room.

The next day I hear that Mrs Bakker has passed away. Christa tells me that she washed her in the evening, dressed her in clean clothes and put on perfume. She had noticed that her nose was very cold. She died that night.

Rosalie saw her at half-past-nine. 'I've seen a lot of people go,' she says. 'And you learn to recognise when their time has come.' She phoned the family and the daughter, son-in-law and son came immediately. They were there when she died. The son was very sad, says Rosalie. Outside carers laid her out during the night shift. Rosalie shuddered: 'None of us were there.'

The death of a resident

Rutger Varenkamp says that he sometimes complains about the carers, but never about the care that they give on the deathbed. Then nothing ever goes wrong. Everyone agrees on that. Carers are extremely motivated to ensure that the deathbed goes well, he says, and they are one hundred percent committed to this. Varenkamp thinks they derive satisfaction from it.

The humanist counsellor Rosan Hüsken also says that the care of residents when they are on their deathbed is good. Carers devote a lot of time to this and are very involved. But in spite of this, she does see a problem. When someone is dying it turns out that things *are* suddenly possible. It is suddenly possible to put them in a separate room, pamper them, and give them full attention. She wonders why this isn't always possible. She thinks that contrary to daily activities, the deathbed is orderly: it is clear what needs to be done and the time frame is relatively short.

Rutger Varenkamp says that he is not emotionally affected by the death of a resident. Usually they have had a good time in the nursing home and their death has been a humane one. Death is part of the business of the nursing home. If that has happened the way it is supposed to, then he is satisfied. Varenkamp also thinks it is important that the relatives are satisfied, and to that end he strives for consensus regarding all decisions.

As a doctor he is further away from the residents than the carers, he explains. And he wants to keep it that way. That's why he never goes to funerals. For the carers things are different. They are more emotionally involved and have a much closer relationship – even a very personal relationship – with the residents. That involvement has two sides. For residents it can be very good, but for their relatives it can sometimes be confrontational. 'Just imagine,' Varenkamp says, 'you come to say goodbye to your dying mother and the bed is surrounded by crying carers. That can be a difficult experience, especially if your own relationship with her is not very good.'

Rosan Hüsken finds it striking that the death of a resident can have such an intense emotional effect on the carers. She was recently involved in the funeral of a woman who had not been in Park House long. 'So no one knew her very well, but there was a whole delegation of carers, all crying. That's how easily the emotions flow.'

Personal loss

Some carers are indeed extremely moved when residents die. Often they have cared for them for years and developed a strong tie. But sometimes it has more to do with themselves. Darah, for example, recently lost her mother and suffered intense grief as a result. When a resident dies, that grief resurfaces, she says. Christa never goes to residents' funerals. It makes her depressed because it reminds her of the death of her parents.

Colette's final thesis, at the end of her training as a carer, was about terminal care. The death of residents exercises her. She sometimes experiences it as a personal loss that makes her grieve and mourn. She finds it very difficult to cope with the fact that the bed of a deceased resident is occupied the very next day by someone else. There is no time for proper closure. She always goes to the funerals, though sometimes it is so busy that she doesn't have time.

The management board of Park House have questioned whether carers should be allowed to attend residents' funerals during working hours. Their position is that, given staff shortages, they should give priority to the *living* residents. But the final word still hasn't been said about this. The relatives appreciate it when staff attend funerals, says the residents' ombudsman, Bob Eelman. Sometimes there is hardly anyone else apart from the carers at the funeral. And after they have cared for someone for years, the carers feel the need to go. 'It's logical,' says Eelman. 'They aren't machines; you can't just flick the switch as soon as a resident dies.'

'The board can decide whatever they like,' says Colette, 'but we'll go anyway, even if it has to be in our own time.'

There are also staff who experience the death of residents as a relief. Assistant dietician Tanja, for example: 'What kind of a life is it here anyway?' she asks. 'They have so little. They have been deprived of everything. When colleagues are so sad that someone has died it's because they are sad for themselves.' She says that she thinks that the situation of residents is so bad that she sometimes has difficulty controlling her tears. Tanja has a euthanasia declaration.[8] Her children know that if she ever becomes like the residents in Park House, then she wants euthanasia. She hopes that by the time she gets that far euthanasia for those with dementia will have been legalised.

None of her colleagues want to end up in a nursing home, she says. 'It's only our Mayor. When he said that during the opening, I thought: Okay, great, come on in and enjoy yourself then.'

Wanting to Die

My child is dead

Darah comes into the room looking shocked and tells me that the daughter of Mrs Wijntak has died. She didn't feel well and called the GP. A bit of flu, the doctor said. She didn't improve, though, and phoned her sister. When the sister arrived her hands were already cold and blue. She phoned the emergency number, but it was already too late.

They told Mrs Wijntak on Sunday, but it seems that it only got through to her yesterday. She started screaming and shouting. She fell onto the bed and tore off her clothes. She was so heartbroken that Darah didn't know what to do. She took Mrs Wijntak in her arms and they both lay on the bed together crying.

As Darah tells me this tears well in her eyes. Mrs Wijntak kept saying in Surinamese: 'Why has our dear God taken Irena and not me? Now I have nobody. My mother is dead and my child is dead.' Darah tried to comfort her by saying that she still had her other children but she didn't seem to hear. Mrs Wijntak had already buried two of her children. She started praying for her eldest daughter and youngest son, because they are also ill.

Darah phoned one of Mrs Wijntak's daughters and told her how distraught she was. The daughter had promised to come and visit her. When Mrs Wijntak heard that she stopped crying. Mrs Wijntak is now going to stay with her children until after the funeral.

Darah is worried about her. Her condition has been deteriorating for a while. Last week she had a bladder infection; and her dementia is getting worse. She keeps saying she wants to go home to her mother. She gets angry when the carers talk about her children. 'Be quiet,' she says, 'please don't let my father and mother hear.' She knows that the children belong with her, but she doesn't see them as her children. She lives increasingly in her own childhood. When Darah asks where she is, she says: 'In Paramaribo [Surinam] naturally.'

Euthanasia requests

Dr Michiel Groothof has received a request for euthanasia from one of the Alzheimer's residents, and it is worrying him. He wants to talk to me about it, so I go and see him. Mr Pastoor has been in Park House about two months, Groothof tells me. His stay in the nursing home was initially temporary, to facilitate recovery from a fracture. It soon became clear, however, that he would not be able to return home due to a deterioration of his dementia, even though he wants to. Initially he tried to adjust to the nursing home; he had decided to make the best of things. But it did not work out. And now suddenly disgust has gained the upper hand. When they were talking yesterday in Groothof's office, Mr Pastoor pointed through the window and said: 'Look at all those old tarts. They poke their noses into everything.' Groothof chuckled: 'He's right, though. They do poke their noses in. You need to be able to cope with that.'

Mr Pastoor is requesting euthanasia, quite explicitly, Groothof says. Groothof tries to avoid the word in discussions with residents. He prefers them to describe what they mean. But he knows what Mr Pastoor means, in spite of the dementia. He is able to express his suffering movingly, Groothof thinks. He says that Mr Pastoor's 'mouth doesn't work' and describes his situation as 'cut off'. Groothof asked him whether he thought he was the same. 'Yes' he said. 'I'm the same, it's just that my mouth can't say that it anymore'.

He is obviously suffering, Groothof says. This is clear from the way he describes his problems and his hopelessness. He finds himself in a situation that he has always feared. He has prepared himself for euthanasia. He spoke to his GP about it a while ago, and he has signed a euthanasia declaration. He is not depressive, but Groothof has prescribed antidepressants nonetheless. The psychologist is to test Mr Pastoor's cognitive capacity and evaluate his understanding of what he is saying.

'What touches me,' says Groothof, 'is the conviction and the hopelessness with which he confronts what is happening to him. The only consolation is that perhaps he forgets.'

Mr Pastoor wants euthanasia, but his wife does not. In a discussion with Dr Groothof about what the treatment policy should be, she had said that she wanted them to do all they could to keep him alive. She visits him every day for four or five hours. They have many friends, who also visit. So he still has a rich social life.

The GP also finds the situation difficult, says Groothof. He wants to explore the issue of euthanasia further, but he can't because Mr Pastoor is now in the nursing home and is therefore the responsibility of the nursing home staff. Groothof doesn't want to allow euthanasia under these unclear circumstances. The policy at Park House is to ensure transparency.

'I could just let the euthanasia request dry up,' Groothof suggests. 'If I wait, then hopefully he will forget it. Soon he won't be able to talk at all, and then I'll have to deal with just his gaze. That's how things usually develop in the nursing home.'

But in spite of this, Groothof is still considering euthanasia, he says. If he decided not to acquiesce, he would say: 'We can discuss it, but I won't do it.'

That morning Rutger Varenkamp had said that Mr Pastoor was not competent, and that euthanasia was not permitted under such circumstances. Groothof doesn't agree. 'Incompetent, rubbish! Yes, maybe regarding the management of his finances. But in this context he knows only too well what he is talking about.'

A tough job

In order to take the euthanasia request further, additional neurological tests in the hospital were required. In addition, Dr Groothof needed to study the GP's reports and await the results of the consultation with the psychologist. Then he would discuss it with Mr Pastoor again, and speak to his family. He had asked Mr Pastoor to write his thoughts down, but he was no longer able to do this. He was considering a video recording. Mr Pastoor had agreed to this. Dr Groothof also wanted to involve one or two other doctors.

He looks at his watch. 'I should have been in the department ten minutes ago.' We leave his office together. In the corridor, as he is locking the door, he tells me that Mr Pastoor used to be a television newsreader. This makes the situation even more complicated, he says. The friends who visit him are also well-known personalities, and Groothof feels the pressure. The policy of Park House is not to implement euthanasia in residents suffering from dementia, so agreeing to euthanasia would bring Groothof into conflict with the management of Park House. He sighs. 'Pastoor is just not your average nursing home resident.'

'He speaks your language,' I say. 'He uses the arguments that you are sensitive to.'

Groothof shakes his head vigorously. 'No, it's not because he speaks my language. No, for me the important thing is how clearly he expresses his hopelessness, that isolation.'

As he turns to leave, I mention that I would like to follow this case, if he agrees. He nods and asks whether I want to be present during discussions with relatives.

'If everyone agrees,' I say.

He says he is not sure whether he should risk it. He wants to know what exactly I am interested in – is it the procedure? I tell him I am interested in everything, and that I am curious how he is going to get out of this dilemma.

'How I'm going to get out of it,' he says, quietly, 'or how I'm not going to get out of it.'

At the end of the day I run into Rutger Varenkamp at reception. He is just leaving. When he sees me he says: 'You've spoken to Michiel, hey?' He tells me that this is not the first time that there has been a situation like this. Last year euthanasia was carried out on a resident with dementia. Or at any rate, he adds, the resident was sent home and the GP carried it out. It was a different sort of case, though. He was suffering from dementia, whereas Michiel's resident is suffering from the *consequences* of dementia: he can't go home to his wife, and that is something different, he says.

When I ask him what he thinks of Mr Pastoor's case he says that it is very time-consuming: in other words, Michiel spends a lot of time on the case when there are other pressing issues to be taken care of. Although he finds it interesting, it isn't *that* interesting. It's a tough job, but if it was in his department it would also be open for discussion, he says. He would at least seriously consider the matter.

Death wishes

Some residents want to die. In some cases this wish stems from before their arrival in the nursing home, and it is usually the relatives who inform staff. There are also residents who say themselves that they want to die, but often their requests are not consistent. Darah says that Mrs Birza said she wanted to die again this morning when she woke up. 'She said it very directly and emphatically,' says Darah. But later, when Darah had come back to wash her, she had said: 'Ach, you know, now that I see you my dear, I don't want to die anymore.'

Mrs Sterk has wanted to die since the death of her husband four years ago. Her sons have raised the issue with Rutger Varenkamp a number of times. He respects that request in the usual nursing home way: the initiation of a policy of symptom alleviation and no interventions to keep her alive. When I first arrived in Park House she was lying in bed calmly, in the process of *versterven*. She refused to eat and drink. Everyone was satisfied with this state of affairs.

One morning she was suddenly in the living room again. She had drunk and eaten everything that had been presented to her that morning, and afterwards requested a slice of bread with chocolate spread. During the rest of the year Mrs Sterk ate so much that her clothes didn't fit any more. She seemed to enjoy life and never mentioned death. When she contracted pneumonia the decision about exclusive symptom alleviation was reversed, in consultation with her sons, and she was given antibiotics and hypodermoclysis.

In Park House there is hardly any discussion of euthanasia. Occasionally a relative will raise the topic, as did the son of Mrs Anjelier one day during a meeting with Rutger Varenkamp. Varenkamp had reminded Mrs Anjelier's son and daughter that she had now been in the nursing home for three years and that her condition had gradually deteriorated during this period, but that she was a quiet resident and no trouble to the carers.

'She could be really difficult with us,' the daughter interrupts. She shivers and describes how her mother can take a piece of bread in her mouth and just leave it there without chewing or swallowing. 'I used to do that as a child, and she used to get angry with me and shout: You dirty child! Swallow it! And now she's doing it herself.'

'You've observed that well,' says the doctor nodding. 'Why do you think that is?'

'She's forgotten, I think.'

Varenkamp confirms that those with Alzheimer's forget. He explains that even sensations of hunger and thirst recede. He looks at each of them in turn, then he tells them that he has asked them to come because their mother is in the final stages of her dementia, and as a result she is eating and drinking less. He says that he can prescribe food supplements and then feed her through a tube later on, but he wonders whether that is what would really benefit her.

They shake their heads.

Varenkamp agrees. He can postpone Mrs Anjelier's death, he says, but he doesn't think it would be in her own best interest.

The son scratches his beard: 'No, that would be humiliating. It sounds hard, but we already took leave of her three year ago. She is there physically, and we will keep visiting her, but the woman in that wheelchair isn't our mother any more.' He doesn't think it is in anyone's interest, including her own, to try and keep his mother alive at all costs. And moreover, they have already experienced the death agony of their father, who had cancer in his lungs and brain. They are very reluctant to go through a similar struggle with their mother, he says.

Rutger Varenkamp nods. He tells them that they have discussed their mother's case in the team and that they all agree. They will take good care of her and continue to offer her food and drink, but if she keeps her mouth tightly closed they will not force her to eat. If she is in pain she will be given an analgesic such as morphine.

The son leans forward and asks softly: 'And speeding up the process, doctor?'

'What do you mean exactly?' asks the doctor.

'Letting her die sooner.'

'In theory we could stop giving her food and liquid,' says Rutger Varenkamp, 'but that isn't a serious option, of course.'

The son looks straight at the doctor.

'Call a spade a spade,' the doctor challenges.

'Euthanasia.'

'We don't do that here,' says the doctor immediately.

'Pity.' The son shrugs. 'I think that's a pity. Especially for my mother, because she never wanted to have the life that she has now.'

Varenkamp explains that euthanasia would not be permitted in the case of Mrs Anjelier even if he wanted to do it. Euthanasia is only allowed in the case of physical illness and when the patient requests it. Mrs Anjelier can no longer do that.

A few residents in De Stadhouder have a euthanasia declaration. Of the sixty-six residents four have an official declaration. Mrs Kok has made her wishes clear in a hand-written note. Assistant dietician Tanja, who thinks that euthanasia should be permitted in the case of dementia, put the note in a plastic cover in Mrs Kok's file so that it wouldn't be missed.

Lying? Who's been lying?

Mr and Mrs Pastoor spend every afternoon and evening in the restaurant. She picks him up and they go hand-in-hand, looking for a free table. He sits down and she goes to get coffee, and then later wine. Usually there are just the two of them, sometimes a large group of visitors, all engaged in animated conversation.

One day I am sitting with Rosan Hüsken and social worker Dina Vogel in the restaurant having lunch. Michiel Groothof joins us, worming in next to me. Straight away he starts to tell me about his conversation, the day before, with Mr and Mrs Pastoor, in his office, with a glass of wine and nuts. They had a good chat, he says. At a certain point, he had said to them that they should talk about dying. Mrs Pastoor had answered: 'Lying? Who's been lying?' The doctor shakes with laughter.

Then his tone becomes serious and he tells me how, once they understood what he was saying, Mr Pastoor had said very clearly: 'Yes, that's what I want: to die.' Groothof sighs. He feels that the law has left him in the lurch here. That there should be clear criteria for cases such as this.

I ask whether Mr Pastoor discussed this with others in the home, carers for example. He shakes his head. He doesn't think Mr Pastoor has a very close relationship with the carers. He thinks that it is because they disapprove of his daily glasses of wine. One of the carers even said that Mr Pastoor has Korsakov's syndrome. 'You enjoy a glass of wine and suddenly you're a Korsakov patient,' says Groothof. He has the impression that Mr Pastoor has his hands full just trying to cope with living in the home. This morning he grabbed the doctor's arm despairingly and said: 'I have to talk to you. It's all so inelegant here.'

After lunch I walk with Rosan Hüsken. She tells me that Michiel Groothof also discussed the euthanasia question with her. He has been touched by this man's predicament, she says, and he feels very involved. He is unhappy that he will be away on leave soon.

Hüsken explains that as a doctor you need to unpick a situation like this very carefully. But by the time that has happened it is often too late because the person in question has sunk too deep into dementia. That's the tragedy, Hüsken thinks. She is a member of the nursing home euthanasia committee. That committee has decided that Park House is not going to play a pioneering role in the euthanasia discussion, and that it should therefore not even be permitted. In spite of this Hüsken hopes that Groothof will make use of the current situation to try and have the decision revised, 'so that it becomes clear that this view is obsolete in some situations.'

I mention that the doctor denies being influenced in this case by the fact that the resident in question is eloquent and highly educated.

'It seems to me that it has everything to do with it,' says Hüsken. 'This resident's choice of words really touched him.' She looks at me: 'You like them as well, don't you?'

A rather frayed end

In the weeks after the lunchtime discussion about Mr Pastoor's euthanasia request I didn't see much of Michiel Groothof. He cancels one appointment, and when I try to ask him about the situation he makes a defensive gesture: he's busy, tired, no time at the moment, and yes another time would be fine.

Four weeks later I hear that Mr Pastoor has died. I phone Michiel Groothof and ask if he will tell me what happened. We meet later that afternoon, and he returns to the meeting he had with Mr and Mrs Pastoor in his office over wine and nuts. 'That was a very good talk,' he says. 'We made an agreement: not to keep him alive. He was very clear about it. He said: Yes, that's what I mean.'

Then his condition deteriorated rapidly and it was difficult to discuss the topic with him any more. The doctor wondered whether Mr Pastoor really wanted euthanasia, because he was making plans for the future, and he kept repeating that 'he wasn't quite ready, that his friends were coming this afternoon.'

His wife clearly didn't want euthanasia. She was evasive when the doctor tried to discuss it with her. Groothof: 'If he had been consistent in his request then I would have done it.'

I ask how he died.

Groothof says that his condition suddenly deteriorated: 'Death was waiting for him, as it were.' He was completely turned in on himself. Then he started to complain of pain. Groothof gave him some light pain medication. That was on Friday. He died peacefully on Sunday.

Groothof says he looks back with satisfaction at the contact that he had with Mr Pastoor. They had some good discussions, and he didn't avoid the issues. But,' he adds, 'he did have a rather frayed end.'

Rough Treatment

There'll be hell!

Loud shouting erupts from the living room. Mrs Walker has taken a bottle of water from the fridge and won't give it to the dietician. 'It's mine, do you hear. Buzz off! Be careful or I'll call my father.' The diminutive woman holds the plastic bottle close. 'Give it to me Mrs Walker. That bottle is supposed to remain in the fridge.' Carer Justine comes out of one of the bedrooms and calls to Mrs Walker: 'Hey, Auntie Miek, what's the problem?'

'Everyone leaves their rubbish lying around. I say: turn the light off first; don't leave it on.' Mrs Walker's tone is indignant. She stutters with agitation.

'I see you've got a nice bottle of water there,' says Justine.

'Yeeees,' Mrs Walker holds up the plastic bottle.

'Are they trying to take it away?'

'Yes, but it's mine. If my father finds out, phew, there'll be hell.'

'Well, why don't you give it to me; I'll look after it for you. I'll keep it in the fridge, then it'll stay nice and cool.'

Mrs Walker gives the bottle to Justine.

'So, that solves the problem,' she says. The dietician turns her attention to cleaning the sink.

'And now?' Justine asks, turning her cheek to Mrs Walker.

'Now you get a kiss,' says Mrs Walker laughing. She plants three thick kisses on Justine's cheek.

To me Justine says: 'Oh, she's such a darling. I have a bond with all the residents, but with her there is really something extra.'

Bruises

Twice a week volunteer Gerard comes to feed Mr Ruiter and put him to bed. Henk Ruiter is forty-eight and suffers from pre-senile dementia. He is divorced, no longer has contact with his children, and never receives visitors. Gerard has offered to be his contact person. He used to be a manager in Park House but he had to retire due to illness and now he works as a volunteer.

Gerard has made an appointment to speak to Darah because he is worried about Mr Ruiter. He thinks that Mr Ruiter is angry and unhappy that his family never visits him. The tragedy is that he can't express those emotions.

Gerard also thinks that Henk has a toothache. When Henk came to live in Park House he had all his teeth done. Now he's got a mouth full of stumps; his teeth have all rotted away. The dentist refuses to look at his teeth because he gets aggressive. Gerard wonders whether anyone brushes Henk's teeth. He wonders whether Henk ever gets washed at all. Darah nods and says that some of her colleagues don't want to get Henk out of bed and feed him because they are scared he will hit them.

'If you're a dear little old lady then they do everything for you,' Gerard says angrily, 'but if you're grumpy, strong and heavy, then it's a different story.'

'We really have the power,' says Darah. 'The residents all have dementia. We can do with them what we want. The carers decide when they have to go to bed; the residents really have no say. You do what suits you best. If you don't feel like it, you don't take a resident to the toilet. Then she just doesn't go, because she can't go by herself. The way residents are treated is sometimes really an abuse of power.'

Darah says that colleagues reproach her for spoiling residents. As an example she mentions a new resident who likes to have a nap after lunch. She used to do that at home. After lunch Darah takes her to her room and puts her to bed. And if she wants, Darah puts on some music. Some of Darah's colleagues don't think it's a good idea to spoil residents like that. They lock the bedroom door so that she can't go to bed after lunch. She then sits in front of the room waiting for someone to open the door. Darah thinks that her colleagues find this resident arrogant. She wears good clothes and is a bit standoffish. 'I don't understand,' says Darah, 'why she's not allowed to go to her bed in the afternoon. It's not as though she's bothering anyone.'

This weekend she was really shocked, she continues. A colleague got very angry with Mrs Walker because she had taken underwear out of the laundry basket and refused to give it back. The colleague grabbed the underwear and Mrs Walker got angry. She raised her hand as if to hit her and the carer grabbed her and shook her and said: be careful, I'm on shift this evening. It happened in the living room, with visitors present. Darah was really shocked and didn't know what to do. She went and sat in the office to calm down. In the end she didn't say anything at all; she was so taken aback. And it was a permanent colleague, not a temp, and someone from whom she had not expected it.

'I start to boil when I see things like that,' says Gerard. He thinks that Darah has certainly taken on a big task as care coordinator. To do her job she needs to be able to be unpleasant and take unpopular decisions, but she will then be doomed to criticism behind her back. If she doesn't do anything then unpleasant things will continue to happen and she will regret not having intervened.

I notice that this is all very open and that the colleague does not appear to think she has done anything wrong. It makes me wonder what happens behind closed doors.

'There are things that can't bear the light of day,' Gerard says slowly. 'We all know that. In the evening and night shifts there is no control.' To

Darah he says: 'You must have come in on some of the morning shifts and noticed suspicious bruises on residents?'

Darah nods. She says that Mrs Walker had a bruise on her arm for a long time; a very large bruise. It was said that she had fought. But Darah doesn't believe it. 'Mrs Walker couldn't say what had happened. She kept saying: She did it. You can tell that there are carers she likes and there are carers she is scared of.'

I ask why this sort of thing happens. According to Gerard it is due to work pressure and also to changing attitudes in society: people generally treat each other more roughly. He says that he regularly sees things in the living room and thinks: Is that really necessary? And he doesn't keep his mouth shut. 'How would you like your mother to be treated like that? You wouldn't? Well then, don't do it to someone else.' Gerard says he often hears screaming in the bedrooms or the showers. Carers say those with dementia scream like that. Gerard has his doubts. 'But what can you do?' he asks. 'You don't have any evidence.'

Pickled mussels

The conversation with Gerard and Darah has given me an unpleasant feeling. I go for a walk to try and get rid of it. Then I go into a café and order a cup of coffee. From my seat at the window I see Mr Nierop getting off the tram. Not long ago he had to have his wife admitted to the nursing home, after having cared for her at home for years. He visits her three times a week. When he comes he stays most of the day, helps the carers to fold up the washing and eats meals with the residents. It is a good remedy against an empty house and loneliness. He and his wife were childless and led a reclusive existence.

Mr Nierop is dressed neatly for the occasion. His shirt is buttoned up to the collar and his hair is neatly parted. He carries an umbrella rolled up under his arm and a plastic carrier bag that swings back and forth as he walks. What could it contain? Home-pickled mussels, in a jar, with a colourful cloth over the lid, held in place with a rubber band? During the introductory interview with Rutger Varenkamp, Mr Nierop asked, in tears, whether he could bring his wife a pot of pickled mussels. He made them himself. 'Please doctor? My wife loves them.' When the doctor answered that he could bring whatever he liked, he answered: 'May I really? Oh thank you, thank you, doctor.'

I recognise other denizens of the nursing home in the street scene unfolding in front of me. Dina Vogel, the social worker with her long black coat, just coming out of the bakery with bread rolls for lunch. And Tineke from admin cycling past. What would I see if I came and sat at this same window a year hence, I wondered. Would Mr Nierop still be there? No, probably not. But there would be another Mr Nierop coming to visit his wife, I just wouldn't recognise him. Then the street scene reverts to its normal state, with anonymous pedestrians passing to and fro, just as it must have been years earlier when, as a student, I had surveyed the street from the same vantage point.

I ask Darah a few times whether she has spoken to her colleague about the incident with Mrs Walker in the living room. No, says Darah, she just never seems to get round to it. First the colleague had a few days leave, then Darah herself. And anyway – she admits reluctantly – she doesn't really dare to. I never ask her again.

Teasing

After the discussion with Gerard and Darah about Henk Ruiter I heard other similar stories. When I was drinking coffee with the dietician Tanja, she mentioned that she doesn't like the way that carers sometimes tease residents. Sometimes, for example, they may talk about a topic that a resident doesn't like, and when they see that she doesn't like it, they don't stop. Then when the resident gets angry but can't express herself, they laugh.

Once Tanja saw a carer push a resident, who then fell. It wasn't on purpose, but it wasn't entirely accidental either. The carer immediately said she hadn't done anything. Tanja had looked at her in silence. The carer flushed and asked whether Tanja would report her. Tanja had said no, but that she would if she saw it happen again.

Colette tells me that she recently heard a colleague say to a resident: 'If you don't shut your trap then I'll open the window and throw you out.' Colette wonders why someone like that works with people with dementia. 'You'd think they'd know that when someone has dementia they don't act and think like you and me,' she says. 'Sometimes they're troublesome, but they don't do it on purpose.'

I tell her that I sometimes think: it's really pleasant here. But then other times I think: it's a struggle for survival.

Colette says that she would never want to live like the residents in the nursing home. 'You have no privacy,' she says. 'Everything is controlled by the carers: they get up when we want them to, they get food when it fits our schedule, they go to the toilet when we take them. They've been put away, by their family, by society, by everyone. Nursing home residents have been abandoned and left at our mercy.'

You have to teach them who's in charge

Leontien and Veronica are in the office. Leontien has been on extended sick leave – a back problem. She is a Surinamese woman in her mid-thirties, with conspicuous clothes, jewellery and make-up. She has sharp eyes and doesn't miss a thing. When I walk into the living room on her first day back she calls me: 'Psssst, nice skirt, very sexy.'

She offers her hand: 'I'm Leontien, the notorious Leontien. You must have heard of me.' I had indeed heard about Leontien. Her colleagues speculate, for example, about where she gets the money to buy all the expensive clothes and jewellery. Rumour has it that she is a striptease dancer.

In the following weeks we speak often. She tells me about her children – she is a single mother – and about the men in her life. She seems to be in control of her life. When I tell her that, she replies that things used to be different. She used to do everything for the father of her children and was 'a dependent woman'. He left her for another woman. She hadn't expected that. Leontien then decided to do things differently. In relationships she is now in charge. She makes the decisions and she controls her own money.

She shows me a case full of creams and make-up, and tells me she is a rep for skin-care products. She takes my hand and starts to massage the skin with scrub. Then she applies two creams. 'Just feel how soft it is,' she says when she is finished. Then she offers to sell me some products. She says she can come to my home and give me a face job.

'That's a good book,' she says when she sees I have Colette's copy of *No Time To Be Nice*. She tells me that when she first started working in the nursing home she also wanted to be nice to the residents. 'I worked really hard. But later you realise that it just doesn't work. You start to slow down. You think: I'll do that one if I have time. You start to think more of yourself. That's because of the pressure of work. You have to work so hard that you gradually start to think like that.'

Veronica agrees. She says that in another nursing home in which she worked, carers put plasters over the mouths of residents who screamed like Mrs Bloem. 'It's true,' says Veronica. 'If they screamed, they were put in isolation. People like that spoil things for other residents. She keeps nagging to go to the toilet but when you get there she doesn't need it any more. You have to deal with residents like that. New carers are initially nice to residents like Mrs Bloem, but you see them change.'

'You have to control them with your eyes,' says Leontien slowly. She looks me straight in the eye and after a minute I look away. She laughs: 'You can't take it, hey? You have to keep looking. That's what I do with the residents. Even if you're getting clothes out of the cupboard to dress them, you have to fix them with your eyes. That cools them down.'

'Yes, you have to deal with them,' Veronica adds. 'Otherwise they'll be bossing you around. I do that with my kids as well. If they don't listen to me, I put them out on the balcony. I don't care whether it's raining or freezing, it teaches them to behave.'

Leontien nods: 'If a resident says she doesn't want to be washed, then I wash her first, I give her a nice cold shower. You have to teach them who's in charge.'

Learning about decorum

Rosan Hüsken nods when I tell her of my conversations with Darah and Gerard, and of the discussion with Leontien and Veronica. The humanist counsellor tells me about a meeting of the discussion group with somatic residents. Hüsken had brought along a coffee grinder and other old-fashioned things. A resident said that she would like to eat at a nicely laid-out table. Hüsken asked what should be on the table. A tablecloth, nice plates without cracks, a butter dish with curls of butter. The residents had a whole list of things.

Then suddenly the mood changed. Hüsken doesn't know why, but suddenly everyone was angry. They couldn't enjoy their meal, they said, because there was always such a lot of noise in the living room. Lots of shouting 'in a language we don't understand.' Their biggest complaint was that everything was so rough. One resident said she couldn't eat because no one said *bon appetit*. And one man said falteringly: 'There's still a lot to be learned here about decorum.'

In the discussion groups with relatives of residents with dementia there is also discussion of the rough treatment of residents, says Hüsken. There are relatives who come and feed residents themselves because they want to be sure it is done properly. Hüsken thinks that some carers don't really understand dementia. She often hears carers say to residents with dementia: 'I already told you that yesterday,' and they get irritated when residents 'can't be bothered to listen'. They also take residents' comments personally. You need to have the capacity to reflect and distance yourself in order to properly evaluate residents' behaviour. Unfortunately that capacity is often absent, says Hüsken.

She doesn't discuss the coarsening in the nursing home. It's taboo, she says. She raised the topic not long ago during a staff dinner. The supervisor of the evening shift became angry and denied it categorically. Others agreed. They were very defensive: 'What do you expect when everyone has to work so hard,' they said.

Hüsken has thought about how she could help residents. 'The best way is to write a book explaining how to be the perfect nursing home resident. Forget about autonomy and being yourself. You have to be nice to the carers. Residents who are happy with cold soup, who don't weigh a lot and who don't complain get the most attention. Remember the names of all the carers, compliment them on their dedication, ask about their children, and don't complain. Then they'll like you. Even better if you smoke, because then you can go with them to the restaurant and drink coffee.'

Behind Jessy's back

When I enter the office Darah is sitting with her face in her hands. She shakes her head. I ask what the problem is. She looks up and has tears in her eyes. She tells me that during the care coordinators' meeting she had talked about the incident in the living room when Jessy shook Mrs Walker. They were discussing how to deal with emotions and everyone had to give an example. Darah had thought that the meeting was confidential but this morning Anna van Raalten had called her and Jessy into her office to discuss the incident. Now Jessy is angry with her. She feels that Darah should have discussed it with her and not behind her back with Anna. 'But that's not what I intended,' Darah says. 'I didn't know Anna was going to pass it on.'

Later that day Anna van Raalten also mentions the incident. She understands that Darah is shocked and doesn't like it, but she couldn't just let it pass. When Darah told her story, Anna felt that she had to intervene. 'I'm supposed to protect the residents aren't I?' she says. 'Who else is going to do it? If someone can't cope with the work here, for whatever reason, then they should go and work somewhere else.'

The care manager doesn't think that dismissal is an option, though. That wouldn't help anyone, and it's the first time she has heard something like this about Jessy. She hadn't expected it from her, and she is otherwise very happy with her work. So she thought that a meeting with both of them would be the best option. She sees it as a learning process for Darah. She thinks that Darah, in her management role, should be able to raise issues like this with her colleagues.

During the meeting Jessy defended herself by saying that she shouldn't have to tolerate being hit by Mrs Walker, because that is what had been happening in the previous weeks. Van Raalten said that she should indeed not have to tolerate being hit, but that in cases like that she could simply walk away. She asked Jessy to show her what she had done to Mrs Walker. Jessy took her wrists and shook her. Van Raalten found the experience quite painful. She suggested that Jessy, who thought giving such a shaking was quite normal, might be used to rough treatment, that it might be a question of cultural differences. 'How do I know how she was brought up in Surinam?' she says. 'Maybe by a heavy-handed grandmother who was quick to hand out corporal punishment? Maybe Jessy has become that grandmother and Mrs Walker that eight-year-old girl.'

Van Raalten asked Jessy how things were at home. Jessy said that everything was fine. Van Raalten said that the discussion should be seen as a warning. They would speak again in two weeks. In the meantime Jessy was to keep away from Mrs Walker.

In the department, and especially in unit C, the collision between Jessy and Mrs Walker is the talk of the day. Various carers say that they have occasionally seen bruises on a resident for which they were unable to identify a cause, because those with dementia can't remember.

'Sometimes it seems as though people forget that those with dementia are also people with norms and values,' says Justine. 'Of course you occasionally have an off-day, but it shouldn't become routine to snap at residents.' When she sees something like that she tries to be constructive and suggest alternatives, but she is often told that she spoils residents too much. 'I don't,' she says. 'I just try and find the right way of dealing with them.'

For example, Mrs Walker has a mania for collecting things. When she passes by with a pile of towels, there's no point saying: 'Give me those; I'm sick of you stealing the towels.' Justine just lets her walk around with her towels for a while, then she asks: 'Mrs Walker, can I put those towels away?'

Femke says that she once almost hit a resident. It was shortly after her mother had died after a long struggle with cancer. 'I suddenly saw myself standing there, with my hand in the air, ready to strike.' She blushes as she talks, and fidgets with her white coat. 'Phew, I still feel embarrassed when I think about it. When I realised what was happening, I just walked away. I asked someone else to look after that resident.'

Femke then reported sick and stayed home for the next six months. She hadn't realised that she was so stressed, after caring for her mother next to her full-time job. 'I never thought that I would ever be capable of hitting a resident,' she said.

Aggression

Anna van Raalten asks psychologist Max Hermann to organise a meeting for the carers about aggression. Two weeks later the psychologist stands in front of ten carers and tells them that the meeting has been organised because a few residents have manifested aggressive behaviour. His job is to teach carers how to deal with that aggression. The aim is to exchange experiences and make this sensitive topic a subject of discussion.

The psychologist points to the text on the flip chart behind him: 'I've put up a few topics here,' he says. 'First, how is aggression expressed? Who has an example?'

Myrna replies that she was recently dressing a resident who suddenly became very angry. She threatened Myrna with the potty and Myrna had to run away. 'I was shocked,' Myrna says, 'because she never does that.'

Christa says that Mrs Gramberg often hits out, or pinches or spits without warning. Often it is painful.

Mrs Birza makes racist remarks, says Darah. For example: 'I just don't understand why God made black people. You're not any good for anything.' Or: 'I hope that you blacks get run over by a car.' Comments like that hit you hard, Darah says. She has the feeling that Mrs Birza knows exactly what she is saying, because she looks Darah straight in the eye when she says it.

The psychologist asks why they think that aggression develops. Christa thinks it's because residents spend the whole day together in the living room: 'They get on each other's nerves,' she says.

'Irritation' the psychologist writes on the flip chart.

Sylvia notes that residents usually get aggressive during care sessions: 'They have all kinds of physical problems and we probably hurt them.'

Mrs Halie has just lost her daughter, says Yvette. Since that happened she gets very angry.

'Pain' and 'bad experience' the psychologist adds to his list.

'A lot of residents don't understand,' says Darah.

'Incomprehension' goes up on the chart.

The psychologist says that it is important to realise that incomprehension and powerlessness go together. Those with dementia don't understand things and therefore feel powerless; and feelings of powerlessness can lead to aggression. So the failing memory of a resident is an important cause of aggression.

Personality also plays a role, he explains. Those with dementia still have a personality. He gives the example of Mrs Goslinga, who was difficult and dramatic all her life, and still is. The psychologist says that aggression never just appears out of nothing, but is always a result of frustration. Unfortunately, the reason for that frustration is not always clear. It is no coincidence that aggression suddenly develops during care sessions, the psychologist explains. It is then that residents are asked to do things they don't like and don't understand. They also have a different conception of time. If it is eight in the morning for us and we want the resident to get out of bed, it might be midnight in their experience. 'It's best to prevent aggression before it develops,' he says. 'Try to intervene as soon as you see the early warning signs. Let them express their anger. Tact and going along with the resident's experience are often the best approach.' The psychologist looks at the carers. 'Questions? No? Then I want to ask you what aggression does to you.'

Christa remembers well the occasion when Mrs Molleman kicked her hard in the stomach. 'I have to kick you to death,' she had said. Christa is convinced that she meant what she said. Christa was very angry and wasn't involved in caring for Mrs Molleman for a year.

Femke says that Mrs de Vos was once angry and chased her. 'She cleared her throat, looked me straight in the eye, and spat in my face. She knew what she was doing.' Christa felt humiliated. Darah recognises the feeling. When Mrs Birza accuses the carers of theft and says: 'You blacks all steal,' she also experiences this as humiliating.

When Myrna was chased by the woman with the potty she wondered what she had done to deserve it. 'A feeling of failure,' the psychologist concludes. He wants to dwell on this some more, to give the carers something that will support them. He says that it is important to remain calm and to radiate understanding. That won't work all the time, he adds, because sometimes a resident's comments will really hurt you. 'If you feel that you're really getting angry, then count to ten before you respond,' he advises.

Walking away is also a good response, he says. So is trying to distract the resident. Carers can also try and find out from the resident what the problem is. Or they could say: 'I don't want you to hit me.' When the situation is really threatening, the psychologist advises them to seek help. 'Call a colleague or even the doctor.'

Then there are things that they should definitely not do. Respond aggressively, for example. That doesn't help, it's not permitted and it is certainly not professional, says the psychologist. 'Discussion usually doesn't help,' he adds.

The psychologist looks at his watch: 'We're over time, so we're going to round this up.' But first he wants to note that discrimination is a separate issue. He points out that most of the residents are white and most of the carers are coloured, and he affirms that discrimination can really hurt. 'And just because the person making the remark has dementia doesn't mean it should be acceptable,' he says. Carers can limit discrimination by answering: 'I don't want you to say things like that to me.' If that doesn't help, just walk away.

After the session the psychologist tells me that incidents like that with Mrs Walker happen regularly. The question is, is that really ill-treatment, he says, though even if it isn't, it does come close to it. Ill-treatment happens, even here in Park House. Especially in the evenings when carers are alone and the pressure of work is high. In other nursing homes it's the same. He hears similar stories from colleagues in other homes. 'We don't talk about it often,' he says, 'because it's taboo. Our response is to organise meetings like this one.'

Reorganisation and Black Magic

Quarrels

Care manager Anna van Raalten doesn't work on Fridays and weekends. The first time I go to the nursing home on one of those days I am surprised by the very different atmosphere. As I come out of the lift I hear Marco Borsato [a Dutch crooner] blaring from the living room.

'It's very jolly in here,' I say. Colette gives me a meaningful look. She says that everyone is always in a good mood from Friday to Monday evening. If they play this kind of music on other days they get told: 'Is that your choice or that of the residents?' Mrs Boshard and Mrs Keizer are smoking in the living room. No one seems to mind the music.

In the coffee break in the restaurant I hear about the tense relationship and the conflicts between the carers and Anna van Raalten. This week things blew up. During an argument Femke threw a tray full of cups on the ground. She shouldn't have done that, she now says, but she was so angry and felt so powerless and it all happened before she realised what she was doing. She feels that her supervisor treats her like a small child: 'It's as though we can do nothing right.'

Femke has her resignation letter in her pocket. After coffee she drops it off at personnel, but they refuse to accept it. They suggest an immediate meeting between Femke and Marco Burgers, Anna van Raalten's line manager, and then a meeting next week between Anna and Femke. Femke agrees. She doesn't really want to resign. She has worked in Park House for fifteen years and has been happy here. She just doesn't want to work like this any more.

Femke is not the only one with complaints about the care manager. The carers call Van Raalten 'hard' and say that she never has much interest in the 'person behind the carer'. Most complaints are about the way she speaks to staff, or rather reprimands them. Darah says that a few days ago she was with the chiropodist, who comes once a month to do the residents' feet. If she has time left she also does the carers' feet, for a fee. Darah had just taken off her shoes when Van Raalten walked past. Darah was summoned into her office and there Van Raalten exploded. Did Darah think it was normal to have a pedicure during working hours when they chiropodist was supposed to be looking after the residents' feet? Darah was shocked. She thought the response was unjustified. She was very upset, she says, because she often works longer hours than she is paid. She had done all her work and had gone to the chiropodist fifteen minutes before the end of her shift. 'It's not that bad, is it?' she asks, indignantly. 'I felt humiliated by the way she called me into her office and lectured to me.'

The carers are irritated by the fact that their care manager never says 'thank you', says social worker Dina Vogel. She is Surinamese and also the ombudsperson for many of the Surinamese carers. The carers complain that their superiors are constantly commenting on mistakes but never see all the things they do well. Dina Vogel thinks this is foolish because it means that carers lose interest in making an extra effort and are more likely to report sick.

Dina Vogel thinks that the incident with Darah and the pedicure was 'terribly silly and short sighted'. Darah has worked in the nursing home for many years. She often works late and is always prepared to do overtime, even though she is a single mother. 'That should be appreciated,' says Vogel. 'You don't summon someone like that into your office and lecture them as though they were a child.'

In the afternoon the living room in unit C is very busy. The laughter and chatter of the carers can be heard at the other end of the corridor. As is often the case, all the carers present are Surinamese or Antillean. They are gathered in the kitchen off the living room.

'And you know why she always wants to sit on the spin-dryer?' I hear someone say as I enter. 'No? It's because it loosens the turds!' Laughter. 'It's true, just ask her. She says so herself!' The carers slap their thighs as they laugh.

The residents sit around the living room table with coffee. They look around and don't say much. Only Mrs Goslinga responds to the laughter of the carers with a smile. When Christa sees me she comes across. 'There you are. I brought you some peanut sauce but I haven't seen you all week. When are you in again? I'll bring you some more.'

Darah slams a game of Ludo on the table. 'Come on, go and join the residents,' she urges her colleagues. 'And play with them, not with each other.'

Carer Justine comes into the living room and claps: 'Ladies, ladies, what a mess! Do you call that tidying up? The cutlery should be in the drawer.'

'There she goes again,' the carers say in unison.

'I'm allowed to comment, aren't I? You could do the same to me if I didn't do what I was supposed to.' Justine points to herself: 'A bit of respect, please, for an older woman.'

When I move away from the table they call: 'We haven't shocked you have we? You're not leaving because of us?'

I laugh and hear Christa say: 'Don't worry, she's always coming and going.'

Community service for the director

In Park House there is dissatisfaction with the director. He is the third in the last five years. 'They actually managed to appoint a catering entrepreneur as director of this nursing home,' says nursing home doctor Rick van Velzen. He says that the director had been convicted of fraud in his previous job. It was on the news, so everyone knew about it. 'How can someone like that have authority?' the doctor wonders. 'He was doomed to fail.'

He had been given community service, and there had even been a documentary about it. The doctor thought it was also 'very comical' because in the documentary you could see the director out in the forest somewhere knocking poles into the ground. He had to do that for sixty hours. In an emotional tone he had said that people don't realise how offensive it was having to do such work. Rick van Velzen slams his hand on the table. 'Can you imagine? And the guy had just committed a crime,' he says. 'Nice guy, by the way, but that statement illustrates how far from reality he is. There are so many people who do jobs like that all their lives. Like most of the staff in the nursing home of which he is now the director, for example! But that doesn't enter his head. So how can he expect to understand those people?'

As time passes the dissatisfaction with the director increases. Finally the whole thing explodes in a conflict with the employees' council. The council gives the director a vote of no confidence and all the members report sick.

The interim manager

The Board of Trustees appoint an interim manager to carry out a reorganisation. 'The advantage of outside administrators is that they can achieve things in a very short time that someone from inside could never achieve,' explains Roderik Franssen, the interim manager. He is in his forties, wearing a corduroy suit and brightly-coloured tie and comes from Westerlaken & Partners, an interim-management agency. He explains that interim managers get the 'tools' from the director or the Board of Trustees that enable them to make quick decisions. Because they don't have a bond with the staff they can easily implement unpopular measures and they are freer to take risks. 'Sometimes that's just what a company needs to get back on track.'

When Westerlaken & Partners are called in they first carry out a 'quick scan': all departments are given a list of questions that they have to answer. How does the organisation work? How is control exercised? What are the procedures? They look at documents – annual reports, budgets, accounts, contracts and protocols. Finally they interview staff. In this way they generate a picture of the organisation, and on the basis of this they develop a plan.

Anna van Raalten is positive about the arrival of the interim manager. She hopes that he will support her in carrying out the changes that she thinks are necessary. In essence the problems in Park House are not very different from the problems in other nursing homes, she says. They are just more clearly visible because there hasn't been good leadership for such a long time. The core problem, she says, is that there is no broader vision among the carers. 'They just do whatever they want. That's why everything needs to be repeated over and over and why we have to impose things.'

The care manager also thinks that the carers do not have a proper sense of responsibility. She says that she has arranged with her colleagues that they will take turns visiting the departments unexpectedly in the evenings. There is a rumour that residents are sometimes put in bed by eight-o'-clock. Not because they are tired, but because the evening shift want to finish earlier. 'Then they can chat and watch television the rest of the evening,' says Anna van Raalten. 'That's unacceptable. Staff who do that will have to go.'

The carers also have criticisms. Robby, for example, is not entirely happy about the way care is provided. 'Residents aren't given any real attention,' he says. As an example he mentions the way in which carers sit together drinking coffee rather than joining the residents in the living room. Carers also talk loudly about topics that the residents might find unpleasant, 'such as sex for example'. He is irritated by the constant complaints. 'It starts first thing in the morning,' he says: 'Oh I'm so tired; the work is so hard.' Robby is also tired sometimes, he says, 'but then that's my problem. It means I haven't been doing things the way I should.'

Carer Myrna is also dissatisfied, but she finds it difficult to talk about, because it may seem like she is criticising colleagues or gossiping. She thinks that things aren't structured enough. At the end of the morning some of her colleagues break for more than an hour. 'I sometimes have the impression that they come here to chat and maintain their friendships,' she says, shaking her head. 'They sit and talk so much.'

Even the transfer between shifts is unsatisfactory, Myrna says. They hardly write anything in the files. How are you supposed to know how things are going with the residents? When relatives ask her something about a resident, Myrna often doesn't have an answer. Complaining is difficult, because then you're seen as an 'eager beaver'. She says that the previous care coordinator tried to change things. 'And that's what got him: he was harassed out of his job, just because he said something when staff arrived late or spent too much time over coffee.' Myrna refused to succeed him as coordinator, as suggested by Anna van Raalten. 'No, I didn't want to burn my fingers on that one,' she says. Myrna doesn't think that the arrival of Westerlaken & Partners will change things: 'That manager doesn't understand the problems here,' she ways.

In fact, none of the carers expect any good to come out of the interim manager's activities. 'In the fifteen years that I've worked here we've been turned this way and that,' says Colette, expressing the general feeling. 'First we had a head of department, then a team leader, then a section head, and now a care manager. I wonder what it'll be next year.'

Rutger Varenkamp is ambivalent about the coming reorganisation. It appears that he is to be a member of the management team. He is not very keen. He enjoys working on the ground with the residents. But on the other hand, something has to be done, he agrees. De Stadhouder was always the best functioning department in Park House. In only six months it has become the most problematic. Varenkamp says that it's difficult to face reality, but that there are things that are unacceptable. He describes how he makes arrangements for the care of residents' injuries. The care coordinator is there as well and it is noted in the file. 'Everyone nods in agreement,' he says. 'But then when the time arrives to actually do it, no one does. You decide as a doctor what needs to be done, but then when the carers take no notice there's little you can do.'

During the initial weeks the presence of the interim-manager is hardly noticed. Then one morning yellow announcements appear all over the nursing home with the text:

> From today not everyone is allowed to park behind the home. An announcement
> will be made as to who is allowed to use the car park.
> Sincerely, Roderik Franssen

On the one in the lift someone has written: *Probably reserved for the Gold Coast!*

A new beginning

Roderik Franssen and Anna van Raalten are to inform the carers of De Stadhouder about the results of the 'quick scan' and the proposed changes. 'Attendance is obligatory,' the care manager warns them when announcing the meeting. 'And you have to be on time.'

When the time comes all the carers and Anna van Raalten gather in the meeting room. Roderik Franssen hasn't arrived yet. Robby is irritated: 'We all have to be on time but Mr Big Interim Manager is late.' After ten minutes Anna van Raalten leaves the room to phone Franssen.

'He's on his way,' she says when she gets back. 'But let's start so that we don't waste any more time.' She starts by saying that there will be a new organisational structure that will be flatter. That means less bureaucracy and less paperwork. Practically it means that the doctors and care managers will join the management team and have more involvement in policy. Van Raalten says that the financial situation in Park House is 'critical, very critical', and if things continue like this the home will be bankrupt in a few months. As a result management will have to take unpopular steps. In the next month no more new staff will be employed, for example. As she says this there is a buzz of voices in the room.

'Can we keep the discussion central please,' the care manager calls above the noise. 'Any questions?'

Myrna asks whether this means that in the coming months the care manager will have even less time for the carers. 'Just look around you,' she says. 'Everyone is burnt out and exhausted. Anna, when we need you we look for you but can't find you. Your room is locked. You're already too busy. We also need a pat on the back occasionally and confirmation that we are doing a good job.'

The care manager confirms that she will have to attend more meetings under the new system, but she will have a secretary for eight hours a week, and that will help.

'It's not nice working here any more,' Myrna continues. 'Even the temps don't want to work here any more.'

'If you have solutions, we'd like to hear them,' says Rutger Varenkamp.

The door opens and Roderik Franssen enters: 'Sorry, sorry, in my diary it said half past three.' He takes his place next to Anna van Raalten. 'May I? For those of you who don't know me, I'm Roderik Franssen, partner in Westerlaken & Partners. I'm the interim director and present four days a week. We have organised this meeting to tell you about our findings. I also want to tell you about our plans, which I'd like to discuss with you.'

He scans the room. 'In brief, care, which is what nursing homes are about, is not central. Or, to put it differently, the support services are not supporting care.'

'Everyone knows how long it takes when something needs repairing,' Van Raalten adds. 'How many memos you have to write, how often you have to phone, how you have to beg, and even then it takes months. That's because the technical support section does not provide adequate support.'

'When in fact the guys in technical support should be thinking: Great, a memo, now I can get down to work,' says Franssen, rubbing his hands. 'We're not saying that this will suddenly improve. But we are going to work on it. That's the first thing.'

The conditions under which the carers have to work are 'plainly pitiful', he continues. They almost always need support from temp staff, who don't know the residents or the procedures, and by the time they are getting familiar with things, they leave, says Franssen.

He says that there is 'a huge amount of illness,' and that carers regularly arrive at work in the morning to find that two or three colleagues are off sick, and those who are at work just have to manage. 'And as soon as your sick colleagues are better and return to work, the next batch falls ill and you are still under-staffed,' says Franssen. 'That all has to change.' He wants to make Park House a pleasant working environment again, so that everyone says: 'Park House, now *that's* the place to work.' He wags his finger to emphasise the point. 'And we have to work together to achieve that.'

In order to do that he wants everyone to agree to certain things. He falls silent and surveys the room, then he continues slowly: 'That means that we have to agree that from now on everyone arrives on time and leaves on time. It means that we turn our mobile phones off during working hours. It means that we point out each other's mistakes, and don't get angry when someone points out our mistakes. It means that we welcome the temps and explain to them what needs to be done and how. Seems only normal to me. We know the ropes, they don't.' He looks round the room. 'Clear? Questions?'

'I think it's a pity that we didn't get any information about what this meeting was going to be about,' says Sylvia. 'It would have been nice to have been prepared.'

'You could have asked,' says Roderik Franssen, irritated. 'You don't have to passively wait until everything is presented to you.' Sylvia turns away.

Tanja says that Franssen has only repeated things that she has been saying for ages. So long in fact that she is starting to feel like an old bore. No one listened to her, she says. 'Take the kitchen, for example...'

Franssen interrupts her: 'I know. Crazy. Getting the dieticians to the kitchen at half-ten, just when the residents are out of bed and there's no one in the living room. That's all going to change, but I can't do anything about that right now.'

'And then there's the fruit,' Tanja continues. She says that the apples and pears that are bought every week are too hard for the residents to eat, and there are only five bananas. She wants to know why they can't buy more bananas.

The interim-manager mumbles that he doesn't understand why no one has informed the person who orders the fruit to change the selection.

Tanja says that she used to have a blender but since that was stolen she can't make smoothies from the fruit any more. She suggests buying a new one.

'That would just get stolen as well,' someone says.

'They steal everything,' someone else says. 'Even the residents' slippers.'

'They? They're your colleagues,' Franssen says sternly.

'Perhaps, but not necessarily,' comes the answer.

'There are so many people coming in and out of the home,' says Tanja. 'We don't know everyone.'

Roderik Franssen bangs the table: 'It's unacceptable that things get stolen here. It makes me furious. From now on we're going to do things differently. We'll forget about the past and look to the future. Has anyone any ideas about how we can recruit new staff?'

Myrna says that in some nursing homes they give you a bicycle if you come and work for them. The interim-manager nods: 'Go on.'

Various suggestions follow: 250 euros for any staff member who brings in a new recruit; asking new staff to approach colleagues from their previous job and ask them to come and work in Park House; information evenings in the neighbourhoods where carers live.

'A crèche would help,' suggests Darah. 'There used to be a crèche where you could leave your children. That would be a solution for some of us...'

'Excellent. Go on.'

'You could let the day shift start at nine so that we have time to take the kids to school.'

'More difficult,' says the interim-manager. 'Okay, thank you. We'll certainly consider your suggestions.'

I walk with Tanja and Sylvia back to the department. I ask what they thought of the meeting.

'Hm,' they grumble. Tanja says she still feels she isn't being taken seriously.

'They've had plenty of time to see the conditions under which you work,' I say.

Tanja: 'Pff! He talks smoothly, but I know from other sources what they think of us. We drink coffee for hours; we're always late, etc., etc. No, I'm not taken in by his smooth talk.'

Summer care

Summer is approaching. It is clear that these will be difficult months. There are already too few carers, with a number on long-term sick leave, and in the summer many take their annual leave, and if the weather is good it is difficult to find temp staff. Last year the situation was described as occasionally tight; this year it is a structural problem. It happens regularly that a carer is alone on a unit with twelve residents. The mood has deteriorated perceptibly. Things tend to go wrong in the weekend.

Tanja tells me that last Sunday was one of those days. Sylvia was on unit A and a temp was on unit B. Each had twelve seriously demented residents to look after. Tanja had fried eggs, but by the time she was finished it was almost lunchtime. Mrs Blauw only got up at half past one. Sylvia was exhausted after her shift and there were still three residents in bed.

Work on units with seriously demented residents is hard work, says Tanja. Many have to be carried and that is almost impossible if they don't cooperate. Two yeas ago one carer was responsible for four residents on average; now it is six. When they have finished the work on their own unit, carers have to go and help out on other units, and in the afternoons there is the washing to sort. There is just no end to the work.

In order to alleviate the staff shortage the management team decides to implement a temporary restriction on the admittance of new residents. They also implement 'summer care'. All non-carer staff and volunteers receive a letter asking them to assist with daily care activities. Rosan Hüsken, the humanist counsellor, excitedly shows me the schedule on which volunteers can fill in their name. She reads it dramatically: 'Who is going to help me get out of bed? The residents of Park House need you!' She shakes her head: 'It's understandable, but it's not really a solution. I sometimes think: better to let everything collapse. It must be very confusing for the residents to suddenly find themselves being washed by the pastor.'

A shower once every three weeks

Anna van Raalten raises the issue of the heavy workload during a meeting. The carers explode and overwhelm her with examples.

'I know that there is a heavy workload,' the care manager interrupts. She says that they are working on a long-term solution, but she wants to talk about measures that can be taken now. Showering is a problem, and she asks how often the residents have a shower.

'When we have time,' the carers say in chorus.

Van Raalten knows that, but wants to know whether the carers keep track of when residents last had a shower. Silence. 'So the answer is no,' she concludes. She asks for an estimate of what is possible.

'No more than once a week,' says Femke.

'We can't do it that often,' says Sylvia shaking her head. 'Our people are more difficult. Maybe once in two or three weeks.'

'Okay,' says the care manager. 'Is it possible to shower the mild dementia cases once a week?' The carers nod. 'And the more serious ones once in three weeks?' The carers nod. Van Raalten says it would be nice if they could at least try to do it more often. She suggests making a showering schedule for each resident.

Then she talks about work pressure. 'It's busiest at half-past-eleven in the morning,' she says. She proposes trying to spread the work out more evenly across the day. 'For example, wash three people before coffee and then help other residents after coffee...'

The carers protest: 'Yes, but then they won't get any food...'

Van Raalten proposes letting them have breakfast first and then washing and dressing them later, perhaps even in the afternoon. Maybe they'd rather stay in bed longer and have breakfast in their pyjamas, she suggests. Anyway, she thinks that the carers do need a break in between.

'I'd rather get everything done before I take a break,' is the response of most of the carers.

But the care manager points out that they don't finish their work in practice anyway. There are always things that remain to be done. So they have to take a break: 'Otherwise you won't be able to keep it up.'

Sitting at a desk is not work

After the meeting with Anna van Raalten there is much complaining on unit C: 'The way she spoke to us!' The carers agree that Van Raalten doesn't understand the situation. She doesn't know anything about work pressure. She doesn't know the residents. She should come out onto the work floor more often, and she should try the work herself.

'She's very busy,' I say in defence of the care manager.

'Poeh,' says Myrna. 'Busy? Don't make me laugh. She arrives at half-past-eight in the morning because she has to come *all the way* from Utrecht. By the time she gets here we've been working for an hour. And no one takes into account the time it takes *us* to get here. Then she spends all day behind her desk with the door closed. And when she does come out she walks around importantly with an organizer under her arm. Busy you say? That's not what you call work.'

'Real' work, according to the carers, happens at the bedside. Sitting at a desk, holding meetings, thinking, is not work in their view, it's cutting corners. As a result the care coordinators have difficulty working on schedules and planning during working time because they feel they are letting their colleagues down by not supporting them in the 'real' work. But if they don't do the organisational stuff, then they are not doing their job as care coordinator properly and get called to account by Anna van Raalten.

Van Raalten says that there are consultations every week during which it is agreed who will do what. But, she adds, the care coordinators often do not stick to those agreements. If a care coordinator is unable to stick to the agreements, then Van Raalten feels that she is not suitable for the job. The care coordinators feel caught between two fires and don't know which way to go. This situation has led to confrontations and tears on more than one occasion.

Social worker Dina Vogel explains that carers have learnt to 'act'; they are doers and that is how you have to evaluate them. 'About policy, abstraction, reflection, they have not the faintest idea,' she says. As a result, you shouldn't expect too much on that level. She thinks that it is not right to ask them how they think certain things should be done. 'They could learn, of course,' she adds, 'but then you have to provide them with the opportunity.'

Plum pudding

Anna van Raalten says that the management of Park House has been trying for some time to change the daily routine in order to spread the workload more evenly throughout the day. The carers try their best to get all the residents out of bed *before* coffee. If they don't succeed then they postpone their break. As a result, residents only get their breakfast at the end of the morning, just before lunch, and the carers have a late coffee break that is often much too long. 'At half-past-eleven they're all exhausted and drop into the chairs like plum puddings,' says Van Raalten. 'They don't have the energy for anything.' It is difficult to break that routine.

'They just won't listen,' says the care manager. 'They just have to get the residents out of bed and wash them *first* and only *then* can they have their food; and all the work has to be done before they will take a break.' She sighs. 'I know how they talk about me, but my days at the bedside are past. Quite apart from the fact that I have too much work to allow that, it wouldn't solve the problem if I went back to washing residents.'

Ambivalence

During the 'summer care' Rutger Varenkamp spends three of his four working days wearing a white apron and washing and dressing residents. In doing so he joins his fellow doctors, the physiotherapists and the social workers. 'Very educational,' he says, winking, after a morning of care on unit C. 'I now see how disorganised the daily care routine really is. I'm constantly running up and down looking for soap, nail clippers, all kinds of things. That wastes a lot of time.'

He says that at the beginning of the year the nursing home doctors sent out a press release in which they expressed their concern about the level of care in nursing homes. They said that they could no longer guarantee an adequate level of care. 'The article in the paper was this small,' he says, raising two fingers. 'This sort of thing doesn't get people's attention. It's not interesting enough.'

Varenkamp describes the attitude of the nursing home sector to the media as ambivalent. On the one hand they complain about not getting sufficient media attention, but at the same time they try their best to avoid that attention because they are worried that it will damage their reputation and bring the sector into disrepute.

I point out that things are not all that good in nursing homes in general. Varenkamp agrees. He is a member of a consultation group that contains doctors from different nursing homes across the city, and the situation in other homes is no different.

Our conversation is interrupted when assistant carer Kim and a temp appear in the entrance to the office with Mrs Grasberg in a wheelchair.

'Rutger, Mrs Grasberg wants to tell you something.'

Rutger Varenkamp kneels next to the wheelchair: 'Good day Mrs Grasberg, what do you want to tell me?'

'Are you the doctor?'

'Yes, I'm the doctor, Rutger Varenkamp.' He gives her his hand.

'They pinch me and they hit me.'

The doctor looks at the two women. 'Was she difficult during care?'

'We didn't do anything,' says Kim indignantly. 'I just said good morning and she started spitting at me.'

'Mrs Grasberg, I hear from the nurses that you were a bit moody this morning. Hmm, what's that I smell?' He sniffs loudly. 'That's very nice perfume you're wearing.' Mrs Grasberg gives a satisfied nod. 'Eau de cologne? 4711? And probably half a bottle by the smell of it. I tell you what: I'll keep an eye on things, Mrs Grasberg. Thank you for pointing it out.'

Leontien and Mrs Grasberg

The incident

'How am I ever going to get through the day?' Anna van Raalten sighs as I enter her office. 'What a morning. And that's without Mrs White, who has just died.'

'Has something happened?' I ask.

She nods and traces circles on her blotter. After a while, without looking at me, she says: 'Leontien spat in Mrs Grasberg's face yesterday.'

Ten minutes later, when I walk into the department, everyone is talking about the incident.

'Leontien is overwrought,' says Colette, clearly affected. She is the care coordinator of Leontien's unit. 'It's all become too much for her, but this is unacceptable, of course.'

I ask what happened. Christa saw Leontien grab Mrs Grasberg by the hair and spit in her face twice. Or rather, spit back, because Mrs Grasberg had started. She spits at all the carers. Christa asked Leontien: 'What are you doing?' Leontien apparently said: 'You're not sticking up for a white are you?' Leontien assumed that Christa would not mention the incident, Darah says, but she was so shocked that she had to tell someone. She phoned Justine, who then told Anna. 'Not to tell on Leontien,' Darah adds, 'but to warn Anna that she should keep an eye on her.' Now Christa and Justine are being ignored by some of their colleagues, because Surinamers are not supposed to betray each other, Darah explains. It's just not done.

There will be serious consequences for Leontien. She will probably be dismissed. She's a single mother and has just bought a house: how will she pay the mortgage and look after the children?

Black magic

A few days later Colette hurries into to the room where I am writing some notes. She says there is going to be an emergency meeting about the incident. Apparently Christa is being threatened by the Surinamese community. There is also a rumour that black magic is being practiced against Anna van Raalten, because she is the one who will probably have Leontien dismissed. Anna van Raalten is on holiday, so the meeting will be chaired by Paula Klaver, one of the other care managers.

Later that morning I am in Rutger Varenkamp's office. He is discussing residents with carers Darah and Robby. Varenkamp says that there have been rituals around Anna's office. 'Something with effigies.' Spells were also cast to ensure that she did not return from holiday; and there were messages on the notice board. Management is taking it all very seriously, hence the meeting later that day.

Varenkamp raises his eyebrows: 'And of course I noticed nothing at all. I have to be informed about this sort of thing. Sometimes I think I walk around with blinkers on.'

'Oh come on,' says Robby cynically, waving his hands. '*Winti*, voodoo, black magic – I've experienced all that in my previous nursing home. One day the head of the department walked up and down the corridor waving a dead chicken, and suddenly the spell was broken.[9]

Varenkamp says he isn't sure what to make of it. How seriously should he take it?

'If you want to know more, you should consult a *winti* doctor,' says Robby, drumming his fingers on the table. 'For goodness sake, don't be taken in. We're too sober for this sort of thing.'

'But if you believe it, then it can be very threatening,' says Darah quietly.

Robby is exercised. He thinks that there is too much gossip; that the carers are winding each other up. And rumours spread like wildfire from one nursing home to another through the temps. They all work everywhere and everyone knows everything.

Rutger Varenkamp takes a deep breath: 'Good thing that you mention that,' he says. He has heard that some of the temps, and even carers with fixed contracts, have parallel jobs in different nursing homes; that they are doing double shifts. He doesn't think that this is in the interests of the residents. He asks Robby and Darah to report to Anna van Raalten if they hear anything. They are going to compile a list of those with double jobs, but it is impossible to screen everyone, he says. He has also heard that some of the carers report sick and then temp in other nursing homes. He looks at Robby and Darah in turn. 'The residents are the ones who suffer, but so do you. You have to fill the gaps.'

'Double jobs are common,' Robby says. He shrugs. 'You can't prevent it. They have debts; they need extra money.' Darah nods but says nothing.

We don't do *winti* here

Roderik Franssen is fifteen minutes late for the meeting. When he arrives, Paula Klaver, who is chairing, taps her pen on the table. 'We're here to discuss Leontien's dismissal,' she says.

'Dismissal? Dismissal?' The interim manager interrupts. 'It's a suspension.'

'Okay,' Paula corrects herself. 'Leontien's suspension.'

The interim manager clears his throat. 'You know that Leontien spat in Mrs Grasberg's face. Christa witnessed it and reported it. This has led to a great deal of agitation. Perhaps we should discuss that first. Who wants to say something?'

After a long silence Colette says that she thought that the suspension was not related only to the incident with Mrs Grasberg, but that there were other issues, and that the incident was only the final straw. She says that Christa has reported sick. She has a headache and feels threatened. She says that many colleagues think that Christa did the right thing, and that carers have to defend the residents. But not everyone thinks so: Leontien has to take care of three children alone. Colette turns to the interim manager and reminds him that he had said that they should all point out each other's mistakes. That is what Christa had done. But Colette is worried that there is now a climate of fear and that no one else will follow her lead.

Roderik Franssen nods. He thinks this is a serious development, especially since the agreements that had been made about 'how we were going to improve things here'. He thinks it should be made clear that 'we are here for the residents, not to drink coffee and gossip'.

He has spoken to Leontien twice – last week and just before the meeting, which is why he was late. Leontien denies spitting. They have also talked to Christa. Whether or not Leontien is dismissed will have to be decided in court. 'If the judge doesn't agree, then we will have to keep her,' Franssen explains. 'That's how it works in this country.'

He scans the circle of carers. 'Look,' he says, grimly, 'I don't care if someone has four children, no husband, or four husbands or whatever. We have all agreed that what we stand for is a certain level of care; that there are limits. Spitting or hitting a resident goes beyond those limits.' He says that this is not the first incident involving Leontien. He scans the faces as though expecting a response, but everyone is quiet.

Then Paula Klaver says, carefully, that she has heard something about voodoo or *winti* being used against Anna van Raalten. She thinks that this is serious and asks whether anyone wants to comment.

I look round the table and see eight Surinamese carers, arms folded, looking straight ahead, faces expressionless, giving nothing away. There is a long silence.

'I don't understand,' says Veronica in a high-pitched voice. 'I thought that that only happened in secret. So how could it happen here in the corridor?'

Roderik Franssen is relieved that someone has spoken. '*Winti*, voodoo, whatever you want to call it. We don't do that here. No way.' Someone stifles a laugh

'What? Who?' The interim manager responds, as though stung by a wasp. Let's keep the discussion central, shall we. He looks from one carer to another. Silence.

Colette suggests sending Christa a card, just to show her that they support her.

'Good idea,' says the interim manager. 'We'll all give something for a bunch of flowers.' He puts his hand in his pocket. 'Shit, didn't bring any money.' He turns to Paula Klaver: 'Can you lend me ten euros?'

'Christa hasn't done anything wrong,' says Colette. 'It's a brave thing she's done, but she feels she's now being punished for it.'

Paula Klaver agrees. She spoke to Christa this morning, and Christa had told her that she doesn't feel safe.

'I hope that this gossiping will stop,' says Colette.

'But it won't,' says a chorus of voices. Myrna reports that she hadn't been at work that day, but she had heard about it at the market.

Robby says that he didn't know about it, even though he works on the unit. But he had heard about it from people working in another nursing home. He shrugs. 'That's how it is.'

Roderik Franssen says: 'As long as we're open and talk about it, and if any of you want to know anything, just come and ask.'

The door opens and Mrs Carpentier enters. Colette offers her a chair. Mrs Carpentier, who was once the head teacher of a girl's boarding school, taps her walking stick on the floor. 'Can I join you? Yes? Much appreciated.' She sits down. 'As long as we're open and talk about it,' she repeats. 'That's the important thing.'

Everyone laughs and nods. Mrs Carpentier: 'Okay, so we agree on that. Good.' She taps the ground with her stick. 'In that case, I think I'll go home. If that's okay?'

'That seems like an excellent way to close this meeting,' says Paula Klaver smiling. 'Thank you for coming.'

Mrs Carpentier walks to the door and turns: 'I would also like to thank you all. Now I'm off to bed.'

I walk with a group of carers back to the unit. I ask them what they thought of the meeting.

'I hadn't heard about the *winti*,' says Rosalie. 'I had to laugh. Who would do something like that?'

'I'm not sure whether it's true,' says Veronica. I don't know much about it. I'm only half Surinamese, and I don't have it in me.' She says that she had encountered it in another nursing home. A team leader had told off staff for arriving at half past ten instead of eight, as they were supposed to. They had glued her desk drawer closed, put glue on her chair, drawing pins under her papers, and nails in her shoes. Then she had acute pains in her chest and had to be admitted to Intensive Care. 'They said she was bewitched,' Veronica says.

Prowling

I have an appointment with Rosan Hüsken, the humanist counsellor. I tell her what I have heard about *winti*, and ask her if she knows anything. She is white, but lived in Surinam until she was twenty. She hasn't heard about any incident involving *winti*, and doesn't know much about *winti* at all. One of the carers, Pearl, has written a thesis about it, she tells me, and offers to introduce me.

A few days later Rosan picks me up and we walk to the department in which Pearl works.

'Now that I know,' she says, 'I keep hearing about *winti* all the time. But Pearl is the one who knows all about it.'

Pearl Chin A Faw is a small, Chinese-Surinamese woman in her mid-forties. After the introductions the three of us walk to the office so that Pearl and I can make an appointment. When we are out of earshot of the other carers, Rosan asks: 'Pearl, do you know anything about the recent *winti* incident?'

'No,' she answers. 'Why?'

Rosan tells her what happened.

'Oh, really?' Pearl responds, shocked.

'Downstairs?'

'Yes.' Rosan nods. 'I think that's going too far.'

'Yes, it's not something to joke about,' Pearl almost whispers. 'Its mostly the blacks, the Creoles, who do it.'

'It was against a white person.'

'If they were white then it must have been a care manager.'

Rosan nods.

'Oh,' Pearl says and shivers. 'What happened?'

Rosan shrugs.

'I heard that they were prowling around, stalking,' Pearl whispers. 'They were watching her.'

Rosan Hüsken calls me a few days later. She had called a group of Surinamese carers into her office and asked them directly whether they knew anything about the recent *winti* goings-on in the House. They were very defensive. She tells me that many Creole-Surinamers pretend that they know nothing about such things. Others might be involved in such things, but not them. She tells me that she knows that some of the carers go to Surinam to undergo ritual ablutions. It is supposed to protect them from evil. One carer had told her that there had been *winti* activities in another department as well. Spells had been cast at night using cigar ash. No one will say what exactly is happening, but Rosan is convinced that there is a lot of agitation and dissatisfaction.

Effigies with needles

A week later I have an appointment with Pearl Chin A Faw to discuss her thesis. When I ask her about the *winti* that is supposed to have been practiced in the unit she repeats that she knows nothing. She asks what happened and what was said in the discussion with Roderik Franssen. She listens attentively. Then we talk for two hours about other matters:

work, her children, her partner, spiritualism. We drink cappuccinos. It's pleasant. When I have long given up any hope that she will tell me anything about *winti*, she asks me if I know Rosalie, an assistant in the unit. I nod. I talk to her regularly. Pearl says that they often take the metro together after the evening shift. Rosalie had told Pearl about the meeting. Rosalie thought it was funny that 'that guy Franssen' hadn't the faintest idea what was going on.

'That's typical for the blacks,' says Pearl. 'They keep quiet and keep it to themselves. They think: 'just wait.' She tells me that *winti* originated in Africa and was taken to Surinam by the slaves. The Dutch colonial authorities prohibited it and there were severe punishments. Even today, Surinamers don't speak openly about it. She tells me that *winti* rituals are performed 'when someone has trodden on your soul'. It doesn't matter what colour they are; it can happen to anyone, black or white.

Rosalie thought that the tone of the meeting had been derogatory. 'And of course nobody said anything,' Pearl continues. 'Of course not. Nobody wanted to get burned. That manager wouldn't understand anyway. He's not open to that sort of thing. He's not accessible.' If Pearl had been in his shoes she would have asked the carers for advice. That would have been the right approach. But at least he *did* talk to them. The problem was, he did it in the wrong way. 'Because,' she says, 'asking someone not to do *winti* is like asking them not to pray, or not to believe in God.'

I ask if she knew what happened. She says that it was 'something with effigies'. Effigies stuck with needles. They were meant to ensure that Anna van Raalten didn't return; that something happened to her. Pearl falls silent. Then she asks whether anything did happen to her.

'I don't know,' I answer, 'but it doesn't appear so. She's back from holiday and at work.'

'Well maybe it's something else,' Pearl mumbles. 'Maybe something else will happen to her.'

Strong Women, Loafing Men

Fatigue and stress

The incident between Leontien and Mrs Grasberg ends up in court and Leontien is sacked. Christa reports sick with a back problem and doesn't return to work for a number of weeks. Then she goes to Surinam on extended leave. She is hardly mentioned and the attention shifts to Justine, who Christa had informed about the incident and who had reported it to the care manager. She is ostracised by the Surinamese community in the nursing home and totally ignored. One doesn't betray a compatriot.

Justine is seriously affected by the response. She never imagined that her warning to Anna van Raalten would have such far-reaching consequences, either for Leontien, for Christa or for herself.

Justine thought that Anna van Raalten needed to know that some residents are sometimes treated roughly, she says, and she wanted her to keep an eye on things. Justine says that she had asked whether she could tell her in confidence, and that Anna had agreed. But ten minutes later she called to say that she would have to act on what she had heard and that she was going to talk to Leontien and Christa. She wanted to know the details, and then Justine knew that things were going to go wrong, she says. She thinks that Van Raalten didn't deal with the situation properly; that she had failed to protect the carers. Justine thinks that the care manager needed the story because she was always having conflicts with Leontien and couldn't cope with her. She had been waiting for an opportunity like this.

Justine had to go back and tell Anna the details, and Anna had then decided that she must speak to Leontien. Then it all went wrong, says Justine. Everything that happens in Park House is common knowledge in the wider Surinamese community. People meet at the market, they chat, they phone each other. Everyone knows everything as soon as it happens.

Justine thought: 'If they send me *winti* then I've had it.' But she is still here. She seriously considered resigning, but she didn't want to just walk away from it. She cried for a long time, she says. Then she sought help. She also spoke to Anna, who wondered whether she was over-reacting. 'It's easy for her to talk,' Justine says. 'I have to work here.'

The problem is still there. When Justine walks through the restaurant she feels all eyes on her. Her Surinamese colleagues ignore her. They don't greet her and they warn new staff about her: 'Are you with her on the evening shift? Then don't put the residents in bed too early, otherwise Justine will report you. Be careful, she's become one of the Hollanders.' Justine doesn't regret standing up for Mrs Grasveld because, she says, that wasn't the first time that something like that had happened.

She has an explanation for 'that sort of thing'. It is due to impatience, she thinks. It's not deliberate. Most of her colleagues experience a lot of stress. She explains that most of the carers are foreign. They had to be independent early on, and adjust in a strange country. Most of them have broken homes and they have to take care of the children alone, without the support of the father. She says that many of them have debts, and various other problems. They take these worries to work with them and they work off the frustrations there. 'I know,' she says, 'because I have done so myself. But over the years I've managed to cope, and I don't have to vent my frustrations on the weak. Because that is what happens if you don't feel good.'

According to Justine, Surinamese women often live above their means. You can see that in the nice clothes they wear and all the jewellery. 'You're brought up like that,' she says. 'It's something you learn to value because you've worked for it. You buy things to prop up your ego. It's not bragging but more symbolic. A Dutch person might work hard and buy a car or a house; Surinamers buy gold bracelets or give big parties. They send money to their family in Surinam and regularly take the whole family back there on holiday.'

Justine has also had to learn how to manage her money, she says. Her current partner explained to her: if you work for 600 euro then you can't spend 800 euro. That sounds obvious, but she says that it is not so obvious for her colleagues. They buy things too easily with the idea that they can pay it off next month. That's how they get into debt, and then after a while they can't get out of it any more. Then they get a double job. That works okay for a while, but sooner or later they need a rest, and that doesn't happen, so they become exhausted, and easily irritated. You are much more resistant to minor irritations and you can cope much better when you are rested, she says. 'Then you can be more diplomatic. It's easier to think: that resident is a bit hysterical. How can I best deal with it? Let me take her for a walk or for a cup of coffee and distract her with a chat.'

I ask why there are so many coloured staff working in the nursing home. Justine says it is easy to get jobs in the care sector because you don't need many qualifications and you don't need to know much: 'You get in through the temp agency, you put on a white dress, and suddenly you're a sister.'

Double jobs

Having two jobs is common, just about everyone in the nursing home agrees on that. But it is against the rules. The law allows workers to have two jobs, but they are not allowed to work more than thirty-six hours a week, and they are supposed to report second jobs to their primary employer. If they do not their employer may be fined by the Inland Revenue Department. For this reason, Park House does not allow employees to have double jobs, and as a result employees do this secretly.

The longer I am in the nursing home the more I hear about double jobs. Colette tells me about a temp who spends the evening shift sleeping because she has another daytime job. Colette had to care for the residents by herself. She says that carers sometimes fall asleep during the night shift because they have already just worked an evening shift. When Colette first started working in the nursing home she didn't understand why everyone was putting on makeup at the end of the night shift until she found out that they were about to go on to a morning shift in another nursing home. She asks whether I know the two girls who prepare the food in the evenings. She tells me that during the day they are tram conductors. Colette doesn't know how they keep going, and she thinks it's irresponsible.

Everyone is very mysterious about the extent of double jobs and who is involved. I am told that many of the coloured staff have double jobs. When I ask people directly whether they have two jobs they say: 'Well, I used to, occasionally'.

Darah is the first one to admit to me that she has two jobs. Or rather, it slips out unintentionally. 'There is a Mrs The in Westerhuis nursing home,' she says. 'Is she a relative? She's such a dear. When I'm on shift I always try and make sure that I get to care for her. I know her very well now.' It is only after Darah has spoken about Mrs The on a number of occasions that I begin to realise that she must see her regularly. Because Darah has a full-time job in Park House I assume that I have not understood her properly. 'When did you last see Mrs The?' I ask.

'The day before yesterday,' she says. 'It was really nice...'

'The day before yesterday?' I say. 'But wasn't that your first day off in eight days?'

'Yes, yes,' she says, looking down.

I ask whether she often works on her days off.

'I used to. I hardly ever do nowadays,' she says quickly. 'Only occasionally when I need something extra for the family in Surinam, or if the washing machine is broken or something like that.'

She won't tell me any more.

I gradually learn more about double jobs, though. One day Darah nudges me and says, giggling: 'Just listen to this. Last week we were changing shifts in Westerhuis and guess who comes in? Michiel, the doctor from upstairs. He recently started there one day in the week. He said: Sister Darah, I've caught you. I got such a fright!'

'Actually almost all of us have double jobs,' social worker Dina Vogel admits one day after I have been badgering her about it. And by 'us' she means the Surinamese and Antillean carers.

At first she shrugs: 'It happens.'

'A third?' I suggest tentatively.

She nods. 'A third, yes.'

'Or is it half?'

'Yes, half,' she agrees, nodding again.'

'Perhaps three quarters?' I suggest.

'Well, yes, three quarters, yes, you're right.'

'So just about everyone?' I venture

'Okay, just about everyone,' she admits. 'We have to, otherwise we can't make ends meet. We all know what everyone else is doing and we talk about it, but we don't shout it from the rooftops.'

Most of the second jobs are in other nursing homes or in home care. 'Yes,' Marcia admits, 'I regularly work consecutive shifts in different nursing homes.' She looks older than her fifty years and walks with difficulty. 'I have to. I have eight children at home and an unemployed husband.'

Myrna says: 'I sometimes work extra. I have four children of my own and my late sister's three children also live with me. How else can I provide for them?'

In addition to the care sector, moonlighting as cleaners or in the catering sector are also popular second jobs. Justine tells me that she has a cleaning job a couple of hours a week. She supports her mother in Surinam with the extra money. Her mother is ill and dependent on her. She tells me that Rutger gave her elastic bandages to send to her mother, who needs them for her leg.

When I get to know Pearl better she tells me that, in addition to her full-time job in Park House she does home care at night. There she earns 500 euro for five nights. 'Not bad, hey?' she says. She also does catering, sometimes when she is supposed to be in the nursing home. Last week she and a friend made an Indonesian rice table for eighty people. To do that she had to take sick leave from Park House. Anna van Raalten phoned her every day to ask if she was feeling better and especially to find out when she would be back at work. 'She was like a strict school mistress,' Pearl says. 'I certainly wasn't planning to come back just for her. Who does she think she is anyway? If she had a bit of respect for the carers it might be different,' Pearl says. 'Van Raalten should try doing some real work herself for a change, instead of faffing around with all those papers behind her desk.' Pearl had coughed loudly into the phone and said: 'Do you hear? I'm still all blocked up. No I really don't feel up to it yet. I think it will be a while yet before it's better.'

Last respects to Mrs Wijntak

One morning I run into Rutger Varenkamp in the lift and he tells me that Mrs Wijntak passed away last night. There was a big fuss around the bed, and Darah was also there. An hour and a half later Mrs Molenaar followed. There were no relatives at her bedside. 'What a contrast,' says Varenkamp.

Darah's eyes are swollen from crying. She describes Mrs Wijntak's death. 'Fortunately I was there,' she says. Her death wasn't unexpected, but Darah still feels upset. She has just been to have a look at her and she looks calm, Darah says, wiping away a tear.

Then she smiles. 'It was a real happening, I can tell you. You really missed something. Have you seen her room and the corridor?' Darah's voice rises. 'It looks like there's been an earthquake!' She says that Mrs Wijntak had been put in a single room, but that this was too small for all the relatives. The whole corridor was full. There were relatives Darah had never seen before. 'When Mrs Wijntak died there was wailing and screaming. Chairs flew through the room, pictures hung skew. Mrs Wijntak didn't want to die, that was clear. Otherwise those pictures wouldn't have been like that,' she explains. She was hardly dead and they all grabbed their phones, Darah says with an amused look though her tears. 'They knew about it in Surinam before they did here in the rest of the unit.'

That evening I meet Darah and Justine at the bus stop and we travel together to the funeral parlour just outside town to pay our last respects to Mrs Wijntak. When we arrive there is a large crowd. We thread our way through and go inside. I feel dizzy. Justine takes my hand and leads me into the room, greeting people she knows as we go. The only person I recognise is Jessy. She comes over to say hello and then disappears again. We are given a hymnbook. Then a door opens and the coffin is carried in by a group of men.

Everyone sings, cries, and wails with abandonment. I recognise a few of Mrs Wijntak's daughters and grand daughters. Rachelle, the daughter who came to visit her in the nursing home most often, is standing erect with a scarf tied round her head and wearing a gown. She looks strong. With a powerful voice she leads the singing, while supporting her two brothers who look on the point of collapse.

After the service Justine, Darah and I take the bus back to town. I suggest a drink. In a café near the bus stop we drink one *pisang ambon* with orange juice after another. The clientele in the cafe is almost exclusively Surinamese. Justine is the centre of attention. She chats to everyone and enjoys the attention. She was divorced years ago, she says. At twenty-five she was alone with three small children to look after. 'No,' she keeps repeating, 'I didn't let them walk all over me. In those days I danced the heels off my shoes.'

Slavery and *'wijverij'*

The next day the Surinamese carers in Park House crowd around me. They want to know what I thought of the service for Mrs Wijntak. When

I say that I was struck by the strength of the women, they all nod in agreement. 'And the men,' I let slip, 'were just, just...' I search for the right word.

'Layabouts?' Jessy suggests.

'Yes,' I say, 'they were just layabouts.' Everyone laughs.

'Or do you mean chin wagging, maybe?' Myrna says, looking at me expectantly. I hear contempt in her voice.

'Chin wagging,' I repeat. 'Maybe that was it.' They all laugh again and pat me on the shoulder.

It's the women who run things in Surinam, I am told repeatedly during the rest of the day. On the one hand the women have no choice, because they are all abandoned by their partners. Darah says that she discovered after a few years that her husband, Morgan, had another woman. *Wijverij* they call it. Most Surinamese men do it, says Darah. By the time she found out she had three small daughters. It turned out that he had other children. Darah knew nothing about it. He couldn't help it, he said. It was because of the legacy of slavery that Surinamese men can't stick to one woman. The slaves were continually sold on and the men learned not to become to attached to one woman. So they had many different girlfriends. Darah laughs as she recounts, but her expression betrays sadness. 'It's three hundred years ago, slavery, but it still affects him.' It wasn't so bad when he left, she says. At least she had the children she wanted.

Darah is not the only one. In the Surinamese and Antillean communities, single mothers are almost the norm. There is a lot of mutual assistance. Darah has a friend who recently divorced and is having difficulty making ends meet. Darah regularly helps her out. She takes her to the hairdresser and does 'double shopping' for her, because she knows what it is like when you can't afford things.

Wijverij is not always the reason for separation. Pearl says that one day she just picked up her son and left. Her husband drank and was violent and she had had enough. She didn't want her son to grow up like that. Her husband didn't agree to her leaving and she had to go into hiding. He kept tracing her and would be waiting for her in the evenings. But she was lucky, she says. She received a lot of help, and after a while he left her alone and she was able to build a life of her own.

The difference between Dutch and Surinamese women is that Surinamese women are not afraid of going through life alone, social worker Dina Vogel explains. 'A Dutch woman thinks that she needs a man. But what do you need a man for?' She looks at me questioningly. Children she already has, and she earns her own money. 'For sex?' she suggests. Dina's motto is: 'You have ten fingers; at least one of them must be nice enough. You have to try them.'

Dina doesn't think she has had a difficult life. It's a question of 'getting on with your work, being organised and bringing up your kids'. Often the eldest child helps with the domestic chores and looks after the younger children. That enables her to have a nap when she gets home, before going on to the next job. Or there is a sister or aunt or friend who helps out. And she tries to explain things to her children: 'When school finishes you have to go to Auntie's house, because I'll be at work, and then I'll pick you up there later when I've finished.'

Dina says that she had a lot of support from supervisors and managers in her previous nursing home. They encouraged her to train to be a social worker. They did that because they knew they could depend on her, she says. She was always prepared to help out. When her son was ill they allowed her to bring him to work so that there would be someone to look after him while she got on with her work. The evening shift supervisor often took her son to the nursery for her, and in return Dina looked after her child if she wanted to go out.

But it wasn't always easy, she adds. When she got divorced, she went to live in rooms with her small child. She was training to be a carer at the time and often had to do the night shift. She would go to bed with her three-year-old son at seven in the evening, then get up quietly and slip out of the house to start her shift at eleven. The whole night she would 'have a double heart' worrying. 'My God, I thought, I've left a three-year-old alone at home.'

Stories like this shed a different light on the illegal double jobs, the high absenteeism, and the struggle that management is having in banning the use of mobile phones. These need to be placed in their wider socio-economic context to be understood. Is the carer who phones home every hour because she wants to check whether the children she left at home alone are all right a bad carer or a good mother?

'No, I'm sorry,' says Anna van Raalten when I raise the question with her. 'We all have our private problems. You have to deal with those yourself. And if those problems impact on your work then you shouldn't be working in a nursing home, and certainly not with people with Alzheimer's. Then you should be working at MacDonalds. Look, that's the big problem: the people who work here don't do anything to solve their problems.'

Limited Labour Market

Poor quality staff

Because the labour market is so limited, 'poor quality' staff have to be employed, says Colette. By poor quality she means that they just work for the money, are not interested in the residents, and as a result have high rates of absenteeism. You can see that clearly, she says. For example when the residents have to be washed and dressed. 'That is an intimate business,' says Colette. 'It's not just anyone who sees you naked.' When Colette cares for residents she tells them what she is going to do: take off your nightdress, wash you, etcetera. Sometimes she sings. Colette says that it calms residents. But, without saying anything, some of her colleagues suddenly 'shove a face cloth in the resident's face' and start undressing them. It gives residents a fright.

Yesterday Colette heard loud screaming coming from Mrs Vriesma's room. She is a nice resident, says Colette, but you have to be calm when you deal with her. She opened the door and saw a colleague lecturing Mrs Vriesma because she was not cooperating. Mrs Vriesma kept shouting: 'She's murdering me! She's murdering me!'

Colette tried to calm things down and then left. A bit later she heard screaming again. When she went to investigate she found Mrs Vriesma naked on the bed and the colleague on the phone to her son. 'Then I really got angry,' says Colette indignantly. 'And she felt I was attacking her. She kept saying: Yes, but my son this and my son that.'

Colette experiences situations like this as confrontational and, she says, it happens a lot. She thinks that the carers should adjust to the needs of the residents, not the other way round. Colette thinks that the current attitude has to change. She wonders what things will be like when her generation is in the nursing home with Alzheimer's. Who will be working in the nursing home then? Maybe criminals doing community service. If it were up to her she would 'throw out everyone who was only in it for the money'.

The 'bigwigs' have got the policy on staff seriously wrong, Justine thinks. They should have been more selective. They should have asked for proper references, because their aim should be to protect the residents. It's their fault that the wrong types have been employed. 'Lets be honest,' she says, 'not everyone is *suitable* as a carer, but anyone can *work* as a carer. Usually you have to know something about the job. When you work for the veterinary ambulance you have to know how to handle sick cats, and when you work in C&A you have to know which products they sell. But when you work in the care sector you are not expected to know anything.'

Social and antisocial

Pearl works as a carer in the department for somatic residents, i.e. residents who have primarily physical impairments. Unacceptable things happen there as well, she says. Residents are snapped at and treated roughly. In the coloured community there is a distinction between 'social' and 'antisocial' staff, she explains. Fortunately most carers belong to the former group. They work hard, and have to cope alone at home. They have a lot of worries and are often tired, but they still care for the residents properly. They love the residents. But there are also antisocial carers who don't love the residents. They only work for the money, says Pearl. Sometimes they are even on permanent contracts. That's because of the limited labour market.

Unlike the Alzheimer's residents, those in the somatic department can complain about the care they receive, though it is doubtful whether this helps. Pearl remembers the case of a couple that were watching football in the living room one Sunday. The Surinamese carers were cooking and making a lot of noise and as a result they couldn't hear the commentary. The woman asked them in a friendly way whether they could make less noise. The carers didn't take any notice.

She asked a second time. Then the third time she said: 'Can you keep it down, it sounds like a chicken coop!' One of the carers subjected her to terrible verbal abuse, says Pearl. The couple reported this to the director. The carer was suspended, because that wasn't the first complaint. When she returned she was transferred to De Stadhouder. She's still here. 'Just imagine,' Pearl says indignantly. 'Now she's working with dementia residents who can't complain!'

Another of Pearl's colleagues had said to a resident, while she was washing her: 'Your cunt stinks'. The resident was very upset and spoke to one of the other carers. She spoke to the first carer, who denied everything. Then she went to the resident and lectured her for complaining about the first carer. 'That resident will take care before complaining again,' says Pearl. She says that that particular colleague smokes a joint every morning in the toilet before starting work. Pearl keeps quiet about this. Why? She doesn't dare to report it, she says, because she doesn't fancy hassle.

Betrayal and punishment

The atmosphere in unit C in De Stadhouder is restless again. There is gossip and bickering. There are 'things happening' in the Surinamese community, says Justine. 'So-and-so is no longer talking to so-and-so, someone has said that someone else has done such-and-such. You know how it is with women. There's always something going on.'

Justine thinks that they should have made more effort to mix the different ethnic groups in Park House. In some units the teams are exclusively black. 'At one point unit C looked like a Surinamese market!' says Justine. 'That's not good, because it leads to cliques. Surinamers tend to form groups anyway. You can't avoid that, it's part of the culture, but you have to try and break through.'

The reason for the tensions on unit C is still the 'betrayal' of Leontien by Justine. The rumour is that Cynthia, a nursing assistant who has recently come to work in De Stadhouder, will teach Justine a lesson for her betrayal. Cynthia is a stocky Surinamese woman of about forty, with six children. She didn't work in Park House at the time of the incident with Leontien and has only heard about it from others.

Darah says that Cynthia and Justine almost had a fight in the office on unit C. Cynthia lured Justine into it, and things escalated. Darah tried to calm them down. It eventually fizzled out. Cynthia left the office and said she would 'prick' Justine if she ever got in her way again. Pricking means stabbing with a knife, Darah explains. That is not impossible, she says in a concerned tone, because Cynthia has fought often, and she always carries a knife in her bag. She says she needs it in the evenings when she has to take the metro home.

Last weekend the tensions surfaced again. Cynthia had been egged on to 'deal with' Justine, and when Justine entered the living room of unit C she immediately felt that something was wrong. Cynthia was bragging loudly and she tried to provoke Justine. She was looking for an excuse to 'rough her up'.

All the Surinamese carers who were at work that day had gathered in the living room with high expectations. 'That's how Surinamers are,' Justine explains. 'They like a bit of sensation. They would have loved it if Cynthia and I had fought in the living room.' Justine, alert because of the previous incident in the office, ignored her. She sat down in a chair and peeled an apple. She ate the slices of apple slowly, all the time returning their gaze. When they realised she wasn't going to let herself be provoked they slunk off.

Anna van Raalten and Roderik Franssen each speak to Cynthia and Justine about the confrontations. They make an appointment to discuss the future with Darah, care coordinator of the unit. Both Cynthia and Justine are permanent staff and as a result will have to work the same shifts. But nothing comes of the meeting because Cynthia is stabbed by her ex-husband in front of the children. She is admitted to Intensive Care and remains in the hospital for months. During this period Justine decides to go and study for a nursing diploma.

The proletariat

'Lets face it,' says Bob Eelman, the residents' ombudsman. 'It's the lower classes, the proletariat, that works in places like this. Why? For the simple reason that no one else wants to do this work anymore. It's too hard, too dirty, too dull and the pay is too low.'

The care sector is following on the heels of the cleaning sector, he says, which has been coloured for years. 'We whites leave the dirty jobs to our coloured neighbours.' In the nursing home, he says, two social problems come together in a rather unfortunate way: an ageing and senescent population in a multicultural society. The ageing population leads to a shortage of staff in the care sector, and the low status of the work results in it being done largely by coloured women. 'But we can't talk about it,' Eelman says. 'And we can't mention the cultural gulf between the coloured carers and the white residents. We can't mention it, but it's there nonetheless.'

Eelman is struck by the fact that violence is so much more normal in the Surinamese and Antillean community than in the white Dutch community. They almost all know someone who has been murdered, he says. In the past two years there are at least three relatives of carers in Park House who were murdered. Not so long ago the brother of one of the carers was stabbed to death. Eelman had gone to see her and found the way they talked about it remarkable. They all said it was 'terrible', says Eelman, but they gave the impression that they thought it was just something that happened, as though that sort of thing is normal. Whereas he thought: How the hell can something like this happen? It's at times like that that Eelman realises how different their lives are to his.

'And now that we're on the topic,' he continues hesitantly, 'you know what I have real difficulty with? The way in which the Surinamese and Antillean carers boss the residents around.' Of course, it's *not done* to say so, he adds immediately, but he often gets complaints from the relatives of residents about this: give me this, give me that. Carers too often think that they know what is best for residents. Obviously this doesn't apply to all the carers, he adds, and the white carers are not entirely innocent, but there is a tendency.

Eelman has spoken to people about it because he wants to understand the process. Now he understands it historically and sociologically. In the past the men worked on the plantations and were hardly ever home, so the women had to learn how to survive with the children. Eelman thinks that that has given them a certain hardness that is passed on down the generations.

Even now life is not easy for the women, he explains. They have children when they are young – often more than they want. The fathers of the children come and go, so the women have to slog away in order to make ends meet, and that contributes to the authoritarian tendency. Otherwise they just won't make it.

He thinks it is understandable, but it is contrary to what the nursing home wants to achieve: taking into account the experiences and the needs of the residents. 'Mrs So-and-so, what time would you like to go to bed this evening?' No one asks a question like that in this nursing home. The carers are not used to asking things like that. They are always critical of those above them, says Eelman: 'My boss just sits behind her desk and decides what I should and shouldn't do'. But that's exactly what the carers do with the residents.

It's also ambiguous, he says. Management tells the carers what to do and won't listen to what they want and what concerns them, but at the same time management expects the carers to be friendly to the residents and ask them what they want and what concerns them.

Eelman sees this as one of the real problems in the modern nursing home, and it is difficult to deal with. He would like management to try and solve the problem. Unfortunately that doesn't happen. Even worse, it's almost impossible to even mention the problem.

'Bossy,' Rosan Hüsken says when I discuss the issue with her. She has often heard about how loud and directive Surinamers are in their communication. Hüsken knows all about it, because she was reproached for this when she first came to live in Holland. She has a partial explanation: in Surinam everything is open – windows, doors – and it's more difficult to hear what people are saying. As a result you have to talk louder than you do in Holland in order to be understood.

But it is also a question of language, she adds. The Surinamese vernacular uses the imperative much more than Dutch. When Surinamers feel at ease, they also tend to use the imperative when speaking Dutch. They translate Surinamese directly into Dutch and leave out the polite forms that we consider normal. They say: 'Sit! Eat! Drink!' when they mean, 'would you like to sit down and eat'. And that can lead to misunderstandings, says Hüsken. Dutch people tend to think: Hang on a minute; I'm not going to let myself be bossed around by you.

Hüsken recognises that cultural differences can lead to tension. The carers do work that goes against their norms and values. They are not inclined to send older relatives to a nursing home, and when that does happen they visit often. They do not understand how the Dutch treat their elders, says Hüsken. In Surinam things are very different. The elderly often live at home with their children or relatives, and the younger relatives look after them.

In Holland carers are also discriminated against. They want to be treated with respect and be 'visible', but they are often confronted with being considered 'nobodies', Hüsken explains. She says that it regularly happens that a relative of a resident wants to find out something. They go into the living room and if they only see a Surinamese carer they leave again because there is 'no one there'. 'Imagine how that must feel,' says Hüsken. 'Surinamese carers take this even harder because of their more general experience of not being taken seriously by the Dutch.'

The Big Problem

Norms and values

'The big problem in this nursing home?' interim manager Roderik Franssen says, repeating my question. He pushes a flask of coffee towards me. To begin with, he says, everything in a nursing home is aimed at optimising the care product. In this home that isn't the case. There are separate 'islands' of activity and little communication between them. At least, that's what it looks like. Moreover, he continues, the care 'doesn't really run smoothly'. Franssen mentions the huge staffing problem. Then there is 15 per cent absenteeism and the 'herds of temps'. When he started reorganising they had spent almost a million euros too much on temp staff. The response to that was a temporary freeze on admittance and the 'summer care' initiative.

Westerlaken & Partners has succeeded in reducing absenteeism and solving some of the financial problems, says Franssen. They are now negotiating a fusion with Westerhuis nursing home. If that goes through then the financial prospects for Park House will be a lot healthier.

Franssen says that the doctors and care managers think that the care product is 'only just acceptable'. It is extremely difficult to find qualified staff, and he thinks that the work ethic leaves much to be desired. He sees too many people hanging around in the restaurant drinking coffee in the morning when they should be at their workstations. 'The working day is eight-thirty to five,' he says. 'But at five they've already all gone, and they take too long over lunch.'

'Moreover,' he adds, 'there are things happening that you don't even want to know about. There is spitting at residents, fighting, trade in beads, mirrors, lipstick and, who knows, even drugs'. He has also noticed that there are tensions between the different ethnic groups: between black and white, but also between the different coloured groups. He often hears people say: 'I don't want to work with her,' or 'I won't accept a black boss'. The carers say they aren't respected, the blacks feel they aren't respected by the whites, the whites feel excluded by the blacks because they speak Surinamese.

Franssen's response was to introduce rules and try and establish common norms and values. He explained to the carers that it is normal for them to have a supervisor, and that they actually have a right to supervision, but that they should also listen to the supervisor. He emphasised that everyone should be treated with respect: the residents, their families, colleagues. He has called staff to account because of their behaviour, he says. He wants to create a culture of accountability. 'That's what they're afraid of here,' he says. 'They want to spare others criticism because they don't want to be exposed to criticism themselves.'

No challenges

The big problem in nursing homes is carers' low level of education and the fact that they get bored with the job after a few years, says nursing home doctor Rick van Velzen. Most of the carers' work consists of washing, dressing, feeding, giving medicine and sitting with residents. It's important work, he says, but understandable that after a while people have had enough of it. The doctor speaks from experience, because he comes from a nursing background himself.

The doctor sees the same thing happening to others as well: everyone wants to get higher up. In his department there is a care coordinator with a university degree. She chose the job because she wanted to work on the ground; she wanted to care for people and did not want a management job. That was five years ago. Now she is talking about doing courses 'because,' she says, 'I don't want to do this work for the rest of my life.'

It's the monotony of the work that makes it difficult, says Van Velzen, the 'devastating repetitive power of a whining child'. Just imagine, he says, hearing 'I need the toilet, I need the toilet' a thousand times a day. Whenever you go to feed someone, they've wet themselves or they've shit themselves. You have to clean it up. You constantly have to tidy up after them, and all the time you have to radiate geniality and warmth. 'Just try it for a few years,' Van Velzen suggests. 'It's difficult, and after a while you think: I want to kill you.'

Whoever has the option, moves on to something else. And whoever stays runs the risk of becoming indifferent, he says. What makes the work enjoyable is the mutual contact, and so carers associate more and more with other carers – more coffee drinking.

But you are not supposed to think such things, and you are certainly expected not to mention them. It is taboo. But Van Velzen knows how it is. He sees the same thing in the care managers. They are all ex-nurses, and they have all 'mentally decided to get as far away from the bedside as possible,' says Van Velzen, 'because it's only then that you mean something. For people working in care, the highest you can aim for is a supervisory function behind a desk.'

Rosan Hüsken also thinks that it is difficult for carers to keep it up. She thinks it is because carers have to divide their attention: going to help one resident means walking away from another. And if they are going to walk away from a resident anyway, they might as well also do so to go and have a chat with a colleague in the corridor.

The pattern is that the carers work hard until about eleven until all the residents are 'polished and ironed'. Then that's it; then they can focus on each other. You hardly see carers outside walking or sitting in the sun with residents. They prefer to do that sort of thing with colleagues. 'Maybe that's just normal,' says Hüsken. 'Caring for your children is natural, but caring for old, unfamiliar people in an institution is about a group and no longer about individuals. It has become dehumanised.'

Hüsken has argued for years that carers should be able to discuss with colleagues both inside and outside the group they work with on a day-to-day basis. She thinks it is necessary, but management thinks it is threatening, complicated and a waste of time. They think that carers should do what they are told and not complain, that the working relationships should be more professional. There should be more distance between management and shop floor, because 'you can only address staff in the right way when there is distance' and that is what is needed to improve the quality of care, in management's view.

Rosan Hüsken doesn't agree. The secret of good leadership, she thinks, is close involvement. She is convinced that that is where the solution lies. The care managers play a big role in the general atmosphere in a department. If the care manager knows the carers and the residents well and knows what needs to be done then they are in control.

Moreover, the care manager should act as an example, says Hüsken. 'If carers are treated with respect then there is more chance that they will treat others with respect. If they are treated like rubbish, then that's how they will treat others.'

Listening

Social worker Dina Vogel sees as the biggest problem in the nursing home the fact that supervisors and management do not listen to staff on the shop floor. That has far-reaching consequences, she says. If carers feel they are being ignored then they are less patient with the residents. If a resident is uncooperative they think: forget the hassle, I want to get this over and done with, and then they start to pull and shove.

That could be different if they could get things off their chest, says Vogel. Many of the carers have problems. It helps if they can say that they have a problem, or a sick child, even if the supervisor says: 'I've heard you, now go back to work, and if it doesn't work out, let me know.' That's why it's important that supervisors are there when they hand over shifts, says Vogel, and that the doors of their rooms are open.

Vogel thinks that the incident between Leontien and Mrs Grasberg is a good example of this. She says that Leontien's private life, which was full of frustrations, played a big role in the incident. The social workers had spoken to her often to try and calm her. She says that Leontien was a nice woman who went wrong because of frustration. She thinks it is a pity that supervisors didn't intervene earlier – they should have spoken to her. They should have suggested that she work less and go on holiday. If they had acted earlier then the incident with Mrs Grasberg might not have happened.

In the past the heads of department worked in the department and worked together with the teams, says Dina Vogel. They knew what was going on. Now the care managers are far from the shop floor. They spend all their time with each other and don't really know what is happening on the ground. As a result staff become demotivated and tend toward absenteeism. Dina tells me about a nursing home in which a care manager decided not to go to meetings any longer but to spend the whole day among the carers. 'She talks to the carers, she advises them and she is available, and as a result the absenteeism there has been reduced to zero!'

If Vogel had been interim-manager in Park House, she would focus all attention on the shop floor and improve the relationship with supervisors and management. She would make sure that staff felt comfortable, that there was the right atmosphere, and that there was cooperation and communication. Vogel is convinced that if that happened then the quality of care would improve drastically.

Care for carers

There is unrest in Park House about the way that Westerlaken & Partners works, says psychologist Max Hermann. He thinks there is even a counter-movement. There are plans, he says, and he is tempted to join in. The interim-management company has been hired in for 25,000 euros per month. That is a lot of money for a nursing home that is on the brink of bankruptcy, and everyone agrees that they are not really solving the problems. They are not really interested in care and are not involved with staff. They're on 'a different track', says Hermann, and he thinks that is detrimental because the fundamental problems are being ignored.

Many carers have worked in the nursing home for a long time but have hardly received any additional training on new ways of treating residents. You would expect, he says, carers to be well-trained in dealing with the kind of behaviour that is associated with dementia, but they aren't. As a result, patterns of behaviour develop that are difficult to break. He thinks that this needs to be taken seriously, because the residents are entirely in the hands of the carers for a large part of the day.

Max Hermann is in favour of further training for carers. Not when things are already going wrong, but on a structural level. He also thinks it is important to devote time and energy to care-for-carers: 'As a gesture from management that would do more good that all the financial overviews that they keep dishing up.'

Carer Justine also thinks that discussion with colleagues, reflection and training for carers are necessary. She thinks that carers need 'nourishment' to be able to break out of the grind of everyday routine. That can be achieved through special training days for carers, in which they are also taught how to work together. 'Staff become quiescent,' says Justine. 'At twelve, once the residents have eaten, they just hang around.'

Justine would like that to change, for example that they did something different at lunchtime. Or that there was somewhere they could go to get away for a moment if they felt the need. She thinks that her colleagues need this. It would enable them to recharge for the rest of the day. But unfortunately there is no space for that in Park House.

Keeping carers on board

Nursing home doctor Rick van Velzen thinks that the solutions that are on offer from management are a myth. On the one hand they want to impose strict rules on the carers – 'Guys, you are only allowed fifteen minutes for coffee, not a minute longer.' But on the other hand they say they are going to provide further training for the carers and make the job more pleasant. They are going to put everything right and everyone will want to work in Park House.

Van Velzen had said during a meeting of the management team: 'So there are no carers working here who live in Almere and who have to get up at five in the morning to be able to get here on time? And there are no carers who have done this job for fifteen years and who think, at ten a. m., after they have washed and dressed a whole lot of residents: I'm knackered and I've had it for today? We don't have people like that working here?'

Those present laughed nervously because, says Van Velzen, there are a lot of people like that working in the nursing home, and management's approach doesn't work with them.

What does work? Telling the carers that they are allowed to spend more time drinking coffee because the work they are doing is so heavy. That they can go home earlier in the afternoon if there is not a lot to do. That already happens anyway, says Van Velzen, but it is done surreptitiously. He thinks that carers should get what they really want, and that what is already happening anyway in practice should be formalised.

The new slogan is 'client-centred care', says Van Velzen, but those who are supervising this spend all their time in meetings. In order to be client-centred you have to have the carers on board. Van Velzen sees that as the biggest problem for the coming years. That is why it is important to pay the carers well and give them a pat on the back when they deserve it, he says.

But that isn't what the management team meetings are about. No, he says, there they talk about 'turning the organisation around'; about who is going to lead and what they are going to do with the finances. Van Velzen remembers a meeting in the restaurant in which Roderik Franssen got up on a soapbox and said: 'Listen everyone, from now on we have a new culture of communication. Have you all understood? Any questions? No questions? Okay, it's a deal then.'

'He thought he'd come to an agreement that he could keep the staff to,' says Van Velzen. 'But of course, it doesn't work like that. The culture here has developed over the years and you can't just change it by getting up on a soapbox. That's a Pyrrhic victory. You lose staff like that. It's damaging and it leads to mutiny.'

The Coup and the Death of Mrs Driessen

The letter

'It's Rutger Varenkamp from Park House here,' the voice says when I pick up the phone. 'I just thought I'd call. Have you heard about what's going on here?'

I've been away from the nursing home for three weeks and haven't heard.

'Have you heard what happened to Anna?' he continues in an excited voice. 'She's received a letter, signed by most of the staff on De Stadhouder, in which they announce that they no longer want to work with her. When she received it she immediately took sick leave. How she's doing? Well, as you can probably imagine, not so good. I thought I'd call and put you in the picture.'

The next day I receive a warm welcome from the carers on De Stadhouder. They tell me how the tension between Anna van Raalten and themselves gradually escalated. Her will was law and, they say, she had her ideas and she followed them rigidly without taking other opinions into account. The carers were unhappy about not being involved in decisions that concerned them. They felt that they were not being listened to.

'I sometimes thought: Anna, you should be running an Internet company, not a nursing home,' Colette admits. 'She couldn't associate with us; she didn't show any emotion.' There were even problems during the care coordination meetings, says Colette. The coordinators wanted to talk about things that were troubling them, but they had to talk about their strengths and weaknesses instead. When they said that they didn't want to talk about strengths and weaknesses and that other issues were more important for them, Van Raalten cut them short, says Colette.

The care coordinators wanted to talk to her about the way she functioned, but she would have none of it. Shortly after that all the carers received a letter announcing that each unit was to do team-building exercises. At the bottom of the letter it said that there would be consequences for those who didn't attend, though the consequences were not specified. The carers interpreted this as a threat and they were angry. That's when they started collecting signatures. 'There was no other way,' says Colette.

The last few weeks have been difficult for the carers on De Stadhouder. Van Raalten's colleagues refused to talk to them because they were unhappy with the way she had been treated. Even Rutger Varenkamp, who was always on the side of the carers, turned away from them, and was even angry with some of the carers. He interpreted their action as a vote of no confidence in himself as well: he and Anna managed the department together. Later he apologised for getting angry. They hadn't seen Anna since sending her the letter, and they were not sure whether she would return.

Now communication with the other care managers and with Rutger Varenkamp has improved. The carers are full of goodwill and want to make things work. They proudly show me the living rooms, which have been redecorated. Each unit chose a colour and the walls have been repainted. With stencils and posters the living rooms and offices have been brightened up. There are plants and the dining tables have colourful plastic tops.

The carers have received compliments from residents' relatives, not only for the new appearance of the department but also for the new atmosphere and for their efforts. Increasingly I hear them say: 'Maybe we can run things ourselves. Maybe we don't need a care manager.'

During lunch Darah whispers to me that she also signed the letter to Anna, but that she would not have done so if she had known that it would mean her having to leave. 'It all happened too quickly,' she says. 'I only wanted her to listen to us, to have a proper conversation.'

Evaluation

Rutger Varenkamp also gives me a report on the events of the previous weeks. He is still unhappy about the way that Anna van Raalten was treated by the carers. That's just not how people should treat each other, he says. But he is nonetheless motivated to get the department back on track, and he has to admit that the staff are well motivated too. The absenteeism has decreased radically, for example. The nursing home doctor is very busy because he has to manage the department by himself, and recent events have added to his tasks because he now has to develop team-building exercises as well.

Varenkamp is evaluating the events surrounding Anna van Raalten's departure with Roderik Franssen. They have spoken to groups of carers and tomorrow Franssen will present the results to the department. Varenkamp has advised the interim manager to speak to me as well.

Roderik Franssen closes his laptop when I enter his office: his report on the De Stadhouder department is ready. During the next hour he explains his conclusions to me. For one thing, communication was inadequate, both with staff in the department and with him. He knew things weren't running smoothly, but not that they were about to explode. If he had realised then he would have acted, he says. He thinks that the way that the carers worded their letter gave very little space for negotiation, and that they put him under pressure.

Anna van Raalten is not the only care manager who has pulled out in the last few weeks. Three of the four care managers have left within a short period of time. For different reasons, true, but their simultaneous departure is not coincidental, Franssen is convinced. He thinks they have made a mistake, that they became disappointed, and that they thought that change was taking place too slowly. 'At least, that's the sort of thing they were saying,' says Franssen. He thinks that they thought that they were supposed to direct policy, but apart from organising training and other things for staff he isn't sure what that policy function was supposed to be. It's a people-managing job, he says, and an important part of it is being present on the shop floor, keeping the morale up and supporting the care coordinators.

Franssen's time in Park House is coming to an end, he admits when I ask him. Once the fusion with Westerhuis has been sorted out they will appoint a new director and the interim manager will leave. He says that he has learned a lot. It wasn't always easy. When you have worked somewhere for years you know the place inside out. Franssen has had to make decisions that he was 'conned into making,' he says, because he simply didn't know enough about the relationships in the nursing home.

He has had to adjust his ideas. Originally he thought: What a mess. Then he realised that most people meant well but couldn't do otherwise. They were caught in all kinds of structures that they couldn't break out of, he concluded. Then he wondered how he could help them to break out of this helplessness, and he gradually got a deeper understanding of the organisation, he says. 'Problem is, it can't all be done at once. It's too much. It's too broad.'

The next day there is a meeting with the staff of the De Stadhouder department. I walk with Rutger Varenkamp, Colette, Tanja and Femke to the meeting. Robby greets me enthusiastically when I enter. I sit next to him. The carers I came in with sit somewhere else. They don't greet Robby. It seems like they are ignoring him.

Roderik Franssen reports on the communication problems he has identified. He doesn't' have any solutions at the moment, he says. It's still too early. The carers are frustrated, the atmosphere is tense, and there is grumbling. They haven't heard anything new, they say. They thought they were going to be told what was to happen: will Anna come back or not? And what is Roderik Franssen going to do if she does come back? 'Listen,' Franssen says sternly, 'Anna is sick. I have to speak to her before anything can be decided. That's how things are here in Holland. People have rights.'

Afterwards I walk with Robby to the restaurant. We join the others at a table and they immediately turn on him: 'Wasn't it interesting enough? You had you eyes closed half the time. If you don't like it, why don't you stay away?' More verbal attacks follow. They sound aggressive. Robby defends himself: 'I think with my eyes closed. Are you all going to observe me now?' Then he slinks off.

'I didn't like him from the start,' says Tanja.

'He was always with Anna in the office,' says Femke.

'She did everything he wanted,' adds Colette. 'He was allowed to spend hundreds of euros on roses for Christmas and that sort of thing.'

Later Robby comes into the guest room where I am typing. He closes the door behind him. He is angry. He didn't sign the letter to Anna van Raalten. They didn't ask him. When he heard what was in the letter he had said to his colleagues: 'Now you've really finished her off. Is that what you want?' They didn't like his comments. He thinks that 'there is now a power vacuum. It's not too bad at the moment, but sooner or later everyone will try and grab power.'

Mrs Driessen goes to the hospital

Daily life in the nursing home goes on. Mrs Driessen has collapsed again. Last week she had pneumonia, for which she received antibiotics, says Rutger Varenkamp. When he returned to work after the weekend she was drowsy and not responding. He carried out tests and found that she still had pneumonia, she was dehydrated, and her blood sugar levels were worrying. He prescribed a different antibiotic and rehydration, and recommended keeping an eye on her blood sugar levels.

Varenkamp discussed this with Mrs Driessen's daughter-in-law, and she wanted the optimal treatment. And it's already Thursday, the doctor muses. Tomorrow it will be the weekend again and he won't be around, and Mrs Driessen will have to see the locum. During the weekend there is also less control in the department because there are a lot of temp carers during weekends. Varenkamp thinks that admittance to the hospital is a safer option.

Mrs Driessen's daughter-in-law agrees immediately. The doctor is surprised. A few days earlier one of her sons was visiting and he had said: 'When I see mother like this then I wonder whether living like this is worth it? Is it necessary?' Varenkamp could understand the son's response, but it is the daughter-in-law with whom he has to make the arrangements because she is the official contact person.

The carers are not keen on Mrs Driessen's daughter-in-law. She accuses them of not taking proper care of Mrs Driessen, explains assistant carer Rosalie. The daughter-in-law had blamed the carers right from the start. She used to call in every morning early to check whether they had got her out of bed and fed her. Rosalie thinks that someone complained, because one day she stopped coming in the mornings. But then she started coming at lunchtime to feed Mrs Driessen because she thought that the carers weren't giving her enough food.

Later the carers' real complaint about Mrs Driessen's daughter-in-law emerges: she discriminates. 'Just listen to this,' says Darah. 'I was working in the living room when she came in. She looked around as though she wanted to ask someone something, then turned around and went to the office to ask Inge how Mrs Driessen was. Inge is just a trainee while

I'm the care coordinator! But then I'm black and Inge is white. First I thought I'd misinterpreted, but it happened a few times. She doesn't see me – or doesn't want to see me. She discriminates. And I'm not the only one who has noticed.'

Rutger Varenkamp listens attentively to Darah. He doesn't think it is necessarily discrimination. He thinks that there are other things as well. He thinks that the carers are too sensitive due to the fact that she has repeatedly complained about the way they keep speaking Surinamese in the presence of her mother-in-law. Complaining about that isn't discrimination, he says, because it is against the rules anyway. Residents don't like it when they don't understand the conversation, and Varenkamp also thinks it isn't nice. 'I'm not saying you've done it,' he says to Darah, 'but we both know that it happens.' He proposes that they have a meeting to discuss the irritations relating to Mrs Driessen.

Meeting with the daughter-in-law

Later that day there is a meeting between the daughter-in-law of Mrs Driessen, Rutger Varenkamp and Darah. 'We thought it would be a good idea to discuss various things,' the doctor says. 'You have not been entirely satisfied with the situation, and neither are the carers. We have to do what is best for your mother-in-law, and we can't do that if there are mutual irritations. Perhaps you can start by telling us what is worrying you.'

'Yes, it's all so... so... how shall I put it,' says the daughter-in-law, shaking her head. She sighs and straightens her back. 'Yesterday mother's dentures were missing. Gone! I thought: How can that happen? You take them out in the evening, put them in a glass, and then retrieve them again in the morning.' And this wasn't the first time, she says. Also, she always rubs her mother-in-law in with lotion, because she gets blotches on her skin from being in bed so long. She frequently asks the carers to keep an eye on this, 'but they just look at me as though I'm asking for I-don't-know-what,' she says. 'But it's a completely normal request, isn't it?' Then the food: her mother-in-law needs to eat something in the morning, but when she has called in she has noticed that her mother-in-law hadn't eaten anything.

'We have discussed this before,' says the doctor, nodding. 'It is indeed important that Mrs Driessen gets her food on time.' He looks at Darah. 'We try and keep an eye on things,' she says, 'but I'm not there all the time.'

'It's good that you are pointing this out to us,' the doctor says. He agrees that 'unfortunately, there are things that go wrong sometimes'. He explains that this is sometimes due to staff shortage, as a result of which they have to employ temps who don't know the residents. 'It's very bothersome,' he says, 'also for us.' He leans toward the daughter-in-law. 'I understand that you cared for your mother-in-law for a long time?'

She nods: 'She stayed with us for three years.'

The doctor says that the care in the nursing home is probably different to the care that she provided at home. The carers have to get to know her, but she has to trust that there are well-trained carers like Darah who are quite capable of looking after her mother-in-law.

The doctor lays his hand on her arm and smiles. 'You know what I think? I think you are a bit worried about handing over the care of your mother-in-law to someone else,' he says. The daughter-in-law flushes. 'It's very understandable,' he adds. 'Many relatives have the same problem. It's difficult to get used to the feeling that you are suddenly on the sideline.'

'Maybe you're right,' she mumbles.

'We have to try and collaborate,' says the doctor. 'That's what is best for your mother-in-law. Let's try and start again.' She nods. 'If there's anything you want to discuss, you can always come to me, but it's probably better to go to Darah because she is involved in the day-to-day running of things.'

The hospital is holy

A week later Rutger Varenkamp reports that Mrs Driessen is coming out of hospital. He raises an eyebrow. Her stay in the hospital has had 'consequences', he says. He spoke to the daughter-in-law on a number of occasions and she told him that the internist in the hospital had said that if Mrs Driessen had been admitted a few hours later she would have died. The daughter-in-law now thinks that Varenkamp and his colleagues had allowed Mrs Driessen to dehydrate; that they had neglected her.

'That reminds me of the newspaper headlines about the Blauwbörgje nursing home,' I say.

'That thought did cross my mind as well,' says Varenkamp nodding. 'There are a lot of similarities.'

I ask what he thought when he heard the internist's judgement.

'Thank you, hospital colleague, is what I thought,' says Rutger Varenkamp, slightly irritated. 'No, my assessment is different. But the daughter-in-law was completely under the spell of the internist. She kept repeating that according to him her mother-in-law was at death's door.'

I ask whether she blames Varenkamp. 'Not in so many words,' he says. 'But she emphasised repeatedly that she had been shocked.' She had also said that to Darah and Jessy. Varenkamp is now trying to determine whether he was at fault.

'And?' I ask.

Varenkamp doesn't think so. He explains that he has to work within the limitations of the nursing home. The lab only does blood tests on Thursdays, for example. In the hospital they do that daily, so they have more information and it is more up to date, so they can act more quickly. That is why you can't really compare hospitals and nursing homes, he says. 'And then it is very much the question whether all those interventions really benefit the patient.' He shrugs. 'Unfortunately these are matters that are often difficult to discuss. For relatives the hospital is holy.'

A different mentality

Mrs Driessen comes back to Park House by ambulance. In the following week she gradually recovers, but she never really reverts to her old self, and her condition gradually deteriorates again. Rutger Varenkamp informs Jessy, who is on the evening shift, about the situation: 'Unfortunately Mrs Driessen has had a relapse.'

'No, don't tell me,' Jessy repeats a few times.

Varenkamp says that Mrs Driessen has stayed in bed; she has a bladder infection and intestinal bleeding. It isn't clear what the cause is. It could be an ulcer, but it might also be cancer. Finding out would require an endoscopy in the hospital. Maybe she needs a blood transfusion. That could be done in the nursing home on Monday. Her kidneys are also playing up, and that could be a sign of dehydration. Varenkamp wants to give her hypodermoclysis during the night. He thinks that her situation doesn't yet warrant hospital admittance. But if her condition deteriorates during the weekend then she will have to be admitted, he says. He emphasises that it is essential that the carers keep offering her fluid, that they make sure that her diet is adjusted, and that they record what she has eaten. Jessy responds grumpily.

'What's wrong now?' asks Rutger Varenkamp after a while.

The carer shrugs: 'I don't know. I have the feeling that she's suffering.'

'Of course she's suffering,' says the doctor bitterly. 'She's suffering because she has all those ailments.'

'I don't know,' she repeats. 'With Mrs Das I think: a little push and things are okay again. After the hypodermoclysis she really perks up. But with Mrs Driessen I'm not sure.' She shrugs and falls silent.

'What do you mean exactly?' asks the doctor.

'Well, Mrs Das is so different. She has a completely different mentality.'

'Do you realise what you're saying?' The doctor's voice is angry. 'Mrs Das is a dear little old lady who you all like and who you would do anything for. Mrs Driessen is different.'

'I mean that she has a different mentality because of her diabetes,' Jessy says. 'It's just different...'

'But we have to try and get her back on top,' the doctor interrupts. 'Because Mrs Driessen has a different mentality doesn't mean that we are not going to give her hypodermoclysis.' Jessy stands up, puts the paper with her notes for the evening shift in her pocket and leaves the office without saying anything. When she has gone Rutger Varenkamp says indignantly: 'Well I never! Mrs Das is a cuddly little granny, the complete opposite of Mrs Driessen. I can understand it, but it's still unacceptable. It's too explicit. But anyway.' He slams his file closed and gets up. 'Carers are also humans.'

Nothing more to be said

Later that afternoon Jessy returns to the discussion with Rutger Varenkamp. 'He misunderstood me,' she says. 'From the first day she arrived here, Mrs Driessen has ailed. I didn't say that because I like Mrs Das more. There is really something wrong with Mrs Driessen.'

'What?' I ask.

'I don't know,' she says slowly. 'You get so little back from her. You have to start the morning with blood sugar pricks. You're busy with her the whole day and at the end of the day you think you're done, but then there are still all sorts of things that still need doing. With Mrs Das things are different. She had a relapse, was treated and recovered. That's what I mean when I say you don't get anything back.'

Darah sits next to Jessy and listens intently. I ask what she thinks.

She says that the hospital admittance was quite drastic for Mrs Driessen. She came back with a bladder infection and pressure sores on her heels and bum. Her body is used up, Darah thinks. Sometimes she says, when Darah comes to prick her: 'Hey, why don't you go and prick yourself.'

Darah wonders what Mrs Driessen would say if you asked her whether she really wants all these interventions. She is eighty-six. 'Are all these tests really necessary? Into hospital, out of, hospital, pffft!' Darah raises her arms in the air. She thinks that Mrs Driessen should have the hypodermoclysis and perhaps a blood transfusion once more if it is necessary. But if it doesn't help, then she should be left alone, says Darah. And there certainly shouldn't be any more radical tests in the hospital. 'There are all kinds of things that you could possibly do with her, but there comes a time when you have to stop.'

My thirst is broken

A few days later Darah and Rutger Varenkamp are in the office on unit C discussing the residents. The doctor says that Mrs Driessen doesn't seem to be recovering, in spite of the antibiotics, the hypodermoclysis and the blood transfusion. Nothing seems to have helped. He has discussed the situation with Mrs Driessen's daughter-in-law and told her that there is nothing more to be done; that all they can do now is leave her in peace – no more radical interventions, and no more antibiotics. The carers will spoil her, and they will let nature take its course. To his great surprise, the daughter-in-law was supportive, says Varenkamp. He had been prepared for a difficult encounter.

Darah says that the daughter-in-law had visited a lot during the weekend, and she spoke a few times to the locum. Darah also spent some time with her at Mrs Driessen's bedside. According to Darah Mrs Driessen had had enough. When the daughter-in-law said that she would get better and that everything would be all right and that she should ensure that she drank properly, Mrs Driessen had shaken her head. I can't go on, she said, 'my thirst is broken'. This remark made a deep impression on the daughter-in-law. From that moment she thought that Mrs Driessen should be left alone. She even said to her mother-in-law: 'Ach woman, I wish you could close your eyes.' Darah had been struck by this change of attitude.

It happens sometimes, Rutger Varenkamp says. Initially the family want you to do everything possible and refuse to accept that father or mother are dying. But after a while they realise that it isn't going anywhere and they gradually accept that the end is near. It takes time, he says. He always tries to prepare the family by talking to them regularly and explaining possible scenarios and potentially difficult decisions that could arise.

In the case of Mrs Driessen things were more difficult because her condition was also medically complicated. And then there were all the family issues. The daughter-in-law's husband, for example, is also very ill, and they no longer communicate with Mrs Driessen's other son. So the daughter-in-law ends up dealing with everything. And then the communication with the nursing home isn't great and things have gone wrong there as well. Varenkamp thinks that that explains why the daughter-in-law is so active and easy to anger. But now he sees that she is resigned to the situation, and he expects Mrs Driessen to pass away soon.

The nursing home doctor was proved right: Mrs Driessen died less than a week later in the presence of her son and daughter-in-law. Darah and Rosalie went to the funeral and received a card from the family thanking them for their care.

A few days later Rutger Varenkamp handed me a piece of paper. He reminded me that we had compared the hospital admittance of Mrs Driessen with the Blauwbörgje case. Fortunately the communication between the family and the nursing home had improved. Otherwise things could have worked out differently, as they did in the Blauwbörgje case, where the family of a resident accused the nursing home of attempted murder. They claimed that staff had neglected the resident and allowed him to dehydrate. Varenkamp had only followed that case from a distance and didn't know exactly what happened. But this week he spent some time reading up on it. In the *Journal of Nursing Home Medicine* he found a letter to the editor by the doctor at the centre of the Blauwbörgje accusations. He had made a copy for me. He smiles: 'After all, it was *versterven* and that Blauwbörgje thing that brought you here in the first place, wasn't it?'

PART II

THE BLAUWBÖRGJE CASE

The Nursing Home Doctor's Husband

The Letter

In the train I am reading a letter published in the *Journal of Nursing Home Medicine*. It is written by the doctor at the centre of the 'Blauwbörgje case':

> Because so many colleagues, throughout the country, have been so supportive during the accusations against Blauwbörgje nursing home, I would like to report on the legal procedure. (...)
>
> In July 1997 a patient was transferred to us from the hospital (...) with advanced dementia and a chronic infection. The hospital had decided not to intervene radically, given the condition of the patient. He was treated conservatively with antibiotics. His wife reported that the hospital had transferred him to the nursing home for revalidation. During his admission I had a number of meetings with the patient's wife. These were pleasant. I never spoke to the patient's daughter, who pressed the charges.
>
> The charge was that the nursing home, or the responsible staff, were preparing to 'terminate the patient's life'. (...) 'Neither the doctor or the nursing staff made sufficient effort to ensure that B. had sufficient food and fluid (for example through an intravenous drip) or to refer him to a hospital.' Even before the decision to abstain from further treatment was taken, the patient's condition was such that he was going to die.
>
> There was no discussion with the family about the decision to abstain because by that time they no longer wanted to talk to us. Before she had even spoken to me the daughter had pressed charges and informed the press. A week after the patient was admitted to the nursing home, he was transferred back to the hospital and put on an intravenous drip, because the family had lost all faith in the nursing home.
>
> In August 1997 both the Inspectorate of Health and the Ministry of Justice dropped all charges. (...) 'In the case of all charges against Blauwbörgje the Inspectorate of Health has found no evidence of negligence in either medical care or communication with the family of the patient. The actions of the nursing home have been found to conform to professional medical standards and no infringements of the law have been identified.'
>
> Unfortunately the family (...) decided to appeal. On the 15th of December 1998 (...) the Court threw out the charges of 'attempted manslaughter and assault'.
>
> The Court did not rule on the charge of insufficient communication with the family, which is a pity. The Court did not mention that there was no communication with the family regarding abstinence because the family had already taken other steps.

After the verdict there was a press statement. Unfortunately, by this time the press had lost interest. (...)

What has frustrated me in this case is that I have not been able to say anything in my own defence, even though the media have reported on the case extensively. I was advised not to make any statements until a verdict had been given. Moreover, I could not discuss the case without breaching the patient's confidentiality, whereas the media were free to discuss such details. (...)

Fortunately a number of journalists and colleagues have discussed the case more responsibly. And many of those who were involved expressed appreciation of the work that is being done in the nursing home. (...)

If anyone has any specific questions then they can contact me (preferably by letter).

L.S. Moorman-Bakker

I write to Dr Moorman care of Blauwbörgje nursing home and ask whether I can speak to her. A week later I receive an e-mail from her husband. He writes that his wife passed away two months previously. She had leukaemia. Although he wasn't directly involved in the case, he is familiar with the events and is willing to talk to me about them. I reply, apologising, and say that he must have other things on his mind than the Blauwbörgje case. No, he replies immediately, he would like to collaborate. We make an appointment for three weeks hence.

In the train I look at my watch. It has just been announced: 'Due to a technical problem this train will have to stop in Hoogeveen. From there you will be taken to Meppel by bus. We apologise for any inconvenience.' The conductor estimates that the train will arrive forty-five minutes late. I phone Maarten Moorman, who had promised to pick me up at the station. 'The trains again,' he says in a friendly tone. 'Have you had lunch? No? I'll arrange something.' It's the first time I have spoken to him directly; all previous communication has been via e-mail.

I was worried we wouldn't recognise each other. I needn't have been. The village station is small. When I get off the train I see a tall man of around fifty waiting on the opposite side of the track. I raise my hand. He waves back. We drive through meadows to a converted farmhouse. In the kitchen we eat fried eggs, freshly gathered. There is a notice board with photos of two young women and an older woman, in her forties, with a lean face. 'Our daughters, and Liset, when she was already ill,' he says, spontaneously.

What happened

After lunch we go into the living room. Maarten Moorman leafs through two files – letters from the lawyer, statements from those involved, a police report. He allows me to have a look, and says I can use it, as long as it doesn't cause problems. Maarten Moorman doesn't want the Bruggeling family to experience any negative effects. Because, even though his wife was very angry with the daughter, she also understood that 'there was a tragedy behind the events,' he says.

Maarten Moorman tells me the story of Mr Bruggeling. The man was relatively young, in his late fifties, and had pre-senile dementia. He was well known and popular in Groningen – a milkman, active in football clubs. Maarten Moorman knew him from when he was a student. He was originally admitted to a nursing home in the south of the city, but there were problems. His relatives weren't easy, and neither was he. The situation became untenable and the nursing home had to get rid of him.

Bruggeling was transferred to Blauwbörgje, where he only came for day care. Liset Moorman was the doctor. She knew Bruggeling and his wife, or rather, ex-wife. Her role was limited to his day-care: because he lived at home it was his GP who had the main responsibility for his health.

Everything ran smoothly until Bruggeling fell ill and was admitted to Liset's department to recover. He was transferred there from the hospital where he had been treated for epididymitis. Liset and Maarten Moorman were on holiday at the time and when they returned Liset was confronted by the sick Mr Bruggeling. He also had signs of late-stage dementia, such as difficulty swallowing. All this was documented.

Liset saw that things weren't going well with Mr Bruggeling. She told his ex-wife that she should prepare herself for the end. It was a 'hard message' says Moorman. Contact between the family and Liset was through the ex-wife. The daughter, Yvonne, was never involved in any of the discussions. Maarten Moorman thinks that she never spoke to staff in the nursing home.

When Bruggeling had been in Blauwbörgje a week, the daughter came to visit her father. She immediately wanted to speak to Liset. The daughter thought that Bruggeling wasn't being treated properly, says Maarten Moorman, and that he wasn't receiving enough fluid. She was very angry about this. It was during the weekend and Liset was on call for a number of other nursing homes in the region. She said that she would check on Mr Bruggeling in the afternoon. She was busy and had a list of priorities.

Maarten Moorman remembers the events well, he says. His wife had just arrived home when the relatives of Mr Bruggeling phoned. They wanted to get him admitted to hospital. Liset didn't think that was a good idea. In the hospital they would probably pep him up with an infusion. The question was: would that be in his own best interests? The nursing home doctor wanted to discuss that with the family, especially the daughter, whom she had never seen. But it never got that far: it was too late for talking. The doctor tried to save the situation on the phone, but events were already taking their own course. Finally Liset phoned the hospital and said that the family wanted a second opinion.

Maarten Moorman says that until that Saturday his wife had had a good relationship with Bruggeling's ex-wife. Some of the carers hadn't been very tactful in their communication with the family, he says. For example, someone had said that it was the end of the road for Mr Bruggeling. Liset had only heard this second hand, as she had just returned from holiday, but it was still her responsibility. She never had any real influence on the situation, but she was confronted with the consequences, says Maarten Moorman.

What happened in the hospital was very unpleasant, says Moorman. The doctor who admitted Mr Bruggeling added fuel to the flames, Moorman feels. He said that Bruggeling's 'life had been saved' by the quick action of his family, because he was 'dehydrated right down to his kidneys'. This confirmed the daughter's impression that he hadn't been treated properly in the nursing home. 'By then things were so heated that she wanted to follow the matter up to the bitter end and get what she saw to be justice,' says Moorman. This all happened on Sunday and Monday. On Tuesday morning Liset and Maarten Moorman were woken by the newsreader on their radio-alarm clock announcing that a family had accused the doctor of Blauwbörgje nursing home of attempted murder.

'It took a while before it registered that they were talking about Liset,' says Moorman. He falls silent and looks at me. 'There was a big fuss. Liset was being accused of murder. She had to go to the police station. They also had to decide whether she could go on practicing, because if she had committed a crime she would have to be struck off.'

Newspaper headlines

Of course, mistakes were made, says Maarten Moorman. The communication wasn't always ideal. But that happens millions of times a day all over the place, he says. Then it's a question of trying to have a proper conversation before things go completely wrong. Unfortunately that didn't happen in this case. But what Moorman considers much worse than the failure of communication, is the fact that the daughter, who had originally not been part of any of the discussions, 'wormed her way in, pushed her mother aside, and then started to try and organise things. She had almost never even visited her father, and then suddenly she was taking things over.' Moorman says that that sort of thing happens frequently in nursing homes. There are relatives who hardly ever visit, and when they do eventually come they are shocked by the situation and feel guilty and their response is: 'What misery! This is unacceptable. Something has to be done now. I'm taking charge.' 'That really stirs things up,' says Moorman.

Mr Bruggeling's daughter imposed her will, says Moorman. 'You could say that she was given the opportunity to impose her will. Why? Well, because it was all too much for Liset that Saturday.' Retrospectively Liset had told her husband that if she ever encountered a situation like that again she would not allow the patient to be sent to the hospital, and she would do everything to come to an agreement with the family.

Moorman sighs. 'If, if, if. I can still picture her here in the living room. She was so tired. She was already sick then, only she didn't know it. After the phone call in which everything went wrong, she was also relieved to be rid of those people.'

One of the things that played a role in the accusation was that the family didn't trust the nursing home, says Moorman. He is convinced that this was related to their experience with the previous nursing home. There was a rumpus there, he says. What was behind it all? Maarten Moorman leans back in the sofa and raises his hands: 'Guilt? Past mistakes? Unresolved conflicts? You can easily interpret it in that way, and I must admit that we did interpret it in that way.' Moorman says that there were also rumours that money played a role in the accusation; that the family had hoped to get compensation from Blauwbörgje.

The case was reported on television and was headline news in the newspapers. Moorman ascribes the media attention to the fact that it was during the slack summer months of July and August when there is nothing else to report. 'At that time of year something like that makes nice headlines,' he says. The daughter was given ample opportunity to present her case, and she did that 'quite reasonably,' according to Moorman. 'She wasn't hysterical, and the average television viewer must have thought: understandable that she is angry. Her father is being killed because staff in the nursing home can't be bothered to take proper care of him. Scandalous!'

Moorman reminds me that at the time there were also reports in the media about doctors and nurses deliberately killing patients. In one case a nursing home nurse had been labelled 'the angel of death' because she had killed at least four patients with insulin injections. And there was a lot of discussion about euthanasia. The time was ripe for something like this, Moorman says.

Moorman thinks that it is unfortunate that his wife was not allowed to make her side of the story public: she was formally suspended and a spokesperson presented the Blauwbörgje case to the media, awkwardly, Moorman thinks. He couldn't deal with the journalists who asked direct questions and demanded direct answers. He was also unable to counter the accusations of the hospital doctor.

Basically it boils down to the fact that the press had sufficient time to present the Bruggeling family's point of view, while the other side, the nursing home side, received insufficient attention. If Liset had been allowed to speak out, things would have turned out differently, Moorman is convinced. Because she had been directly involved she would have been able to clarify what had actually happened; she would have made an honest impression, says Moorman.

Mr Bruggeling recovered in the hospital and was discharged and went home, Moorman says. Everyone wondered what would happen to him now. 'He was incontinent and could no longer communicate, so it was impossible to care for him at home. And there wasn't a nursing home in the vicinity that would have him.' Moorman doesn't know whether Mr Bruggeling is still alive. He certainly lived longer than anyone expected, he says. He sighs: 'He had that in common with Liset. In the autumn of 1997 she was diagnosed with leukaemia. After the diagnosis she lived for another three and a half years.'

The Ex-wife

A week in the nursing home

I also wrote to Mr Bruggeling's ex-wife, Mrs Koster, and her daughter Yvonne Bruggeling, asking if they would be willing to talk to me. 'My daughter works and has a son, so she is busy, but I have time,' says Mrs Koster when I phone her. A week later it is a neat woman in her late fifties who opens the front door. She starts talking immediately. 'What happened is really unbelievable,' she says. She 'can't find the words' to tell me, even now after all this time. And just imagine, her husband is still alive, after almost four years!

'Pity,' says Mrs Koster when she returns with coffee a few minutes later and tells me she has just thrown away all the documents relating to the court case. Otherwise she could have shown me. I could call their lawyer, she suggests. He probably still has all the information. As far as she is concerned I can see everything, and she's willing to sign if necessary.

She tells me that Koen Bruggeling, her ex-husband, attended the day-care centre at Blauwbörgje three times a week. That was good, she says, and doesn't want to comment on it further. Her ex-husband had enjoyed it there. One day Mrs Koster wanted to go on holiday. Because she took care of Mr Bruggeling she hadn't been able to go on holiday for eight years. The social worker at Blauwbörgje said that it should be possible. All they had to do was admit him for a week.

If Mrs Koster had known what would happen then she would never have gone, she says. She says that before all this happened her ex-husband could walk normally. They used to stroll in the park or go shopping. In any case, the holiday didn't happen, she doesn't remember exactly why, so she said to her daughter: 'Shall we go and get Papa or shall we leave him there?' Her daughter said: 'Leave him there, then you can have a week's rest.'

Mrs Koster says that she visited Koen Bruggeling every day in Blauwbörgje. One day she said to her daughter: 'Don't you think Papa looks unwell?' 'Ach, you're always worrying,' the daughter had answered. But Mrs Koster thought that he looked at her 'strangely', as though 'he realised that he was in the wrong place'. She saw on his face that 'something was wrong', says Mrs Koster. 'As though he wanted me to take him home. But he couldn't say that, because he couldn't talk any more.'

One day Mrs Koster came to visit and found Mr Bruggeling in bed under two blankets and wearing jeans and a thick sweater. She asked a carer what was happening and the carer said that he was cold. 'Why can't he wear his pyjamas if he's in bed?' she asked. 'You can't just put him in bed in his clothes, it's too hot.'

The next day she saw the carers giving him a very small bowl of porridge. She asked for some bread but they refused. 'I said: Pardon? I'd like a few slices of bread, one with jam and one with cheese.' When they continued to refuse she said: 'Now listen here, if I don't get two slices of bread within the next fifteen minutes I'll go to the kitchen and get them myself.'

Later the supervisor arrived and asked to have a word with Mrs Koster and her daughter. He took them into an office and asked them whether they realised that Mr Bruggeling was seriously ill. 'My father isn't sick,' Yvonne answered. 'I don't know what you're up to.' According to the supervisor Koen Bruggeling couldn't eat bread any more otherwise he would choke. Mrs Koster had answered that he had been living at home until a couple of days ago and that he had eaten bread every day. 'And now suddenly he can't eat bread anymore? That's inconceivable.' Finally she got the slices of bread and a cup of tea. 'Koen ate everything,' she says. 'You can be sure of that.'

The next day, Wednesday, her ex-husband's condition was even worse, she says. He had terrible thirst. She gave him a glass of water that he gulped down. So when she and her daughter were in the nursing home he drank, and when they were not there he received nothing, she says. Mrs Koster doesn't know why. She thinks that there was a communication breakdown between the doctor and the carers; that the carers thought that he had come to the nursing home to die. 'It must have been that,' she says. 'What else could it have been?'

Thursday things were worse still. She saw a carer with a plate of food and asked whether it was for Koen. Yes, the carer had answered, but she says she now doesn't believe it was for him. 'They obviously didn't want to admit that he wasn't getting anything,' she says. Koen Bruggeling refused to eat that day.

Mrs Koster asked whether she could feed a woman who was with Koen in the living room. She had seen that the woman was trying to eat but that her plate had been taken away after she had only had a few spoonfuls. 'That's how little time they had for the people,' she says. The woman ate a whole plateful and then devoured a desert as well. The following day Mrs Koster fed her again.

On Friday she again asked Yvonne whether she thought things were okay with her father. Yvonne didn't think so. She thought that the glass of water they offered him was the only drink he had had all day. On Friday evening Yvonne was visiting her mother. 'Because I was agitated,' Mrs Koster says. At about twelve, Yvonne phoned Blauwbörgje. She was told that Koen had high fever and that he had been given Paracetamol. 'Just imagine,' says Mrs Koster. 'If we hadn't called we wouldn't have known.'

More dead than alive

The next morning, Saturday, at about ten, Mrs Koster had the feeling that 'something was wrong', and so she went with her daughter to Blauwbörgje. When they arrived they found Koen in bed, 'more dead than alive'. She went to ask the supervisor what was wrong. He said that things were not going well for Koen and that he would come and speak to them shortly. After a while one of the other carers came by, and she also said that things were not good, and that they should be prepared to accept that 'things wouldn't get better'. Mrs Koster couldn't understand why. She said that her ex-husband wasn't drinking and asked whether he could get fluid through a drip.

'No,' the carer had said, 'because we're implementing a dehydration policy'. 'A what? Dehydration?' Mrs Koster had asked. 'You can't be doing that to Koen?'

'Oh yes we are,' the carer said. 'The doctor can tell you more about it. She'll be here between twelve and one.' It was eleven. Mrs Koster and her daughter went home and planned to return later.

Just before one the phone rang. It was the doctor. Yvonne had asked how her father was and was told: Your father is dying. Mrs Koster says: 'Bang! Just like that, over the phone. I can still see Yvonne's face going white.'

'No way,' Yvonne had said. 'My father isn't dying.' Yvonne said she wanted nothing more to do with the nursing home, that she would call an ambulance and have her father taken to the hospital.

'There was a whole circus,' Mrs Koster says. 'Because you couldn't just do that. They had to call their GP, but he was away, so they had to speak to the locum. He arranged everything. Then finally at half-past-four 'that doctor' from Blauwbörgje phoned to say that the ambulance had arrived.

The hospital

In the hospital Mr Bruggeling was immediately given an infusion with liquid, says Mrs Koster. The doctor examined him. He had said that Koen was 'dehydrated right down to his kidneys'. Mrs Koster is convinced that if they hadn't transferred him to the hospital he would have died.

The doctor had a long discussion with her and her daughter. He didn't understand why things had happened this way, she says. After the discussion she went to see Koen. 'He'd already had a glass of water and some custard,' she says. 'And they said he wouldn't eat and drink! The next morning Koen had a bowl of porridge and a cup of coffee. So he was recovering.'

After Koen was admitted to hospital Mrs Koster and her daughter contacted a lawyer. 'Because,' she says, 'what happened shouldn't be allowed to happen. Someone is admitted to a nursing home for a week's holiday and by the end of the week he is almost dead.' And even if that was really the case, she adds, then at least the doctors should inform the relatives.

Koen Bruggeling was in hospital for three weeks. When he was discharged he could no longer walk. In fact, Mrs Koster says, he was never the same after the incident in the nursing home. Initially he came back home, because after all the publicity they couldn't find another nursing home willing to take him. He was eventually admitted to *De Merenberg* nursing home, in a village near the city of Groningen. Initially he was there only for day care, but two years ago he was fully admitted.

They made clear arrangements with the doctor in De Merenberg, says Mrs Koster. If he refuses to eat or drink, then he is to be given a fluid drip for fourteen days. If that doesn't help, then they will remove the drip and he will be allowed to die. The family also agreed that he shouldn't be resuscitated if he had a heart attack. 'He's so thin that any attempt at resuscitation would crush his chest,' says Mrs Koster. 'We have agreed that if things get worse he should be allowed to die peacefully. It's what he deserves after all he's been through.'

Whether Koen Bruggeling now has a good life Mrs Koster can't say. 'Actually he doesn't really have a life,' she says. 'He sits, he lies in bed, he eats, he drinks. That's it.' She says that he is now very thin; he only weighs 48 kilos. That's why she can now accept it if he passes away. But she does want to be kept informed. She doesn't want them to just 'abandon him to dehydration' as they did in Blauwbörgje.

Mrs Koster's mother

Mrs Koster tells me that her mother died last year. She lived in a nursing home and couldn't stand it. When she had been there a year the doctors thought she had had a heart attack. She refused to eat and drink. Mrs Koster accompanied her to the hospital. The doctor there said that her mother was healthy and that he could find nothing wrong but, he added, he thought that she no longer wanted to live. 'So the only thing we could do,' says Mrs Koster, 'was to let her go.'

Mrs Koster thought the nursing home in which her mother stayed was terrible. 'It was impersonal,' she says. 'They didn't do anything with the residents. No walks, because no one had the time. So they just sat there in their chairs all day. They went from chair to bed and then the next morning from bed to chair. That was it, day-in, day-out.'

Mrs Koster had to admit that in the final weeks before her mother died, they had cared for her very well. 'They were really very kind to her,' she says. 'Yes, I really have to admit.' Her mother was in bed and refused to eat and drink and she dehydrated. Initially the doctors and the family had decided not to give her fluid through an infusion. 'Later they gave her those needles in her leg,' Mrs Koster says. 'That didn't help, so they stopped. But that was a completely different experience to the one with Koen, because my mother wasn't suffering from dementia. She made it clear that she didn't want to go on. She could eat and drink and she was capable of making the decision not to.'

The Nursing Home Doctor

The charge

I read and re-read the documents that Maarten has given me. There are newspaper cuttings with sentences underlined by Liset Moorman. There are cards and letters from friends and strangers who express their sympathy. There are letters from lawyers, copies of documents from medical records, and police statements.

The police notes

On Tuesday 29 July 1997, at about 10:40, I, JANSSEN, PETER KAREL, Brigadier of the Regional Police Force of Groningen, took the following statement from the accused, MOORMAN, LISETTE HENRIETTE, born 15 April 1951, in Groningen, at the Central Police Station, Groningen. (...)

I am a doctor working at the Blauwbörgje nursing home, situated here in Groningen. I have known Mr Bruggeling approximately one year. I work in the day-care centre at the home, from where I am familiar with Mr Bruggeling. In Blauwbörgje people suffering from dementia are cared for. Since 1996 Mr Bruggeling has been attending day care three days a week. (...)

During day-care it became clear that Bruggeling needed a lot of care. This was discussed with his ex-wife and with home care staff. The ex-wife (I will refer to her as Mrs Bruggeling) insisted repeatedly that she could cope with caring for him herself and wanted to continue doing it.

I was on holiday from 5-14 July 1997. When I returned to work on Tuesday 15 July I found that Bruggeling had been admitted to the home for a period of recovery. He had previously been admitted to hospital, referred by his GP, for epididymitis. On Friday 11 July, Bruggeling was admitted to Blauwbörgje, after consultation with the hospital and the admittance committee of Blauwbörgje. (...)

On Tuesday 15 July 1997 I saw Bruggeling for the first time since his admittance. I was only able to establish minimal communication with him. He was very drowsy. The hospital had advised that he could be allowed out of bed two hours a day. In Blauwbörgje that turned out not to be possible. Bruggeling was extremely drowsy and he indicated that he was in pain. Given his physical and mental condition it was decided to keep him in bed. Mrs Bruggeling repeatedly stated that she would prefer her husband to be out of bed. An attempt was made to explain this to her. I had the impression that she did not understand the reasons for this. I discussed this with her on Thursday 17 July. I had already discussed the decision to keep Bruggeling in bed with staff on Tuesday 15 July. I wasn't able to discuss this with Mrs Bruggeling on the same day because she was out of town. I had heard from the nursing staff that Mrs Bruggeling had had a conversation with Fred Beekhuis, the care coordinator, on Monday 14 July. This conversation had not been very agreeable, and I received a request from Mrs Bruggeling for a meeting. This happened on Thursday 17 July.

Bruggeling's treatment with antibiotics, that was initiated in the hospital, continued in the nursing home until Monday 14 July 1997, when that course of treatment was completed. On Tuesday 15 July I prescribed a new course of treatment. Because the drug was not available at that moment, the treatment started on Thursday 17 July 1997. I had consulted my colleague Tom van Bokhoven regarding this course of treatment.

I prescribed this treatment because in my opinion Bruggeling was not recovering. When someone is admitted to Blauwbörgje it is usual to take a blood sample for laboratory tests. I think that this happened on Tuesday 15 July in the case of Mr Bruggeling. The result did not give any cause for concern.

On Thursday 17 July I saw Bruggeling again. He was drowsy and inattentive. I found that his condition had become more worrying. I discussed this later with Mrs Bruggeling. I want to note here that Bruggeling, when he had moments of lucidity, did consume amounts of liquid and food that were presented to him. During the meeting with Mrs Bruggeling she claimed that her husband was always lucid during her visits. That morning I accompanied her to visit her husband. Bruggeling was lucid, or rather, he was responsive. Whether or not he was responding to his wife, I do not know. It is difficult to judge this in patients such as Bruggeling. Mrs Bruggeling interpreted this as a direct response to her. This discussion was held in the presence of Ans Vroom, one of the carers. The daughter of Mrs Bruggeling was not present.

I also told Mrs Bruggeling that her husband's condition was not a consequence of the infection, because that had stabilised. I also discussed her husband's medication with her. We also discussed the possibility of his death. In the latter case she wanted to have him at home so that she could care for him to the end. She wanted to arrange for a bed to be installed at home. That was postponed because I suggested that he first finish his course of treatment in the nursing home. Mrs Bruggeling agreed to this.

On Friday 18 July I had another meeting with Mrs Bruggeling to discuss changes in Mr Bruggeling's condition. As there were no changes, this was a brief meeting. We did agree to wait until Tuesday 22 July, which is when the antibiotic treatment would be completed. The daughter was also not present at this meeting.

On Friday 18 July I stopped the administration of Rivortril. This medicine can cause drowsiness.

In the night of Friday 18 July to Saturday 19 July I was telephoned at home by the head of the nursing staff, Maria Gonzales. She told me that Bruggeling had fever. On my advice he was given Paracetamol. I was on call on Saturday 19 July and intended to see Bruggeling then.

On Saturday 19 July I phoned the weekend supervisor, Gerard Vos, and informed him that I would be in Blauwbörgje at about 13.30. I first had to pay a visit to another nursing home. The supervisor mentioned that the Bruggeling family were worried about Mr Bruggeling's condition. I did not discuss Bruggeling's condition with the supervisor.

At 13.30 I arrived in Blauwbörgje. I examined Bruggeling. I found that he had fever. I thought he possibly had pneumonia, or blood poisoning. This was speculation rather than an accurate diagnosis. I thought that the situation warranted concern and I wanted to discuss further treatment with the family. I wanted to discuss terminating further treatment with them. I had heard from the nursing staff that Mrs Bruggeling and her daughter had already been in Blauwbörgje that morning and that they (the family) had been in contact with the locum GP. The GP had also called the nursing home. I telephoned Bruggeling's daughter. From her I gathered that her mother was very upset but that I could speak to her. This conversation was very difficult. She insisted that Bruggeling receive an infusion. I told her that this was not possible at home, that Bruggeling would need to be admitted to hospital for this. I suggested that Bruggeling could receive fluid subcutaneously through hypodermoclysis. For that he would have to remain in Blauwbörgje. I had gathered that the family were trying to have Bruggeling removed from Blauwbörgje. My suggestion of giving Bruggeling hypodermoclysis was not considered to be an option.

According to the daughter, we were allowing her father to die. Given the daughter's response I repeatedly asked whether they had understood what I was saying. I think they had already made the decision that Bruggeling should be taken out of Blauwbörgje. I then said that I would contact the locum GP, which I did. He then contacted the internist in the hospital, Dr John Meijers. Around 14.00 Bruggeling was transferred to the hospital. I didn't speak to the family again that day.

I know that the daughter has laid a charge of attempted murder through dehydration against the staff of Blauwbörgje, who are under my supervision. I deny the charge. Bruggeling was given food and liquid whenever he wanted to, and could, consume it. Regarding the lemon swabs [that were on his bedside table and on which the daughter had commented], these are used to keep the mouth moist and for oral hygiene.

Notes

On a separate sheet Liset Moorman has made notes, based on three key words:

Abstaining: My thoughts were as follows. I wanted to suggest a policy of abstention to the family and discuss this with them. No decision had yet been made. This was thwarted by the daughter's attitude. At a certain point this could no longer be discussed with them. Referral to the hospital meant that Bruggeling would be treated.

Second opinion: I couldn't treat him any more because the family no longer had confidence in me. I would rather have kept him in the nursing home. I was curious about the internist's opinion. It was clear that they would give him an infusion in the hospital – i.e. that they would treat him. But they didn't know the patient.

Reason for referral: The family no longer had confidence in the nursing home. I would rather have treated him in the nursing home with hypodermoclysis. My doubts related to this being a short-term remedy and that the same problem would soon arise again. The situation would be repeated. Referral to the hospital is strange. There was no medical reason for his reduced lucidity. There was a new infection. Treatment with Rocephousein (cefalosporine) was initiated. Reason for the referral was therefore the conflict with the family. They had already taken a stand before I had spoken to them. They no longer wanted to speak to me even though they knew what I wanted to do. The nursing staff had also already stated that clearly.

The stories

A few days after I had spoken to Maarten Moorman he sent me a story that his wife had written about the Bruggeling case. The story describes the case from the point of view of the various parties involved.

Writing about the discovery that charges had been laid against her, the nursing home doctor wrote:

> The newspaper headlines screamed: Murder in the nursing home? The content of the articles almost didn't penetrate her mind. She quickly read on. 'Daughter of a patient who was admitted to nursing home B accuses staff of wilfully allowing her father to die. Without consulting the family the nursing home decided to stop giving the patient food and drink. The family insisted that the patient be transferred to a hospital where, the daughter reports, her father rapidly recovered. The doctor in the hospital confirmed that the patient was dehydrated. He said that the patient was too young to die ...' It gradually became clear that the article was about the nursing home in which she worked. She read the article again. There was no doubt about it: it was about her and her patient.

Regarding the meeting that she had with the director of the nursing home, an economist, shortly after charges were laid she wrote:

> He asked her how it was possible that one moment it seemed like the patient was at the point of death, but then a moment later, after a small intervention, he appeared to recover. She interpreted this as an accusation. She was inclined to say: Aren't people allowed to die any more? Is it not possible that sometimes it might be a blessing to be allowed to die? But she repressed the thought. She realised that the remark could be construed as too noncommittal. She always found it difficult when people didn't understand how difficult it was for patients in the final stages of dementia. How variable

their consciousness could be. How they sometimes survived a collapse, without any real intervention, and then lived on for a year without any real complication, but with their competence gradually declining, until they were like totally dependent newborns.

'May I ask something, as Devil's advocate?' the director asked. 'Why didn't you give him the infusion a day earlier yourself?'

She knew that the question was coming. 'We have a conservative policy when it comes to the artificial administration of food and liquid. That is described in the information leaflet that is given to relatives when we first admit someone. We always first see whether they recover by themselves first.'

In Liset Moorman's story the care coordinator knew Mr Bruggeling from earlier. The patient had taught him swimming and used to be a sports hero. Liset Moorman describes how the care coordinator saw Mr Bruggeling and his wife:

When his wife was there he was always clear-headed, she said. Why was it then that he was always so drowsy? She wanted to demonstrate how happy he was to see her. She overwhelmed him with kisses and hugs. He looked at her with the same surprised expression that he had when he looked at staff members. But for her it was proof. For him it was a strange experience seeing the former sports hero lying there passively in bed, being ostentatiously kissed and cuddled by his wife. Would he have enjoyed it? Was she happy now that she had a man who had become a large teddy bear?

The last perspective is that of the brigadier of police:

The daughter and spouse had been to the police station together. The daughter was indignant. She said that it was the order of the day in the nursing home. They just let people die by withholding food and water. A friend of hers had said that they had let her mother die there. The daughter did the talking. The mother just looked upset and nodded and sniffed. There was something wrong with the story. The daughter had never spoken to the doctor or anyone else who had been involved in her father's care. She just bluntly intervened and took over from her mother. The brigadier still didn't have a clear picture of the relationship between mother and daughter. What were their motives? He wondered how the daughter could be so angry now without ever having expressed this before. No one seems to have anticipated this reaction. Was this panic or the result of poor communication? Was it an expression of the daughter's general dissatisfaction? Maybe they should question her about this at a later stage. What was the role of the nurses? He couldn't see any clear evidence of euthanasia, let alone murder. More likely barely recognised emotions boiling to the surface.

The Colleague of the Nursing Home Doctor

A sad man

Nursing home doctor Tom van Bokhoven phones back five minutes after I have left a voicemail message. He is keen to speak to me. He shared an office with Liset at Blauwbörgje for fifteen years and discussed the Bruggeling case with her intensively. He saw Mr Bruggeling when Liset was on holiday. He also knew him from earlier periods that he had spent in the nursing home. He is free next week and has plenty of time to meet me and discuss things.

A few days later we meet in the modern house that he and his wife have built in Groningen. Van Bokhoven describes Bruggeling as a man who was completely turned in on himself, and with whom it was hardly possible to communicate at all. He walked around a bit, says the doctor, and said 'tuttuttut'. At home he will have recognised things and had routines. 'But communication, no, that wasn't possible any more,' says the doctor. 'He was sixty-two and in the final phase of dementia.'

Bruggeling had been in the day-care 'crèche group' at Blauwbörgje. The crèche group is primarily intended to offer support to home-carers. Six months before the *versterven* incident, Mr Bruggeling was admitted to Van Bokhoven's department for a short 'holiday' stay. The doctor says that Mr Bruggeling didn't cope very well with changes in his environment. It made him restless. Van Bokhoven had advised the family to leave him in Blauwbörgje. 'But they insisted that he go back home,' Van Bokhoven says. 'His wife felt that she had to take care of him herself.'

Van Bokhoven thought that Bruggeling was 'a sad man' who was struggling to understand what was happening to him. Then suddenly he would want to get out, to go outside. At moments like that he became angry and aggressive. Whether or not he wanted to die, Van Bokhoven can't say, just as he can't say whether Bruggeling wanted to live. Liset Moorman and Ton van Bokhoven agreed that Mr Bruggeling was someone suitable for a 'symptomatic approach' – forgoing treatment that would extend life. Not because his physical condition was so bad, but because of the advanced dementia that he suffered from. The doctors thought it was inhumane to extend a life like that. That was, Van Bokhoven thinks, also one of the underlying problems: 'In the back of my mind I hoped, and I think that Liset did as well, that his life would end.'

Jumping the gun

In July 1997 Van Bokhoven encountered Koen Bruggeling when he was standing in for Liset Moorman. Bruggeling had epididymitis that had made his general condition much worse. That had already become clear in the hospital, where they were not keen to do much more with him. Bruggeling had been transferred to Blauwbörgje to recover. When Van Bokhoven examined him, he had thought: I'm not going to fiddle around too much with this one.

The catch is, says Van Bokhoven, that as a doctor you tend to jump the gun. He tells me that he has been guilty of this himself, most recently with his own mother. She is now dead, but she had had dementia. In the early stages of her disease, whenever she had a cold almost, Van Bokhoven had thought: This is such a poor quality of life, it's not worth it, we must stop the antibiotics. His brothers, on the other hand, had not reached that stage yet. He now thinks that he was a bit over-eager. One of his brothers took the responsibility for their mother over from him. He thinks that that is where the mistake was made: that the doctors hadn't taken sufficient note of which stage of the coping and working-through process the Bruggeling family were in.

During Bruggeling's last days in the nursing home mistakes were made, he says. Not medically, but in the communication. 'We never succeeded in making our policy clear to them,' he explains. 'These are common situations that every nursing home doctor is familiar with.' Recently Van Bokhoven had reduced the medication of an 88-year-old women 'much too radically'. 'It was one of those addictive tranquillizers.' The woman was really addicted, and things didn't work out well. Her husband was terribly angry. Fortunately the carers warned him and Van Bokhoven went in on his day off to talk to the man. 'Talk, talk, admit, say sorry, adjust,' he summarises. 'Often you can get things back on track like that. Generally nursing home doctors have a sixth sense in that respect. You get the feeling: be careful, things can go wrong here, make an extra effort to communicate with this family.'

Liset didn't have that alertness, Van Bokhoven thinks, because she was exhausted. On that Saturday morning, when it all went wrong, she was on call in another nursing home. She was too weak to react adequately to the situation; to come to Blauwbörgje and talk things right. She said she'd come later but, with hindsight, that was too late. If she had been here, Van Bokhoven thinks, then she could have saved the situation, by giving Bruggeling hypodermoclysis and thus giving herself time to come to an agreement with the family.

Liset did suggest hypodermoclysis that afternoon, but by then the situation had already exploded, says Van Bokhoven. The family no longer wanted it. Van Bokhoven thinks that they were fixated on the infusion that could only be given in the hospital. He doesn't know whether Liset would have admitted that she was tired. She did admit that she had lost control of the situation, and that when everything became public the nursing home did not respond adequately. But Ton van Bokhoven thinks that Liset's disease and the concomitant fatigue did play a role.

A chance to die

Ton van Bokhoven says that during the week that Koen Bruggeling was admitted, the carers had spoken about his condition to his ex-wife. Carers are quite capable of initiating fruitful discussions with relatives on this kind of issue, says the doctor. That is, as long as it is along the lines of agreed policy. Their role can be preparatory: 'Talk to the family, assess their thoughts and opinions, massage things. Would abstaining from life-prolonging treatment be acceptable, or do they need more time?' The carers can be more noncommittal and less threatening than the doctor.

The carers from Liset Moorman's department were a headstrong lot, according to Van Bokhoven. They did things themselves. Sometimes that is problematic, he says. They are not always very diplomatic and they can be stubborn. Once they have an idea in their heads, then that is reality for them, says the doctor, even though they might have the best intentions. What he is trying to say is that he isn't surprised that the communication between the nursing home and the Bruggeling family went wrong.

The doctors in Blauwbörgje give hypodermoclysis to rehydrate; it says so in the brochure for relatives. The doctors think that hypodermoclysis is justified in the case of an infection, to help the patient to recover. But they do not give tube feeding, or percutaneous endoscopic gastrostomy (PEG), says Van Bokhoven. When people with dementia no longer eat or drink then they are dying. The doctors in Blauwbörgje had agreed that when that stage had arrived, patients should be allowed to die. Bruggeling's infection could probably have been suppressed with antibiotics and hypodermoclysis, Van Bokhoven thinks. But he thinks that there comes a time that you should be able to let the patient die. Bruggeling's situation in that week was one that Van Bokhoven would describe as the chance to let him die.

He says that the case led to changes in the way doctors communicate with relatives. They have become more active, and they now raise end-of-life issues with the family when the patient is first admitted. There was already a trend in the direction, says Van Bokhoven, but due to the Bruggeling affair this became official policy more rapidly in Blauwbörgje.

Letting go

The family's picture of Mr Bruggeling was completely different to that of the nursing home doctors, says Ton van Bokhoven. They thought he was still all there. 'He goes everywhere with us,' they kept repeating. 'Well,' the nursing home doctor continues, 'in the nursing home there are so many people who go everywhere behind their walking frame. That doesn't mean much.' He explains that Bruggeling's behaviour was the result of reflexes that could be influenced by those around him, but that the man himself had no control over his movements. He was, in the words of the doctor, 'completely empty'.

That the family sees the patient's situation differently to the doctor is very common, says Van Bokhoven. The family has more room for interpretation and can read more into the patient's behaviour. He just has to raise an eyebrow and his loved ones read five or six sentences into that one gesture. Professionals don't have a shared history with the patient from which to derive such interpretations.

'I don't want to harp on about my mother,' he says, 'but we also denied for a long time that it was Alzheimer's. A friend of my mother thought it was incredible that in a family of two psychologists and a nursing home doctor no one had noticed.' On Sundays his mother could keep up the act and fool everyone, says Van Bokhoven, the children invented the rest. And when she couldn't manage something? 'Ach,' he says, 'my mother was always a bit clumsy. I had an interest in keeping up that facade. Why? Because I didn't want a mother with Alzheimer's.'

The nursing home doctor has learnt over the years that people who really love each other are also capable of letting go. It becomes difficult, he says, when there are complications: rancour, vengeance, guilt; past events that haven't been worked through properly. There may be a debt that still needs to be repaid, and in such cases the person can't be allowed to die until things have been put right.

Or sometimes there is resistance to you 'taking away their toy'. Van Bokhoven sees this often in the husbands of women with dementia. Women are the basis for many men, the doctor explains. When they fall away men can lose their way. Men like that come to the nursing home endlessly to feed their wife, sometimes several times a day. Sometimes the doctor has to intervene and forbid it because the patient is in danger of choking. The husband then naturally thinks that his wife needs tube feeding. 'His wife has to be kept alive. What is he to do otherwise?' Van Bokhoven finds situations like that complicated. 'It's a situation that's intangible for outsiders,' he says.

He can well imagine that things from Yvonne Bruggeling's past played a role. With much fuss she took her father into her home, but it didn't work out. So Pa had to be chucked out again and taken in by Ma, says Van Bokhoven. The doctor thinks that Yvonne felt guilty about this.

When things didn't work out in Blauwbörgje either she thought: Now I can do something for my father; I can save him, I can show them.

Van Bokhoven thinks that Yvonne ascribed herself the role of saviour. He is convinced that Liset would have been able to sort things out with Bruggeling's ex-wife. They knew each other from the day-care centre and there the contact between them had run smoothly. In that week in July 1997 they also spoke about Bruggeling's deteriorating condition. His ex-wife was very understanding, Van Bokhoven remembers. In a conversation she had suggested that she would like him to die at home. Liset wanted to help arrange that, but she first wanted to wait and see how Bruggeling responded to antibiotics. They were going to assess the situation after the weekend. Van Bokhoven thinks that the home-care people had already been contacted. Liset had the impression that Mrs Koster understood her husband's situation.

The problem was, says Van Bokhoven, is that Yvonne tended to show up at inconvenient moments. She hadn't been in the nursing home all week, but then Friday evening or Saturday morning she appeared and, the doctor says, 'like a devil popping out of a box, she forced the hospital admittance.' In retrospect Van Bokhoven thinks that perhaps Mrs Koster didn't really understand the situation, and that she was influenced by her daughter. 'By the weekend she was being pulled in a different direction,' he says. 'Under the spell of her own emotions she followed Yvonne. She didn't want to be seen as the 'killer' of her ex-husband. Should this all have been recognized earlier? That's a good question,' says Van Bokhoven.

Wounded animals

The period after the weekend in question overflowed with misery, Van Bokhoven sighs. Mistakes were followed by more mistakes. Fear and emotion ruled. There was no clear line. In the nursing home a crisis team was created. For months there was a crisis meeting every morning. 'Consultations about the battle plan, as it were.' Van Bokhoven was not involved in these meetings and doesn't know much about them. Liset had been given leave to prepare for the trial and Van Bokhoven had taken over her work, so he was very busy keeping everything running.

Van Bokhoven still wonders why the management team of Blauwbörgje let things get that far. 'It was almost masochistic,' he says. 'Everything had to be presented to the press. We were running round like wounded animals, and the press rolled right on over us. No one in Blauwbörgje applied the brakes. The reason they gave was confidentiality. Of course you have to respect that, but that doesn't mean that you can't tell your part of the story.'

Much later, says Van Bokhoven, PR people evaluated the situation for nursing home doctors. Their conclusion was that Blauwbörgje allowed things to take their course. Van Bokhoven agrees. They should have been much more proactive. They should have invited the press in. Liset Moorman should have been allowed to give an interview to the right newspaper, and they should have approached the right television channel; they should have countered the 'spinach-and-custard' story.

Liset Moorman should have been allowed to tell the real story, says Van Bokhoven: that Mr Bruggeling was suffering from his dementia, that the family interpreted his situation differently, partly because of the facade that Bruggeling maintained; that that was a common response when a loved one gradually sank into dementia; and that *versterven* is a natural process in patients with advanced Alzheimer's disease.

But what actually happened was that the story gradually leaked out. And they kept getting bigwigs out of the stable to explain about *versterven*, Van Bokhoven sneers. And they always started their explanation with: 'Well, I don't know the details of the situation, of course, because I wasn't there, but...' And why? Because the nursing home didn't produce any news itself, says Van Bokhoven. The other side of the story that the Bruggeling family were telling was never heard.

Nursing home world

Holland was scared, Van Bokhoven thinks. The Blauwbörgje affair resonated with unconscious fears – 'Oh, we're all getting old. What will happen to us?' That in combination with increasing media coverage of the failing health system. The same applies to the euthanasia discussion – 'Is that how they are going to deal with the failings of the health sector? Is that how they want to deal with the waiting lists? We have to act! We can't let them treat the elderly and the dependent like that, can we?' Whereas, in fact, you should be grateful that you have someone like Liset Moorman at the bedside of those with advanced dementia, says Van Bokhoven.

He explains that everyone in the nursing home makes the best of the situation. There is no alternative, after all. In the nursing home it is possible to have a good life. Usually families learn to accept and come to terms with the situation. There are peaceful moments that should be cherished, says the doctor. But he also thinks that death can sometimes be a blessing for the patient.

The nursing home doctor says that the Bruggeling affair, or rather, the aftermath of the affair, was a disaster for Blauwbörgje. There was a new director, who didn't survive for long as a result. They were in the middle of a reorganisation that ended up derailing. Staff left. They didn't talk about anything else for ages. They suffered the effects for years after. And it cost a fortune. Before the affair things were already difficult, and Blauwbörgje had an eventful history of reorganisations and changes of routine – from social to medical models, from Formica to old wooden tables, and so on and so forth.

But in spite of the trouble, the Bruggeling case also helped the nursing home world, says Van Bokhoven. He thinks that it is a sad club that operates in the margins. In 1997, at the time of the affair, there was a strong inferiority complex. Nursing home doctors were afraid to progress. There was the feeling that 'we can't do anything right anyway'. When Van Bokhoven started as a nursing home doctor in 1982 everyone said: 'And what are you going to do *after* that?' You weren't taken seriously, he says. It was like that for a long time.

Partly as a result of the Bruggeling case the nursing home sector went through a period of development. Nursing home doctors are now more knowledgeable, there is proper training, and doctors have become more articulate in presenting their case. Geriatrics is now on track and there is a wider interest. In short, says the doctor, nursing home doctors are more accepted.

Not long after the Bruggeling affair, Van Bokhoven left Blauwbörgje for a rehabilitation centre. That wasn't because of the Bruggeling affair, but he was sick of the 'endless pushing and pulling with relatives'. It's one of the downsides of the profession, he says. Usually he managed to avoid problems, but it took four or five discussions, and that was exhausting.

Van Bokhoven worked in Blauwbörgje for a long time. He felt secure there. With Liset he had a fantastic relationship, he says. He thought she was an extraordinary woman with a lot of ideas. Warm, enthusiastic and involved; one of the better nursing home doctors, from whom he learned a lot. He thinks that it was cruel that she of all people was attacked like that. They were friends. He had other contacts like that in the nursing home. Work and private life tended to mix – 'a bit like a family'. That also had its downside though, the doctor now thinks. It obscured: colleagues tended not to give feedback or criticise. It was a question of: if you're not too hard on me, I won't be too hard on you.

Van Bokhoven thinks it is very sad that Bruggeling is still alive. He thought that a 'symptomatic approach' – not implementing treatment that would extend life – was justified in his case. Not because of his physical condition, but because of his dementia and his mental suffering. He is surprised that Bruggeling is still alive. He doesn't think that they acted wrongly at the time, he says, but maybe the family experienced things differently. Maybe they had a fantastic time together, and the extension of Bruggeling's life had a function.

If he ever spoke to Yvonne Bruggeling he would like to ask her that. And also why she had done what she did: 'Is it really so great that your father is still alive? Is it really that bad that you couldn't take care of your father? Were you really a hero?' But he doubts whether she would be able to think in those terms. He also doubts whether the extension of life has been pleasant for Bruggeling himself. 'But, ach,' he says, 'I suppose that you need to suffer to ensure a good reincarnation.'

Van Bokhoven says that he is glad that I am researching the topic in order to solve the mystery. He still doesn't understand how things went so wrong, even though such good people were involved. The affair was never discussed afterwards. He thinks it would be useful to do that. He sees a pattern that recurs regularly in the nursing home. He thinks that doctors in the nursing home tend to go along with the family too long in an attempt to spare them. They want the family to like them and because of that they are unclear. He learned from the affair that you have to draw the line earlier, that as a doctor you have to say: 'This is possible, but this is not. And if you insist, then we have to part ways.'

The Daughter

A loving father

It proves difficult making an appointment with Yvonne Bruggeling. Her family and her work take up all her time. When we have finally agreed a date, she cancels. And when she opens the door for our next appointment her hand shoots up to her mouth. She forgot; she is expecting visitors. A blonde woman in her early forties, Yvonne Bruggeling looks me straight in the eye each time I ask a question. She thinks before formulating her answers. She sounds concerned about her father and becomes emotional several times during the interview. We talk for three-quarters of an hour, then her mother arrives and, shortly after, her expected visitors.

Yvonne says that her father was always busy – a hard worker, a sportsman. He cared for his children. He was a loving father, she says. Then he started forgetting things. When he went to the shop to buy coffee, he came back with toilet paper. He started driving through red traffic lights. At first the family didn't notice, but it gradually became worse. They went to the doctor, and after examinations he said that her father had Alzheimer's disease. She hadn't expected that because he was so young, about fifty. 'That was really bad,' says Yvonne. 'You have a father and at the same time you don't.'

Her father's condition deteriorated and the time came when he couldn't take care of himself. That's when he moved in with Yvonne and her family. In those days her parents' relationship wasn't very good. 'Things had happened' between them and they had divorced, but they still saw each other regularly at Yvonne's, and those meetings were good. So good in fact that when it was no longer possible for her father to stay with Yvonne, her mother took him in.

Bruggeling lived with his ex-wife for about eight years, with the assistance of home carers. That also became more difficult and he was then sent to the day-care centre at Blauwbörgje. 'My mother didn't want that,' says Yvonne. 'She wanted to keep him with her. So did I, you know, but my mother was alone, so it was different for her.'

The end of the line

Yvonne says that her father was admitted to hospital with an infection. When this had been treated he was transferred to nursing home Blauwbörgje to recover. The first day he was fine, says Yvonne, but then he deteriorated rapidly. He refused to eat and drink and became bedridden.

From the first day that her father was in the nursing home, Yvonne had the feeling that he would not get better, that he was in the wrong place. The staff didn't understand him, she says. She also thought that the staff didn't listen to the family, even though she and her mother had taken care of him for a long time and knew exactly what he needed. 'But no,' she says, indignantly, 'they knew it all better. They were trained, and we weren't to interfere.' She considered taking her father out of the home, but didn't want to be difficult.

Yvonne and her mother visited him almost every day. Sometimes she took her son along. The staff didn't like this. They thought he was too noisy for the residents. Yvonne thinks that old people like to have children around. 'You could see it on their faces,' she tells me. 'It brought them some excitement. Otherwise they were just sitting there.'

Because things weren't going well with her father they had regular discussions with the doctor. The only thing that they were told was that this was the end of the line. She had the impression that they were supposed to just accept this and not make a fuss. But Yvonne couldn't accept it. She knew that it wasn't true, she says. She just couldn't accept that he was going to die: 'He wasn't even sick'.

Yvonne is convinced that he deteriorated so rapidly because he wasn't given any food or liquid in Blauwbörgje. They couldn't get him to eat or drink, though she thinks that he wanted to, 'because he was terribly thirsty'. His lips were dry and she moistened them with some water. She thinks he deteriorated because the staff in Blauwbörgje didn't look after him.

When staff told her that he was dying and that they were not going to administer any fluid, that was the final straw. She requested that he be given fluid through a drip but the carer told her that this was not possible because it wasn't nursing home policy. She demanded to see the doctor but was told that she would only be available later in the day. Yvonne managed to speak to her on the phone, but she just repeated what the carer had already said: her father was terminal and there was nothing more they could do. And they would not give him an intravenous drip.

So Yvonne called an ambulance and had him taken to the hospital, where his condition rapidly improved, according to Yvonne.

Injustice

Yvonne was extremely angry at the injustice of it all. 'That they just left him without a drink and refused to put him on a drip; that they refused to do anything to save him; that they continued to insist that he was dying. If they'd have kept him there then they would have succeeded: they would have murdered him.'

After they had transferred him to the hospital the family consulted a lawyer, who advised them to press charges for attempted murder.

Yvonne tells me that the Ministry of Justice eventually decided not to bring the case to trial. The family found this unacceptable and appealed. Unfortunately they lost the appeal, she says. They then considered a medical malpractice suit, but this never got off the ground. She doesn't remember why exactly. Their lawyer told them that there was no chance of compensation, so they eventually gave up.

It was a very bad time, Yvonne says: the legal proceedings, the media, the interviews. She went along with it all because she thought that people needed to know what was happening, but retrospectively she thinks that it didn't achieve much. She had really hoped that things would change; that nursing home practices would be more closely scrutinised. But that didn't happen. She has the impression that everything has remained pretty much the same. 'The papers and television were continually on the phone, but after a while they lost interest,' she says sadly. 'They were no longer interested in how my father was doing. They weren't really involved at all.'

In the street, in shops, all over, people came up to Yvonne and told her of similar experiences, and she would think: Well, do something about it! It's your mother or father, after all. Yvonne is surprised how much people are prepared to accept, passively, even though it is 'so unjust'. It's a long time ago, but she still gets angry thinking about it. She will never forget. She still gets upset... She covers her face with her hands. 'Sorry,' she says. 'It's okay.' She gets up and goes into the kitchen. After a while she comes back with coffee. 'I'm okay now,' she says.

I ask her what it was exactly that she found so unjust.

'That they don't believe you. That they won't let you do anything. That they don't involve you.' She struggles with her words. When her father was in Blauwbörgje, she says, she also saw how they treated other residents: 'Don't want to eat? Well okay, don't eat then.' She says that her mother sometimes fed other residents because staff didn't have the time. There wasn't enough staff, but even then, that's no way to treat people.

I ask her whether she thinks she saved her father's life by taking him out of the nursing home.

'Yes,' she says, nodding. 'A lot of people think that he died shortly after, but he's actually still alive now.'

I ask whether she thinks her father had a good life after he left Blauwbörgje.

She replies that he was not in pain, and that he was happy in his own little world. That she still talks to him, and that he still recognises her. When she asks for a kiss, he kisses her. Occasionally he laughs. He's in a wheelchair and can't do anything himself. Still, Yvonne is satisfied with the situation, and when the end comes, she won't mind. He is now well looked-after. In Blauwbörgje he didn't have a fair chance, she says. If they had given him the drip and he had died, then the situation would have been different.

A life as empty as that of a vegetable

Yvonne Bruggeling says that the nursing home in which her father is now is very good. When they visit they get a cup of coffee and a piece of cake, Mrs Koster adds. And they have good contact with the doctor. He says: 'If there is anything, we'll call you straight away.' And that's what they do, Mrs Koster confirms. 'Even if it's something small, they always call.'

'They treat the people properly. They do nice things with them,' Yvonne says. 'There's music and it's pleasant there.'

'Papa is doing a cooking course,' Mrs Koster adds. 'Well, he can't really do anything, of course, but he's there, and I like that.'

'On the Queen's birthday they decorate the home and hang up pictures of the Queen' says Mrs Koster.

I ask Yvonne whether they feel the need to talk to the people in Blauwbörgje about what happened.

'No,' she says, 'that is past. I sometimes wonder, though, whether those carers regret what they did. Whether they ever realised that they were treating those people wrongly. And whether that one carer ever regretted telling those lies. She later denied having said anything about dehydration.'

'If I were like Yvonne's father, I wouldn't want to live anymore,' says Yvonne's husband, who has just entered and sat down on the sofa. 'I think it's a life as empty as that of a vegetable.'

'He *is* a vegetable,' says Mrs Koster.

'Why's that?' Yvonne asks.

'Well, he just sits there.'

'But he still does everything himself?'

'No, he can't do anything himself anymore.'

'He doesn't have tube feeding, he doesn't take any medicine. There's actually nothing wrong with him.'

'Indeed,' Mrs Koster nods. 'There's nothing physically wrong with Pappie, but he's still a vegetable.'

'Well, we'll just have to agree to differ,' Yvonne concludes. She thinks he's more aware of things than everyone thinks, because sometimes she tells him about something and he answers: 'Oh yes, oh yes.'

'He recognises Yvonne the best,' says Mrs Koster proudly.

'Yes, but I have normal conversations with him,' says Yvonne. 'I don't speak to him as though he's no longer there. I tell him all kinds of things. I joke with him: 'All those nice nurses here; I hope you can keep your hands to yourself? And he laughs. Yes, we still have good contact.'

The Managers

The director

Sofie van der Kamp, head of the nursing service at Blauwbörgje at the time of the Bruggeling affair, isn't sure whether it is a good idea to talk to me about the case. Maarten Moorman said that it was okay, she says, but a lot has happened. And she no longer works in Blauwbörgje. She asks whether the current management knows that I am doing this project. No? That seems like the appropriate route to her. She says that the director at the time is no longer there, but I could phone Frank Verkerk. At the time he was the director of one of the branches, and he is currently the director of the foundation of which Blauwbörgje is part. If he agrees, then Sofie van der Kamp will speak to me.

Frank Verkerk doesn't have a problem with me speaking to the staff that were involved in the Bruggeling affair. 'Why would I have a problem with that?' he asks inquisitively at the other end of the line. He's even willing to discuss the issue himself, even though he only followed things from the sidelines. Next week he has time. I make an appointment.

Frank Verkerk thinks that the Bruggeling case was caused by a confluence of events. Initially it had to do with communication, he thinks. They should have been more alert to the dissatisfaction in the family. He also heard that the carers had made undiplomatic comments. He isn't sure what they were, though. He shrugs. 'Whatever they were, the woman had heard something about dehydration,' he says. 'Maybe that word was actually used.' The woman probably thought: 'Hey, they're letting my husband die.' She didn't want that to happen, and she wanted everything possible to be done to prevent it. Verkerk has the impression that the response was too slow. Eventually the family got their way. Mr Bruggeling was transferred to the hospital. The internist there said that he was dehydrated and they knew very well what they were doing in the nursing home. That supported the suspicions of the family, and they took legal steps. That is Verkerk's interpretation of the events.

Verkerk says that as a result of the Bruggeling case another seventeen or eighteen complaints were made. He was the director of Blauwbörgje for seven years. There were a lot of complaints in those years. He new many of the cases and hadn't expected complaints. On the other hand, he isn't all that surprised. People make use of that right because they have started to have doubts. Verkerk can empathise. And you can't do anything about it anyway. Anger is pointless, he says. He is always struck by the 'forced way that doctors respond to the workings of the legal system'. Then he thinks: You did your best, you acted conscientiously. Of course, you made a mistake, but you won't be put in the pillory for it.

Verkerk thinks that doctors respond as though that is the case. He thinks that the doctors let emotions run too high. They had a hard time, they thought what was being said and written about them was terrible. They thought they were being wrongly quoted and that the reporting in the papers was selective. And they were disgruntled about the appeal.

The debate that came out of this focused on *versterven*, whereas in fact it should have been about communication, Verkerk thinks. Communication with the family can be extremely difficult. If people are as tense as a spring and you express yourself clumsily then that can lead to a lot of misery. One good consequence of the debate is that people know more about the dying process. People hardly ever experience a deathbed nowadays; they only see spectacular deaths on television. They don't know any more that it can be a slow process.

Verkerk comes from a conservative background in the neighbourhood of Staphorst, in the middle of the Dutch Bible Belt. He found it striking how people there responded to the affair. They thought it was a storm in a teacup. 'My boy, that's how your grandmother and grandfather went,' he was told. The phenomenon of *versterven* is much more normal there, he says. It's because of the strong Christian culture. People accept that sort of thing more easily. They are less likely to take something like that to court.

The head of the nursing service

Sofie van der Kamp says that the Bruggeling case had an enormous impact on the staff. Those involved felt they were being personally criticised. They were also accosted outside work, and sometimes openly accused. Some of them stopped going to birthdays and that sort of thing. Van der Kamp remembers carers getting into arguments with their husbands, and there were even relationships that broke up, she says.

Management asked the social work department to speak to those directly involved. Later the Victim Support Service also became involved. That helped, even though it was a bit late. And it led to new problems. Some felt that only those directly involved were recognised as having the 'right to sorrow and anger,' and that they were being neglected because they weren't 'really victims'. They felt left out.

In the summer of 1997 staff had to deal with this full-time for a few months. Sofie van der Kamp was 'completely burned out' after that, she says. She thinks it is a pity that the affair was never completely closed. That was partly because Liset fell ill and because other problems developed within the organisation.

Problem families

In the Bruggeling affair, communication played a central role, says Sofie van der Kamp. She thinks that staff focused too much on the ex-wife. In retrospect she thinks that it would have been better to focus more on the daughter, because she had the decisive role. That wasn't recognised at the time. Sofie had the impression that Mrs Koster didn't always agree with her daughter, but that she didn't have the courage to oppose her.

As a result of the case, staff in the nursing home decided to communicate more broadly. If there was a hint of communication problems with a family, then various family members were invited for a talk, not only the main contact person. If there was a division in the family, then two contact persons were nominated. Staff also made more effort to use language that relatives understood. They didn't only speak about medical matters but also more generally about what was being done with the resident.

This policy was discussed in the nursing home's family council, and the members were positive, though they did warn that problem families like this could be difficult. Sofie van der Kamp thinks that 'problem family' is a strange expression. It implies that things only go wrong on one side, and it isn't really like that. But it isn't entirely inaccurate either. It wasn't just the Bruggeling family, and when she looks back at which other families pressed charges then she has to admit that there were similarities. 'They were all from the lower classes,' she says. That also says something about the nursing home staff, she thinks: that they were not as good at communicating with such people.

Communication with the family is the most essential part of her job, Sofie van der Kamp says. It's all about the resident, but because they often can't say what they think, it's the family that they have to communicate with, and as a result it is perhaps the relatives who are the real clients of the nursing home.

In families there are a lot of emotions relating to coping with the illness and taking leave of a loved one. Sofie van der Kamp experienced this herself when her father-in-law was admitted to Blauwbörgje. Her husband and brother-in-law came to the family meetings. Her brother-in-law is a GP and quickly understood the issues, but she noticed that her husband felt that things were being left out. Because she knew the situation, she could explain things to him, but she realised how easily professionals can become blind to certain issues that might exercise lay people.

Dare to look into your own heart

About the team in the department where the whole affair happened, Sofie van der Kamp says that there had been a difficult history of cooperation and poor relations with management. They weren't very good at critically evaluating their own actions, says Van der Kamp. She adds that this is a general problem among carers, because they don't learn to think critically about themselves during their training. That makes it difficult to discuss things openly in the work setting.

When her husband criticised carers about the treatment of his father they did not like it. Were they not doing their best? Were they not doing their job properly? The carers found her husband difficult right from the start. There were already things happening in the department that were difficult to discuss. You couldn't say to someone: 'Hey, you've worked here so long, maybe it would be good to try a different environment.' If you suggested something like that then you were in trouble, Sofie says. The Bruggeling affair didn't improve things.

She thinks that the carers in question would still argue that they behaved correctly in the Bruggeling case; that they wouldn't dare suggest that things might have been better if they had acted differently; that things might not have escalated if they had had an extra meeting with the family, for example. To be able to admit that, 'you have to be able to look into your own heart,' she says.

She thinks that the carers do know, deep down inside, that they played a role. It's different when someone gets shot, she explains. Then you can say: I couldn't do anything; I just happened to be there'. But in the case of Bruggeling, where the whole thing hinged on communication and care, but where it all went so wrong, we missed the daughter, Yvonne.'

The Internist

The saviour of mankind

Internist John Meijers e-mails in response to my letter, saying it would be an honour to speak to me. He is the doctor who admitted Mr Bruggeling to hospital and announced that the family had saved him from certain death. We meet a few days later in his office in the hospital. As he warned me at the start, his pager keeps beeping: he is on call.

John Meijers remembers being called by the GP, who said that there was a man in Blauwbörgje who was dying and that his family didn't want him to die. 'Maybe it's a strange question,' the GP had said, 'but could you admit him and evaluate whether they should let him go, or whether we should do something to keep him alive.' The internist admitted Bruggeling. He had signs of serious dehydration, says Meijers. He was hardly conscious, and it was clear that if the internist did nothing he would die.

Meijers spoke to the family and two things became clear, he says. The first was that the family was not yet ready to take leave of their loved one. The second was that when Meijers tried to find out how Mr Bruggeling functioned before the current episode, the family described him as having a very bad memory but otherwise functioning reasonably. They said he was in the nursing home to recover from a minor ailment. 'An infection or something.'

The family had thought that he would recover in the nursing home and then come back home. He wasn't a permanent resident in the home. On the basis of these two facts, the internist decided that he had to treat Bruggeling, so that when everything had calmed down it would be possible to sort out with the family what was to be done next time something like this happened.

The family, says Meijers, was agitated, very agitated. They had the feeling that treatment had been unjustly withheld from him in the nursing home. What came as an unexpected blow was that the nursing home was not prepared to give him a fluid drip and tube feeding. Maybe things would have turned out differently if they had discussed this with the family first, says Meijers. He says that the family saw him as 'the saviour of mankind'. In their emotionally charged state, he was the one doctor who did exactly what they wanted.

The nursing home doctor called the internist later. She explained that the policy in Blauwbörgje was not to give tube feeding and fluid to terminal dementia patients, but that they had not yet had the chance to discuss this with the Bruggeling family. She thought that that was the cause of the family's agitation, says Meijers. He thinks that she was correct in that assumption. He hopes that they learned something from the affair, which he thinks was all about poor communication.

Sitting on God's throne

The decision not to give a fluid infusion is a difficult one, says the internist. When you do, you place yourself on God's throne and give yourself the right to decide on the value of the life of someone with dementia. If the patient has a heart attack you can say that it is the will of Our Lord and that you have decided not to get in His way. Things are different when someone is in a different environment and stops eating and drinking because he no longer has his wife next to him all day to spoon-feed him. If you then say as a doctor: we'll let him go, then that is an arbitrary decision. He can imagine that the situation would have been different if they had encouraged Mrs Koster to come in to the home to feed him at every mealtime, as he had been used to for years.

Meijers thinks that it is important to discuss things with the family straight after the patient has been admitted, to explain in an intake interview exactly what you plan to do, what the visiting times are, which weekends the patient can spend at home; but also to discuss serious issues like resuscitation and what to do if the patient refuses food. You have to inform the family about these things, he says. They have to understand that refusing food and fluid leads to a mild death, and they have to agree and accept.

The internist doesn't think that the family should make the actual decision, though. How can you expect a woman to decide on the life and death of her husband? He sees that as a burden that she shouldn't be expected to carry, because she will be haunted for the rest of her days by the question of whether it was the right decision. Meijers thinks that such decisions should be made by people who have a more objective distance. But they have to support the family in such a way that they accept the decision and can live with it. And that was absolutely not the case with the Bruggeling family, he says.

In his job in intensive care, Meijers is often confronted with issues of life and death. It is especially important to support and inform the family in situations in which you decide to terminate a medically pointless treatment, as a result of which you expect the patient to die within hours, he says. They have to understand that extending futile treatment will only extend the suffering of their loved one.

In the experience of the internist guiding the family though the process leading up to the death of a loved one often requires precision. You can't suddenly stop treating a patient who you have been treating for three weeks without preparing the family. He thinks that it is essential that you discuss things with the family during those three weeks; that you indicate that 'there is slight improvement, but also slight deterioration'. In that way they get involved in the process, the internist explains. You can't avoid the family for three weeks and then suddenly say: 'Come, let's sit and talk. I'm sorry Madam, but it's not working, so tomorrow we're pulling the plug.'

Meijers says that some families are easier to guide to this point than others. He also sometimes thinks: 'Oh no, this is going wrong. This family doesn't understand what is going on. They protest, and emotions percolate to the surface that I never expected'. When this happens it means that he has done something wrong, he says, because it is the final result that counts. In the case of Mr Bruggeling those responsible have to be judged on the final result. True, it was a difficult family that needed a lot of attention. But the final result is that they didn't understand and were not yet ready. Meijers's conclusion is that the guidance of the family failed.

The internist explains that there are differences between nursing homes and hospitals. In the nursing home, the doctors are more focused on remedies to improve the life of the patient. In the hospital, the emphasis is on looking for the cause of the complaint. But these days the differences are becoming less pronounced. He is seeing more and more elderly patients and is increasingly confronted with the question: how far should you go? Nursing home doctors are capable, he says, but they don't have the pace of the hospital. It is apparently not unusual, says Meijers, for someone to have been in a nursing home for a week without a meeting with the family having taken place. 'The idea that you can have that meeting as soon as the patient is admitted is apparently strange for them,' he says.

The Monday after Meijers admitted Mr Bruggeling, he received a phone call from the family lawyer. The lawyer said that he was calling with the family's permission. He had one question: would Mr Bruggeling have died if he hadn't been admitted to the hospital? The internist had answered: yes. 'Well,' he says, 'that put things in a pretty pickle.' The next day the papers were full of it. The internist also had visits from the police and the Inspector of Health. 'I wasn't aware of any wrongdoing,' he says. 'Then the whole discussion exploded in the press, and that new word *versterven* was invented. I thought it had to do with hanging game after you'd been hunting.'

The Head Nurse

Heavy work

Carer Ans Vroom worked regularly in the week that Mr Bruggeling was in Blauwbörgje. She was the one the family had accused of saying that Mr Bruggeling was being dehydrated (*versterven*). When I ask her she says she can't imagine ever having used that word, because, she says, the word didn't even exist. Ans Vroom remembers that Yvonne Bruggeling asked why her father did not have a fluid drip. She had answered that she was going to discuss this later that day with the doctor, who would make the final decision. Yvonne Bruggeling said that she was alert because the mother of a friend had died in Blauwbörgje because she wasn't given fluid and had dehydrated. The carer still finds it difficult to understand what went wrong in the case of Bruggeling. She gives me the phone number of her colleague Fred Beekhuis; maybe he can tell me more.

Fred Beekhuis lives far away, on a farm in the Flevopolder. The route he has given me takes me along country lanes and through small villages. In his kitchen garden, under a large tree, we talk for three hours, eating butter biscuits and drinking tea.

The team in that section were known to be difficult, says Beekhuis. There had been problems with superiors. Beekhuis was asked to become a unit leader. He did that with pleasure for a few years. Actually he was a sort of mediator, because as team leader he had a position between team and management.

It was possible to work well with the person in charge, he says. But just before the Bruggeling affair the manager left and a new manager was appointed. He was difficult, says Beekhuis. He tried, but his good intentions didn't come across. Some of the staff were scared of him. 'Everything was running smoothly, and then he started pulling the rug from under my feet,' he says. 'He didn't like the way I was running things. I had a nasty premonition. As a result of these frictions I realised that I was going to end up either on sick leave or in a power struggle.' Beekhuis didn't fancy either option, so he left.

Beekhuis says that the work in a nursing home is heavy. You wear yourself out running up and down and you are often impotent. Those with dementia are completely dependent on care. The sad thing is that you can't really care for them properly due to the pressure of work. The basic package is that you wash them once a day, feed them and help them to drink but, Beekhuis says, to be honest, you often don't even get round to that. When it's really busy and a resident is being difficult with eating, then you give him two or three spoons and move on to the next one, because his food is also getting cold. It's difficult to get staff. Some-

times they don't even bother to advertise because no one will apply anyway.

Difficult communication

The news that Bruggeling was to be admitted to the nursing home was
not well received, says Beekhuis. He had been admitted once or twice
previously and on those occasions the family had criticised the nursing
staff. They had claimed that Bruggeling had been left to sit in his own
excrement, and that they hadn't changed his shirt when it had a stain.
Things like that happen to patients in the later stages of Alzheimer's,
says Beekhuis. As a result of those complaints it was decided to place
him in a different section this time – Beekhuis's section. They were told
that he had been in the day-care centre and that he had just been discharged from hospital. 'There was also something about the spouse,'
Beekhuis remembers. 'I think she needed a rest, and the hospital
wanted to get rid of him.'

Bruggeling was admitted on a Friday. Beekhuis was on the day shift.
The family said that he needed to convalesce. The hospital advised us to
sit him in a chair twice a day. That was only possible with a lot of effort.
It wasn't possible to communicate with him any more. Sometimes you
can read things in the eyes of advanced Alzheimer's patients, but with
him there was nothing. He was too far-gone. You put someone like that
in a chair and stuff food in his mouth, and you wonder: what am I doing
to him? He had a temperature; he was just out of hospital. Should you be
messing around like that? That and the fact that he had been in day-care
for years made us think that it might be the end of the line.

Beekhuis worked that weekend. On Monday he was on the late shift.
He had the impression that the family didn't realise how bad his condition was. They kept saying: 'Two weeks ago he was still playing football.
There's nothing wrong with him. He just needs to convalesce, eat well,
drink enough and get out of bed.' Beekhuis wanted to make clear to
them that what they expected wasn't going to happen. His colleagues
warned him: be careful what you say, these people are on edge, they're
not easy. 'I took that into account,' says Beekhuis. 'You do your best,
naturally, but you don't have a sea of time either. There are fourteen
other residents with relatives that need attention.'

Beekhuis told the family honestly that he thought that things were not
going well. They didn't take that very well, he says. They didn't understand. The family was dissatisfied about everything. That happens sometimes. If the family can't accept the approaching death of the patient
then they start to blame others. If you've known the family longer then
you can steer them in the right direction, says Beekhuis. But he didn't
know the Bruggeling family, so the conversation didn't go very well.
They insisted on seeing the doctor, but they couldn't manage the follow-

ing day. 'They were going to some sort of amusement park,' Beekhuis says. They could only do Wednesday, but Liset Moorman worked half days on Wednesdays. Eventually an appointment was made for Thursday.

Bruggeling's condition deteriorated rapidly that week, says Beekhuis. He didn't eat well and he continued to have a temperature. At the end of the week, Beekhuis thinks it was Friday evening, Bruggeling contracted pneumonia. That's always a risk with advanced Alzheimer's patients. On Saturday the family were worried. Beekhuis promised to call the doctor, but otherwise avoided contact with them, he says, because the meeting on Monday evening had been so awkward. He didn't want to irritate them any more. 'They were so critical that it almost felt like they were accusing me personally,' says Beekhuis. That's why he asked his colleague Ans to speak to them. They asked her what the lemon-flavoured cotton buds on the bedside table were for. She explained that they were used to moisten dry lips. They probably interpreted that as 'dehydration buds', says Beekhuis. They accused the nursing home of letting Bruggeling dehydrate, and the buds were meant to alleviate his experience of this. That's how Beekhuis sees the course of events.

Villains and murderers

The family claimed that the way in which Bruggeling had been treated in the nursing home amounted to 'attempted murder' – they had tried to dehydrate him without consulting the family. In their perception there was nothing seriously wrong with Bruggeling one minute, and the next minute he was on the point of death. That had nothing to do with his infection, or his Alzheimer's, says Beekhuis, no, it was all the fault of the nursing staff. They didn't get him out of bed, and they didn't feed him or give him anything to drink either. They interpreted the hospital doctor's comments as confirming this. He said they'd saved him from certain death.

Fred Beekhuis thinks that the daughter was the villain. He had the impression that she was pushing the mother into it, and the mother went along because she was loyal to her daughter. Beekhuis thought that the mother was 'rather vague,' and didn't entirely grasp what was going on. Perhaps that was because she had been taking care of her ex-husband for years, says Beekhuis. That is hard work, he knows, and after a time you start to go into decline yourself.

Given the patient's history, Liset Moorman had wanted to come to an agreement with the family about abstaining from life-extending interventions. But as far as the family were concerned it was much too early for that sort of thing. Usually that process is much more gradual, Beekhuis explains, and you have time to guide the family toward a final joint decision. That happens all the time in nursing homes all over Holland, he says, and it has been happening for years. Unfortunately, though, no one seems to know that.

Beekhuis thinks that it is ironic that this had to happen to Liset Moorman. She was always very careful, she listened and she stood behind her decisions. She had a good reputation and she was really the best doctor in the nursing home. But she was going through a difficult time, he says: two or three months after the Bruggeling affair she was diagnosed with leukaemia. You don't get an illness like that suddenly, and it had probably been affecting her all that summer. He remembers one occasion that she became really angry with the Bruggeling family, and it struck him because it was so uncharacteristic. When the Bruggeling family decided to press charges some people suspected that there were financial motives. Beekhuis isn't sure.

So the family made the case public, and that also had consequences: tabloid photographers with enormous telephoto lenses hiding in the bushes and camera crews camping on the nursing home parking lot and shouting 'Look, there are the murderers!' every time they caught a glimpse of us, says Beekhuis indignantly. And on a television talk show he heard all about 'that head nurse who refused to give Daddy any food'. 'That nurse was me,' says Beekhuis. 'The family wanted him to eat, whatever the cost, even though he kept choking on it because he couldn't swallow properly. I suggested giving him only soft food, but they left out that bit of the story.'

The Journalist

Spinach and custard

Journalist Mark van Driel wrote the article with the title 'Mr Bruggeling enjoys a meal of spinach and custard,' that both the widower of Liset Moorman and her colleague Ton van Bokhoven had referred to. Van Driel hesitates when I call him. What kind of book am I writing exactly? When was the Bruggeling case? It was a long time ago. He isn't a specialist in healthcare issues. He's also moved to another paper. Finally he agrees to see me. He won't talk about the actual case, he warns, but about how things work in a newspaper office. We arrange to meet in a café.

Mark van Driel can't remember the details of the case. He thinks it all began with a news item about attempted murder in a nursing home. Items like that always get picked up. The reporter who usually did health-related topics was on holiday so Van Driel received instructions to cover the story.

Journalists work with tight deadlines, he says. You get an assignment in the morning and your article has to be ready by the end of the day because it has to make the next morning's papers. Van Driel contacted Blauwbörgje, but they didn't want to comment. You try and try again, but if they keep refusing then you have to look elsewhere, he explains. The next group you approach are the experts.

Van Driel had once read a book written by a nursing home doctor called Bert Keizer.[10] He phoned Keizer, who told him that *versterven* was normal in nursing homes. He made some very controversial statements in that interview, says the journalist. For example, he said that he doesn't inform families about the existence of percutaneous endoscopic gastrostomy (PEG), a procedure for placing a tube into the stomach through the abdominal wall for nutritional support, because it causes 'a load of trouble without being of any benefit to the patient'. He thought that giving families alternatives only fuelled unrealistic hopes. On the basis of those statements it was decided to put Van Driel's article on the front page. He didn't have any input in that decision.

The story remained newsworthy and the following day Van Driel wrote another article. He continued trying to contact the nursing home and speak to the doctor in question, but in vain. He tried to find out whether they had read his first article and what they thought of it, but Blauwbörgje wouldn't comment.

The slack season

Because Blauwbörgje wouldn't comment, Van Driel phoned other nursing homes. A nursing home in Utrecht responded positively and he went for an interview. It was the first time he had ever been in a nursing home. The doctor confirmed that *versterven* was normal practice in nursing homes. His report on this visit was his second article relating to the Blauwbörgje affair.

The following day Van Driel made some international phone calls to find out what the position was on *versterven* in other countries. He first had to explain what happened in Holland. He received critical responses, he says. In other countries they are much more inclined to give patients artificial food and fluid. Van Driel said he had looked at the issue from all angles.

A few weeks later Van Driel travelled to Groningen to interview the Bruggeling family. He thinks that it was at the time that Mr Bruggeling had just been discharged from the hospital. He can't remember much of the interview.

He thinks that the summer – the slack season – made it possible for the Bruggeling story to make the front pages. Later he re-read his articles about Blauwbörgje and he was satisfied. The articles led to his nomination for the 'young journalist of the year award' (which he didn't get).

Van Driel never had a response to his articles. He adds that journalists usually only receive comments if their articles are very bad. If you don't hear anything, then you can assume you've done a good job, he says. The nursing home doctor in Utrecht said that 90 percent of patients with dementia in her nursing home died as a result of *versterven*. He thinks it is likely that that is also the case in other nursing homes, otherwise someone would have responded to the article. So he is satisfied that his report represents what actually happens.

Speaking to the media

Speaking about the fact that he never managed to speak to anyone from Blauwbörgje, Van Driel says that this is common, that organisations are often closed bastions. He's not sure whether a closed approach is the best one. He explains that there are theories about this. The most common is that it is best for the accused intuition to go public and be honest straight away. Then the storm blows over the quickest. If you keep quiet then you create the impression that you have something to hide. That usually doesn't work out well in the long run. Van Driel thinks it is possible that people living in the vicinity of Groningen will always have the impression that strange things happen at Blauwbörgje.

Van Driel never got to speak to Liset Moorman. He doesn't know what her reasons were for avoiding the media. If she had told her story in a newspaper or on television then she could have explained herself, he says. If she was convinced that she hadn't acted wrongly, then it would have been good to seek publicity, says Van Driel. And even if she thought she had made a mistake, then it would have been better to acknowledge this publicly.

Van Driel admits that speaking to the media is risky. It can lead to more discussion. It can be used against you. But, he says, you can also let it work to your advantage.

Shock

What struck Van Driel in the Blauwbörgje case was the closed mentality of the nursing home. The way in which they deal with death has a long history that has unfolded behind the closed doors of the institution. New norms and customs gradually develop and what was unthinkable ten or twenty years ago has become acceptable. Practice changes; boundaries shift.

Then suddenly these gradually developed practices are revealed to outsiders and those involved don't understand why everyone thinks what they are doing is strange, because for them it appears normal. Doctors have developed those practices bit-by-bit, and each little step was in itself justified. But does this also apply to the cumulative big step that is the result of this gradual process?

As a journalist, says Van Driel, you have to expose these processes. You try and ask the questions and express the concerns that might exercise the reader, such as, in this case: Shouldn't you be able to just grow old? Shouldn't doctors be helping to keep people alive? Then it turns out that things don't work like that in nursing homes, and that comes as a shock to those who have no experience of them.

Mr Bruggeling

Large eyes and thin as a rake

The De Merenberg nursing home is situated in a village twenty kilometres from the city of Groningen. Mrs Koster phoned ahead to inform the home of our arrival. When we arrive, Mr Bruggeling is in a wheelchair in the living room. His hair is wet and combed back from his forehead. He is as thin as a rake, with large eyes that stare straight ahead. Mrs Koster kisses him a few times. She greets the carers warmly and ushers me in the direction of a woman with short blonde hair. 'She's the boss here,' she says. 'You can ask her all your questions.'

The woman isn't very accommodating. She is busy, she says curtly. She'll be with me in a minute. Mrs Koster adroitly steers the wheelchair out of the living room and into a quiet corner in the corridor. We drink coffee and wait for the supervisor.

When she arrives she ushers me into her office and says that my visit has taken her by surprise. She feels she is being put under pressure and doesn't want to discuss Mr Bruggeling now. She's not sure whether she is allowed to. She thinks it would be better to get permission from the director. She says that when Mr Bruggeling was first admitted to De Merenberg the director had to promise not to reveal anything about this to outsiders, 'otherwise we'd have all those gossip magazines constantly bothering us.'

I explain how I want to write about Mr Bruggeling. She calms down and explains that her response was not personal. 'It has to do with the way that Mrs Koster communicates,' she explains. 'She confronts you with things unexpectedly. Speak to the director and if he agrees then I'll talk to you.'

In the corner in the corridor Mrs Koster asks how the interview went. She nods understandingly when I tell her that I first have to speak to the director: 'That's much better,' she says. I sit down, and she starts to tell me about the relationship with her ex-husband. When they were married she was alone a lot because her husband worked and spent his spare time at football. He was a kind and sensitive man who was always ready to help others. That also contributed to him being away from home. They gradually drifted apart and eventually decided to divorce. They never really had arguments, though. Things just didn't work out.

When he fell ill and Yvonne could no longer look after him, Mrs Koster took him in. She didn't want him to have to go to an institution. She repeats several times: 'He was a kind man and he didn't deserve that.'

Then she shows me round the nursing home. She is full of praise for the home and the staff. 'We made good arrangements when Koen was first admitted here,' she says. 'Because of everything that has happened he is not an ordinary patient. We can't let things go wrong a second time.'

The director of De Merenberg is on annual leave, his secretary says. It ends up being almost a year before I have the chance to return to De Merenberg. I give birth to a daughter later that summer and when I return from maternity leave work at the university keeps me occupied.

Six months later I receive a phone call from Mrs Koster to say that her ex-husband has died. 'We wanted to let you know,' she says. 'Koen's condition had been deteriorating and he only weighed 45 kilos. He had earned a rest and he died peacefully.' Mrs Koster feels sad and lonely, but both she and Yvonne are satisfied with the way things went.

The Doctors at De Merenberg

The disadvantages of extending life

The director of De Merenberg still remembers my letter. Unfortunately he doesn't have time for a meeting: the summer holidays have arrived again. He agrees that I can speak to the doctors and carers. He will inform Erik Vroom, the head of medical services, of my plans.

Erik Vroom proposes that I put all my questions to him first, and if he can't answer them then he will ask Mr Bruggeling's doctor, José van Spiegel, to join us. After half an hour he calls her and a few minutes later she hurries into the office pushing a trolley full of medical files and wearing a stethoscope around her neck.

José van Spiegel admits that she was initially afraid when she heard that Mr Bruggeling was going to be admitted to the home and that she was going to be his doctor. She says that De Merenberg was already a nursing home that tended to ask for trouble by admitting just about anybody: 'Come along, don't worry. We'll take care of you.' But the Bruggeling family had a crisis, and from a humanitarian perspective someone had to help them, she explains. For staff here at De Merenberg it was a question of forewarned is forearmed. Right from the start we tried to 'repair' the Bruggeling case by being very clear about everything, she explains. We wanted to avoid risks, so we built in lots of safeguards. They had been informed by Blauwbörgje about what had gone wrong there and about the role that Yvonne had played in this. As a result they decided: no meetings without Yvonne. All meetings were with mother *and* daughter. And there were always two representatives from the nursing home.

José van Spiegel explains that they try and do this with everyone, but in practice, if there is a sudden crisis, then they often speak to the spouse first, with a family discussion following later. If they hadn't been aware of the history of the case, it is quite possible that staff here might also have only communicated with Mrs Koster. 'And that could easily have gone wrong again,' she says.

The doctor says that she has spoken to the family a lot, and she has invested a lot of energy in trying to understand their situation. But she has also made clear agreements with them. José van Spiegel picks up Mr Bruggeling's file. She pages through it and reads an excerpt:

> November 1997. Do not resuscitate. No probes. Hospital admittance only for things like fractures. Don't force medication. Don't force food or drink.

This is standard procedure in De Merenberg, she explains. The only thing that was different in his case was that if he fell ill he was to get a fluid drip for a week. If that didn't help, it was to be stopped. That was the most we could do, she says. That was the drip that they had fought for. Strange really, that there was no discussion about a probe, because that would have been more useful and less trouble than a drip, the doctor says. But that drip was holy for them, and they would not be persuaded. She thinks it has to do with the mother of the friend of Yvonne who didn't get a drip in Blauwbörgje.

José van Spiegel pages through the file. She says that she has discussed this policy countless times with the Bruggeling family. In September 2000 something changed, says Van Spiegel. There was some family issue, something to do with the death of Mrs Koster's mother taking too long. The family regretted how they had dealt with things, and suddenly they no longer wanted the fluid drip or the hypodermoclysis for Mr Bruggeling. 'Through what happened with the mother, they suddenly got insight into the disadvantages of extending life,' she says.

Victims of the media

José van Spiegel purposely never discussed Blauwbörgje with the Bruggeling family, she says. She wanted to make a new start. So she doesn't have any direct information on the case. But she has thought about it, especially when she got to know the family better. Van Spiegel thinks that the doctors in Blauwbörgje thought that they had made clear agreements with Mrs Koster about the policy they were following, that they had made it clear that they thought that Mr Bruggeling's Alzheimer's was so advanced that they should allow him to die. Things went wrong, according to Van Spiegel, because Mrs Koster 'just didn't get it'. Mrs Koster has difficulty seeing the bigger picture, she says, so she couldn't communicate it to her daughter.

As a result Yvonne was not prepared for her father's death. She didn't have the time to work it through and accept it. She was overwhelmed by his sudden deterioration. She felt like an underdog and decided that she wasn't going to let it happen, that she would fight for her father's rights. She thought that he had the right to treatment, and the best treatment in her view was the fluid drip in the hospital.

Mr Bruggeling's family wouldn't allow him to die, says Van Spiegel: 'They were clearly very attached to him.' Yvonne always said he had been a very good father, and the doctor could see no reason to doubt that. She had never noticed any 'hints of trauma or other complicated issues'. 'Yvonne didn't have an easy time,' says Van Spiegel. 'I suspect that her father had always supported her. When he needed support himself, Yvonne would have had the feeling that she was his saviour.'

The doctor thinks that Yvonne was shocked by the deterioration of her father's condition, and that that is the reason she made such a fuss. Then one thing led to another and after a point there was no way back.

Van Spiegel thinks that she became a victim of the media. 'There was a bit of a witch-hunt and she was being pushed to enflame things further. Initially it was all about care, but then financial issues also got dragged in – I think that there was a second trial in which the financial question was fought out. The family was being provoked by people who didn't understand the issues.'

Van Spiegel knows that her colleague in Blauwbörgje thought that Bruggeling was in a very advanced stage of Alzheimer's and that he could hardly do anything himself, while his wife and daughter were convinced that he was fine and could still do things. Van Spiegel thinks they had the idea that they would still be able to do all kinds of nice things together. Like the spinach-and-custard story in the papers: that he was enjoying his meals, that he still played football with his grandson. In their perception it was really like that, says the doctor. That difference in perception surfaced occasionally in De Merenberg. They thought that we should do more therapy with him, for example. That was sometimes difficult for the nursing home, but they never forced the issue. It was always a bit of give and take.

Yvonne is often considered to have been the malefactor in the Blauwbörgje case. But Van Spiegel doesn't think she is really bad. She says she found Yvonne 'reasonable'. Yvonne listened to the doctor if the doctor also listened to her. Van Spiegel describes her as a fierce and emotional woman who stood up for her father. Yvonne was more consistent than her mother, says the doctor. You could come to an understanding with her. In discussions about serious issues, the doctor focused on Yvonne. 'Mrs Koster often didn't get the point,' she says. 'She was also capricious and suggestible. You could persuade her to agree to one thing and then get her to agree to the opposite as well. So you couldn't depend on her when it came to agreeing on what to do. That was where the case went wrong in Blauwbörgje. Liset Moorman *thought* that she had discussed things properly with Mrs Koster, but the messages hadn't been received.'

Taking leave gradually

Sometimes Mr Bruggeling gave you a radiant smile, but he didn't actually feel very much anymore, says Van Spiegel. He just sat in his chair unable to communicate. He spent more and more time in bed, lost more weight, but was never sick. He just went on living. Van Spiegel doesn't think he suffered. She didn't feel sorry for him because he held on to life, but she didn't think it was a benefit to him either. The doctors didn't do anything to keep him alive, but they didn't do anything to speed up his death either.

She says that Yvonne's views developed during her father's stay in De Merenberg. She learned that not everything that could possibly be done for her father was necessarily also good for him. She had plenty of time to realise this because his illness developed so slowly.

Van Spiegel remembers that one day Mrs Koster said to her: 'Things are not going well with Koen, are they? Yvonne and I discussed it and we think that he won't make another six months.' Mr Bruggeling died exactly six months later, says the doctor. He died peacefully and the family were satisfied.

Because they cared for Mr Bruggeling for so long in De Merenberg they developed a relationship with the family, says the doctor. They had good contact, very good in fact. When the doctor moved to a different department just before Mr Bruggeling died, Mrs Koster gave her a huge bunch of flowers. 'I think they felt listened to,' she says. 'And for them that was important.'

'I don't mean to say that they weren't taken seriously in Blauwbörgje,' she adds hastily. She thinks that she did exactly the same as Liset Moorman. She also would not have sent Mr Bruggeling to the hospital. So she wonders what went wrong with the communication at Blauwbörgje. Van Spiegel says that this sort of thing often happens in the weekend when the doctor has less control over things. 'If Mr Bruggeling's condition hadn't deteriorated so rapidly and if there had been time for the family to take leave more gradually, then things would probably have worked out in Blauwbörgje.'

Conservative policy

José van Spiegel says that the Blauwbörgje affair was a case of derailed communication. But it also represented something that is common in all nursing homes. She says that when a 'conservative policy' is implemented in which patients are not treated curatively for illnesses or complications, but only receive pain and symptom alleviation, most people have no idea what this entails and have never thought about the related issues. During the Blauwbörgje case, Van Spiegel thought that it would have been better to have explained to relatives in simple terms what a 'conservative approach' entails and explained that doctors implement this because they think that it is better for the patient's quality of life.

Most people in Holland don't know that it is normal practice to abstain from treatment in nursing homes, says Van Spiegel. 'When people are first confronted with this idea it is when it relates to their own loved one, and they get a shock. Especially when you have never realised that it is also an option *not* to treat someone.' She explains that the Bruggeling family thought that you always had to do what was possible, that it was bad not to try all possible treatments. And that didn't fit with the policy in Blauwbörgje. And if you already have a rather suspicious nature, or you feel that you are an underdog, then its grist to your mill: 'If this is possible, then why can't my father have it?'

The Researcher

Hidden reality

The Blauwbörgje question intrigued me from the moment that the journalist phoned me and asked for my views. What was the whole affair about? Was it really about *versterven*? Why did it all go so wrong? Because it all did go very wrong.

Things went wrong in the nursing home: Mr Bruggeling's family transferred him to a hospital against the wishes of the doctors and charged the nursing home with attempted murder. Things also went wrong outside the nursing home. The initial media response had been negative toward the nursing home, but the case developed a life of its own, over which the participants seemed to have no control.

How did this happen? It is clear that something went wrong in the communication, but perhaps there is a deeper reason. The case occurred in the context of a society obsessed with physical appearance and with the belief that everything is possible. Medical success stories are popular, and whether in serious documentaries or soap operas, the narrative is always the same: yesterday the patient was fine, today he is gravely ill, but tomorrow he will be better again thanks to the marvels of modern medicine. The recovery narrative is saturated with scientific research, medical discoveries and, of course, the devotion of the doctors and the perseverance of the patient.

We are becoming less inclined to accept the finiteness of life and the limitations of medicine. It is striking how little people know about dying. They don't realise that most deaths are not 'good' in the way they are portrayed in films, without suffering and misery. We would rather not be confronted with these aspects of existence that do not conform to ideals of beauty and control. We only experience real death when it affects us directly, through the death of someone we know. And when a father or a mother dies we are shocked – we have to cope with the death of a loved one *and* the death of an illusion.

The nursing home hides the suffering of those with dementia, a suffering that we do not want to see. The nursing home contains a hidden reality, and in an almost contorted manner nursing home staff try to keep it hidden. They think that outsiders do not understand, and that they can't explain. Staff already assume that they will be the misunderstood victims. That was probably the reason that the management of Blauwbörgje abstained from commenting: they wouldn't have been understood anyway.

Although we don't know what life is like in a nursing home, we have thought about it to some extent. We have filled in the unknown with negative images. In reality everyone has an opinion about death's waiting room, because when the Blauwbörgje incident occurred all the pent-up preconceptions came to the surface. The media were full of examples. For example, one weekly wrote about the 'Dutch cellar,' in which everyone knew terrible things were happening. We tend to hide problems that we can't deal with, and that has consequences. In the Blauwbörgje case this was an unfamiliar way of dying – *versterven* – in a hidden space – the nursing home. The outside world didn't realise that *versterven* was a normal way of dying. The Bruggeling family didn't know that. They had the wrong expectations.

The doctors and carers in the nursing home were not heroes in a medical success story, but carers for the dying. Their job isn't respected. They don't get much state money. One day in an academic hospital costs 800 euros; a bed in a nursing home costs 175 euros per day. Nursing home doctors are the poorest paid medical specialists. Staff have an ambivalent role: on the one hand they like their work, but on the other they have a problem with the whole idea of the nursing home.

Zeitgeist

The Bruggeling case awakened something that had been dormant in society: feelings of uncertainty, dissatisfaction and discomfort. Why, the psychiatrist B. Chabot asked in an essay in one of the newspapers, have all the published facts and experiences regarding how people actually die not reduced the general fear that patients with dementia are dying of neglect? I see a number of reasons, but they all have a common denominator: serious doubt as to whether the welfare state is capable of caring for its most vulnerable members.

We know little about the daily lives of those in nursing homes, let alone about *versterven*. We read in the papers about the privatisation of nursing homes but we have no idea what effect this is having on care: how reorganisation and merging works, how management is changing and everything is becoming more businesslike, how less educated staff are being recruited to reduce costs. We know nothing about the coloured carers who have to cope with poverty and single parenthood.

We know that many of the more unpleasant jobs are increasingly carried out by people from the Carribean. It's a public secret that this happens in nursing homes, but we try to ignore it. It is an embarrassing thought that our coloured fellow citizens not only clean up for us but also take care of our parents when they have dementia because we find that task difficult and unpleasant.

We worry about an ageing population and increasing numbers of Alzheimer's patients. The Netherlands Alzheimer's Foundation estimates that in 2010 there will be about 300,000 people with Alzheimer's disease in the Netherlands. How are we going to care for them? Or, to put it more personally, how are we going to care for our own parents if and when they have Alzheimer's? To what extent is it our responsibility as their children? How can we live our own lives and be responsible for the needs of our parents when they become helpless? These are questions we would rather not think about.

Usually reality overtakes us when a loved one is admitted to a nursing home and we are seldom well prepared. There is a discrepancy between how we imagine care to be and reality. Most nursing homes cannot fulfil our expectations of made-to-measure care, and that is frustrating for nursing home staff, because they can't make this explicit. They cannot say: 'I'm sorry Madam but we can only give your mother a shower once a week and don't have more than ten minutes to feed her. We can change her nappy three times a day, but if you want anything more then I'm afraid you will have to do it yourself.'

This is not the sort of information that families want to hear, and it is certainly not client-friendly. But it is reality. Doctors should be able to discuss these limitations more openly with families at the time of admittance and explain to them what they can and cannot expect, and what the family can do to improve the resident's quality of life. As long as that openness is lacking there will always be the possibility that things get out of control, as they did in the Blauwbörgje case.

Communication and respect

Nursing home staff are confronted with an immense task. Understanding and caring for those with Alzheimer's and their families is complicated and difficult. They have to identify the family, estimate which phase of the coping process they are in and decide on how best to approach them. They have to ensure that the family understands the patient's condition. In some cases they have to be more directive than in others. In the case of Mr Bruggeling, there was distrust and a lack of respect right from the start. The two sides were opposed from the moment he was admitted. Nursing home staff can be pedantic. Carers often feel that they understand the needs of the resident better than the family. They often do not realise how difficult it is for families to hand over the care of a loved one after having coped, in some cases for many years, independently.

On the other hand, the Bruggeling family already had a reputation for being difficult. They did not hold nursing homes in high regard and they had little respect for the staff at Blauwbörgje in particular. They noticed that carers hardly had time for the residents and they were openly critical. Their tone was accusatory, and this must have irritated staff, who were even more overburdened than usual because it was during the summer and many were on leave.

Yvonne Bruggeling felt that staff in Blauwbörgje did not respect her. Those involved tactfully explained that the difficult families, those thought likely to complain, were often those who felt under-privileged: those from the lower socio-economic classes, from the poor neighbourhoods. Sofie Kamp had said, quite accurately, that nursing home staff were not very good at communicating with 'that type of family'.

Carers are usually the main point of contact between the nursing home and the family. With the increasing work burden, lower levels of training, and carers coming increasingly from ethnic minority groups with their own problems of poverty and deprivation, these problems are likely to increase, exacerbated by black carers feeling discriminated against and white families feeling ignored or misunderstood.

Mr Bruggeling lived for another four years

Mr Bruggeling lived for another four years without complications after the Blauwbörgje affair. That raised questions. How bad was his condition really in summer of 1997 when he was admitted? Nursing home doctor Van Bokhoven knew Bruggeling from the day-care centre and from previous admissions. He thought that he was in an advanced stage of Alzheimer's and that he was a 'sad figure' who was confused and aggressive and who had lost touch with reality. Van Bokhoven thought that Bruggeling's life was an agony. When he saw him in the summer of 1997 he found that his physical condition had also deteriorated radically and didn't want to 'fiddle around' too much with him. His colleague Liset Moorman probably thought the same.

In Park House, residents were described as 'serious' when they reached the final stages of Alzheimer's. Sometimes the term was also used to refer to someone who was suffering from their condition. Mrs Prins, for example, who was agitated, aggressive and afraid. When she contracted pneumonia the doctors decided not to treat her. They thought that it was inhumane to keep her alive and thus extend her suffering. The Bruggeling case resembles that of Mrs Prins.

It is not uncommon for Alzheimer's patients to live longer than expected, or to die unexpectedly. The disease trajectory is uneven. That Bruggeling lived so long was probably because he was relatively young and physically fit. He would probably have died in the summer of 1997 if he hadn't been transferred to the hospital. Many relatives of Alzheimer's patients are grateful for the conservative treatment policy because it spares their loved one further suffering and misery. But in order to experience it in that way you have to be ready for the death of your loved one. That was not the case with the Bruggeling family. They thought that they could still communicate with him. The situation surprised them, and perhaps the doctors did 'jump the gun,' to use the words of Van Bokhoven. Maybe the family assessed Bruggeling's condition differently because they didn't want him to have Alzheimer's and die, and so repressed the reality. This often happens, as the nursing home doctor Van

Bokhoven described in the case of his own mother. He didn't see her symptoms because he didn't want a mother with Alzheimer's.

Could it happen again?

Could there be another Blauwbörgje case? The simple answer is: yes. The communication problems that formed the basis for the crisis are common in nursing homes and probably recognisable for every nursing home doctor. Moreover, the underlying cause hasn't been removed: the idea that we can control everything. We don't want to be confronted with suffering that we cannot alleviate and death that we cannot conquer. As a result we know little about dementia and how those with dementia die, and we know less about refraining from treatment and *versterven*. When a loved one is admitted to a nursing home we have to catch up and fill this information gap, and during this hasty process misunderstandings can easily develop.

Staff have less and less time for residents and this has consequences for feeding residents and making sure that they drink enough. In the Blauwbörgje case this made the family suspicious. When Bruggeling became seriously ill they attributed this exclusively to poor care. When he recovered in the hospital this confirmed their suspicions. If they had understood more about the way patients with Alzheimer's die then things might have turned out differently.

Regarding the quality of care, the future does not look bright. Cutbacks continue, staff shortages are increasing and the educational level of staff is declining. Because of the increase in the numbers of coloured staff there is also a cultural and socio-economic gap between carers on the one hand and residents and their families on the other. This also increases the likelihood of another Blauwbörgje.

The case also span out of control because the time for something like that was ripe. Maybe the affair was a symbol of some of the things that are wrong with our society and of the concomitant process of becoming conscious of the problem. My description of Park House started with the festive opening of the new building. The residents were not invited to the party. Why not? Were the demented being hidden from the view of the bigwigs? Would it have been embarrassing if they had been there? There is a parallel here between nursing home and society. We hide away unpleasant things and when things go wrong we blame others. We need to see the reality for what it is and delineate responsibility: who is actually responsible when our parents have Alzheimer's? Is it the nursing home, the politicians, or ourselves? We make up the individualistic society of which this problem is part. And we allow the embarrassment about – or maybe it is contempt for – insoluble suffering to exist.

How It All Ended

Coming and going

One day I bump into Max Hermann, the Park House psychologist. He is still working at Park House and tells me about the latest developments. The merger that Westerlaken & Partners tried to bring about fell through at the last moment. They did manage to appoint a new director, though. Initially it seemed that they had made a good choice, but the tensions between him and the management team are increasing. He seems to be fully occupied with a new merger and as a result is not available for daily management issues. There are rumours that he is planning to leave.

Staff continue to leave. Rutger Varenkamp, Femke, Dina Vogel and Michiel Groothof have all left. Bob Eelman's health has made it impossible for him to continue and Colette is on sick leave. Anna van Raalten did not return after her sick leave. Two of the newer care managers have already left – one of them was sacked. 'She was even stricter than her predecessors, but then she was from South Africa,' Max says, laughing. 'The carers called her "the warder".'

The work burden in Park House has increased. There are increasing numbers of untrained assistants replacing trained carers. The supply of trained staff on the labour market has increased, but in Park House they haven't noticed this because the dire financial situation of the nursing home means that staff that leave are not being replaced. So the pressure on the permanent, trained staff has only increased.

When I was in Park House I often wondered whether I had chosen a time of extremes, but it now seems that that was the normal state of affairs. The psychologist confirms this: 'There were all kinds of things happening when you came and they continued to happen after you left. Things are always extreme.'

I visit Park House occasionally and keep in touch with some of those I met there. When I visit the humanist counsellor Rosan Hüsken in the nursing home just before completing the Dutch edition of this book, she proudly shows me the new 'silence centre'. With paint and curtains from a cheap shop and second-hand chairs they have created a wonderful serene space where residents, family and staff can retreat.

On a lectern there is a commemorative book. I open it and read the calligraphic names of those who have died. Almost all the residents I knew are there. Mrs Bloem, Mrs Melkman, Mrs Walker, Mrs Carpentier, Mrs Prins, Henk Ruiter. I see them in my imagination, shuffling down the corridor or sitting in their chairs.

Notes

1. Roeline Pasman (2004). *Forgoing artificial nutrition and hydration in nursing home patients with dementia. Decision-making, clinical course, and quality of dying*. PhD dissertation, Amsterdam Free University Medical centre.
2. Peter Kloos (1981). *Culturele Antropologie*. Assen: Van Gorcum.
3. Robert Pool (2000). *Negotiating a Good Death: Euthanasia in The Netherlands*. New York: Haworth.
4. This discussion of the term *versterven* is based on Robert Pool (2004), 'You're not going to dehydrate mom, are you? Euthanasia, versterving and good death in the Netherlands.' *Social Science and Medicine* 58 (5): 955-966.
5. People of mixed Dutch-Indonesian descent.
6. A secular equivalent of the pastor and the priest.
7. She is referring to the prostitutes who sit behind large windows in the red light district in Amsterdam.
8. 'Euthanasia declaration' is a literal translation of the Dutch *euthanasieverklaring*, and is used here rather than 'living will' or 'advance directive' as these terms (for which there are also Dutch equivalents (*levenstestament* and *niet-reanimeerverklaring*) do not refer to euthanasia.
9. *Winti* is a form of traditional religion with West African roots, similar to voodoo, that is practiced in Surinam.
10. Bert Keizer (1994). *Het refrein is Hein*. This has been translated into English as *Dancing with Mr D*. (1997).